Beautiful acts of debatable conseque
thinking nonsense..

"GIVE UP YOUR DAY JC

----- Email ----
From: Colossus Sosloss
To: All Staff
Sent: 26th May 2004
Subject: GIVE UP YOUR DAY JOB

Dear management.

I'm sending this email to everyone in the world of banking, everyone on the COUTTS and RBS email list, staff in the UK and abroad, customers and millionaire clients.

If reading this sitting in the London office, you're about to see me stand up from my desk, hear me emulate the mating cry of the polar bear, and walk out of the office.

I will not be returning because I hate my job, everyone I work for, and with.

I can't take another second staring at patronising motivational posters.

The kitten gazing into the mirror seeing a lion, the words scrawled underneath *what matters most is how you see yourself.*

What terrible advice, because by using the word *most*, the poster confirms through what it doesn't say how everyone else sees you *does* matter, and *how they see you probably matters a great deal.*

The poster is on the wall in front of my desk and rips away my will to live through tired eyelids, leaving the fingerprints of who I could have been implanted on my chin.

Not because of the poster, which is stupid, but because the manager has put the poster up because he thinks it's brilliant.

I have a repetitive black and white dream of the kitten who thinks it's a lion trying to eat a dog.

I stand in the rain by the kerb, suit wet, witnessing; the kitten roars in mind, but the small ball of fluff meows on the outside, the kitten lashes out at a dog with large paws the kitten doesn't have, and angers the dog, a beast five t mes the kitten's size.

The butchering is short, knifeless, the kittens head rolls towards me and rests at the feet of terrible shoes I never clean; because only fuckwits base opinion on feet.

The kittens eyes are gone, black holes, two magic eight balls filled with blank triangles.

What matters most is not visual. What matters most is not how you *see* yourself or how others *see* you.

The entire thought process behind this motivational poster is wrapped around suits and hair gel, around make up applied without thought, about not rocking the boat; the poster tells people to stay in chairs and work hard, to not act out of place, because what we do changes what people think of us, and what we do is who we are.

What nonsense.

What matters most is how you feel.

We are not what we do, but how we feel about what we do, and all too often how we feel is a thought we don't action.

And therein lies the problem.

The brains behind these motivational office posters don't want you to think how you're feeling, they want you to focus on the irrelevant, on the ego, to make you think reputation is important.

They keep you in your job.

They make you embarrassed to think alternatively.

They keep aging bums in creaking seats.

Besides management: motivation is your job, not the job of posters.

How does it affect your motivation, management, that you can be replaced by a poster? I imagine that must make you feel quite sad, quite defeated, quite unmotivated.

Why don't we let the posters do other jobs like photocopying?

I'm tired of being treated as an idiot by a bank full of idiots, who only pay enough for my left testicle.

This company makes me angry.

The longer I stay here the more I destroy any chance I have of understanding the bigger picture; like a caveman bashing an abacus into his face over and over again until one day the concept of maths is eradicated from existence.

This place makes me a paper boat; the water we're born to float on is slowly absorbing me until, one day, I'll forget life is not about folding to someone else's desires, but about creating your own.

You have taken away our internet access, what do you take next?

We already have grey walls.

Perhaps you'll paint grey over the sun and invent a rule banning us from leaving the building to prevent the colours making our brains breathe in.

Maybe next year you'll pass a rule stating we can only talk about work and our voices will be monitored to make sure we do.

Perhaps you'll ban smiling, or laughter. After all, if the staff are laughing and smiling we're showing a human side, and that can't be good. If the workers have emotions, we are harder to control, What if we became 'free thinking?'... But hey, it's only business.

No it's not; your business is *my* life!

Life does not have to be a series of events ours to experience not ours to control.

If a rainbow worked here for a day, by five past nine the rainbow would've signed paperwork to have its gold legally stolen, and by nine thirty the rainbow would be black; throwing up colours into one of the toilets surrounded by cardboard cubicles.

The grey carpets, grey walls, grey faces, grey voices.

The room nobody is allowed to go in? I know you have Joseph and his multicoloured raincoat tied to a chair, and you punch him in the face daily to feel alive again.

We all hear him screaming.

Make sure you continue with the free coffee because if the caffeine wears off we might slow down to feel. Make sure the soup, the tea and hot chocolate are all composed of the dust collecting on the top of the PCs to ensure nobody has a choice but to drink the coffee, or risk spending their evening throwing up plastic hoops and solid peas tasting of plastic and retired museum curators.

On Mondays there's less dust on the monitors and the drinks machine is magically full again; the tears from the cleaners in the soup.

Your philosophy is *you can't make people work but you can stop them having fun* and you've taken this philosophy to new levels.

If I had children and decided to raise them with this ethic they would be taken away from me, but a bank not only gets away with it, it makes us pay to travel and sit down for a day to do perform repetitive tasks degrading our intelligence, hacks away at our dreams, takes us away from loved ones and adds years to our faces; yet somehow we do not complain, we say thank-you.

The greatest trick the devil ever pulled is not making people think he doesn't exist, it's saying I'm here, you all hate me, now drink from my nipple.

And we do.

A message for anyone working in this office: leave whilst you can.

Life is better than this!

There will always be another exam; there will always be a reason why they cannot give you a pay rise.

There will be another "independent" pay review next year magically deciding the minions are already overpaid whilst still managing to find enough room in the finances to pay the RBS bosses millions of pounds in bonuses.

A pay review only shows the tip of the iceberg and we are plankton at the base of the iceberg, wiggling around brainlessly, bumping our small heads repeatedly against ice, grateful for its existence because we believe it gives us purpose.

Wake up fellow co-workers! This does not give us our purpose but takes our purpose away.

You could be a polar bear if you want.

You just have to turn around and swim away from the iceberg because every dead end, if you turn around, is a way out.

Yours Sincerely

Colossus Sosloss

Former plankton.

*Hits send on this email. Stands up. Roars like a polar bear, and heads for the door.

"NINE PENCE CURRY SAUCE"

Saturday 14th August 2010

I have been in my new studio flat for four days.

My flat is small; one main room, a kitchen and shower but it's all I need. The main house is owned by an old guy who is lonelier than I am and twice as creepy. He lives downstairs and owns the property.

The building is his house and he's converted his spare rooms into studio flats. The flat is in Willesden Green, London, only a fifteen minute tube ride to work.

To enter my studio flat I have to open the coffin-shaped main front door then head past his smoke-hazed home and up the creaking staircase.

My door is the first door at the top of the stairs.

He fears he's going to be killed by *bloody Somalian's* so has a rule the front door must be bolted from the inside at all times.

Locking a sturdy bolt that could hold off an army makes a lot of noise and little sense; because his front door to his actual apartment is adjacent to the main front door every time I finish locking the door I turn around to find him standing behind me, blocking my way with his crooked frame; staring intently at me with his long nicotine stained fingers and his perfectly groomed white hair, side parted, sitting above his paranoid milky eyes like a flat cloud ironed out over a dark day.

The year is 2010, I am 29 years old.

Six years have passed since I sent my email and walked out on my job in the bank with youthful determination and dreams of becoming a Polar Bear.

This is the story of how in those seven years I rose to the top of my iceberg as plankton. How I felt the sun on my back as I lay on cold ice, eating penguin heads and chasing seagulls as a Polar Bear; and how I sunk back down to being the rising plankton I am today.

*

I'm sitting on my bed staring at the white painted wall; the bland, safe, non offensive colour all landlords decide to paint their homes when enticing new tenants and I'm thinking the wall would be so much better painted with anything other than the bland, safe, non offensive colour landlords choose when enticing new tenants.

My phone rings, an annoying ring I've been meaning to change for months but have never grasped the moment to change. The ring always reminds me I need to change it, but after each phone conversation I have forgotten again.

My phone will remind me again next time it rings I need to change it, and so the circle of my annoying phone ring continues.

I should have turned it off or followed through with the thought of leaving it in the fridge.

I answer the phone.

My mum's voice rattles pleasantly along; a child naively smiling at the gates full of excitement on their first day of school, not grasping they're being pushed into a wood chipper by their own creator.

I agree to go to my mum's house on Sunday to fix her computer. The problem will no doubt be some major malfunction like she isn't sure which finger is best to turn the computer on with; or she can't see the screen because she's in another room looking at a painting of cooked sausages.

I tell my mum I have to go, end the call, and put my phone in the fridge next to a bottle of wine.

The bottle of wine is a good listener, far better than the self-indulgent grains of hard rice indiscriminately scattered across the lower shelf of the fridge, dying French soldiers caught in no man's land during battle.

I close the fridge door and return to my bed relieved I don't have to worry about being contacted by people.

I won't hear my phone if it's in the fridge.

I am alone; all one.

That's why I have moved here.

Maybe the lion in the cage doesn't dream of escape, maybe the lion doesn't dream at all. Perhaps to not dream, is to find true freedom.

I don't have a chair which is frustrating because my bed is the only place I can sit down and my computer is on top of a chest of drawers in the corner, so I have to either sit on the wood floor looking up at my PC like a child clumsily clawing at candy floss being held by a teasing sibling, or, bring the bed over and sit on it like I'm preparing to make money by touching myself whilst laying back on my bed for potential webcam viewers.

A simple chair would resolve both of these issues and I could then spend endless hours on-line being sociable by avoiding real people.

And then the internet was turned off; and all the people left their houses and stared up at the sun;

"I think I'm your neighbour" said one.

I look around my new flat: lipstick on a pig. A large pig, made from decent wood but carved by a once skilled labourer who lost both arms in an incident with a faulty bread maker, and, after stubbornly refusing to give up the practice he loves, was forced to carve wooden sculptures and studio flats using only his teeth under the careful watch of Roman guards.

The floor and the kitchen look new, and the materials used probably are. They look expensive, but if I look closer I see the gaps; like staring at an office worker after lunch on a

Friday. They look on the most part respectable, but if you get up close you can see the wobble.

There is one bump in the corner where the wooden floor doesn't quite fit together and the oven, meant to be state of the art, fails to provide the basic facility of temperature control and lacks a timer.

In the kitchen the white shelves are a little crooked and out of place; the teeth of an old cat with a monkey on its back bashing a symbol repeatedly to the theme of *my old mans a dustman* and the fake tiled floor curls up at the edges as, day by day, the floor shrinks away under the icy breath of the two large kitchen windows.

The two large windows stretch across the entire wall of the kitchen, revealing the concrete, functional garden below.

The glass is single glazed and not properly sealed, loose glue flaps along paint chipped windowsill, cold wind grips the kitchen with invisible fists.

If I stand in the kitchen for too long I see a child leaving fingers out of the top of a fast moving car window, until tips turn blue.

Even if I don't touch the sink in the day, overnight black stains appear mysteriously across its chalky surface as if at night pixie slaves are forced to march across the sink in dirty boots returning from mining jewels for evil fairy overlords.

The shower my landlord assures me is a power shower, but it's only power seems to be precisely emulating the functions and water pressure of an ordinary shower that doesn't work.

I decide to go to the shops to buy a tin of curry sauce to go with the rice I'm having for dinner. I'm not a great cook and lately I'm only eating rice, in curry sauce, with tuna and sometimes sweet-corn. I know it doesn't sound appealing but for five years all I lived off was pasta, tuna and sweet-corn all mixed up with salad cream and I think rice, tuna and sweet-corn in curry sauce is a small step in the right direction.

I leave my flat in silence so my landlord doesn't hear me; the best chance of making it down the stairs and out the building without being cornered by a lonely old man.

I quietly close my front door but he's already at the bottom of the stairs, walking alone in tight circles. He looks up at me, a vulture flying over a lost man in a desert.

He watches me like a hawk; his head bobs feverishly, his tongue a manic, twitching mouse hanging out from his beaked mouth.

I've only known him for four days and he is intense and paranoid. I think he's from Pakistan.

I have never met a more racist person.

He is so racist he even hates people from Pakistan and he is Pakistani; but he isn't just racist – he's homophobic, sexist, against men with long hair, girls with short hair, piercings, tattoos, loud noises, unlocked doors, the weather, bright colours, any expression of individuality, accents not his own, silence, the wall at the end of the drive, both neighbours, buses, cars, leaves, stairs, his own ideas, being a landlord, his own accent, animals (including dolphins) and, not last I'm sure; he harbours a special obsessional hatred towards Somalians.

I know at his age he's from a different generation and I'm not going to change his views, so instead, when he corners me, I listen and nod my head and hope the pain is over soon.

The unfortunate aspect to this survival tactic is because he's so lonely he can, and does, talk for hours. He also forgets what he's saying and has a habit of telling me the same story five times from five different starting points.

His mind is as small as his world and so everything he says is about somebody else in the studio flats. Information I don't want to hear or know about; it would be okay if he had a nice word to say about anything or anyone – but he doesn't.

It's all negative.

If I take away his political views he is a lost old man fearful of the Somalians inside his head living outside his triple locked door who sees in me someone he can talk to. I understand that, but what he doesn't know is I want to be left alone to drink myself into a magic roundabout because I didn't move here to be alone to find company; I moved because I wanted to get to know me.

As if sensing this, he is insisting on friendship.

Not the neighbourly friendship where you say a quick hello, but the type of friendship seen floating on the surface of lost marriages and abandoned sons. The type of friendship based on letting love slip through your fingers, justified if you can find another guy to hang out with.

I'm at the bottom of the stairs and Mohammad, his name, stands in front of me.

He's a thin man, weight maintained by his smoking habit. He must smoke sixty cigarettes a day yet his teeth are perfectly white and straight and there are few lines on his face.

Although thin, he has a perfectly formed round belly making him look constantly six months pregnant.

His fingers are too long and when he talks he uses them to point out moments in his sentences. When he does, as the tips of his spindly fingers touch the words his mouth forms, his words turn dark before my eyes and disintegrate like twisted people caught touching the metallic surface of a detonating atomic bomb; then his breath blows away the ashes making way for fresh words.

His skin is light brown and he would be taller except for the hunch in his stance which puts his large head down lower than his shoulders.

He wears glasses and his eyes are too milky, he is losing his vision, and in one corner of his left eye is a big wart. I don't stare into his eyes for too long.

His ears are a notable feature, large, but his earlobes larger.

When he gets angry (often because age has chomped his patience) his face shudders and his earlobes wobble against the side of his face, like two fat naked adults with no facial features swinging back and forth on small swings into chocolate pudding.

His voice is a marvel. He has a beautiful Pakistani accent and pronounces words with a curious pattern of self encouragement and rhetoric, like he's constantly checking what he just said; only I know he isn't, because he only talks to himself and uses my stupid nodding head as the medium to validate himself.

He is quite deaf and suffering from memory problems so when I do talk he asks me to repeat what I have said back to him until he can hear me but, because a few minutes have past, by the time he hears me he has no idea what I'm referring to because he can't remember why I'm talking.

His pride means he cannot admit to not knowing he can't remember what we were talking about, so when he forgets what's going on he hides it by continuing with what he thought he was saying, either from the place where he left before I started talking, at a random place in the same story, or he will start a different story entirely.

I'm too polite to tell him I've already heard what he's saying. So I stand in front of him, in the hallway, or on the stairs, or in the front of the house, staring into his too milky eyes and praying for an intervention that never comes.

I'm slowly starting to hate his block-shaped head and his dull stories, wonderfully packaged in his amazing voice.

That's my problem, avoid Mohammad and all is well, become embroiled in a conversation and it can be a crazy, draining adventure, lasting hours because he's so old he can't remember how long he's been chatting for or what about.

As I reach the bottom of the staircase I try and avoid him but it's impossible.

As my landlord he holds some power over me and seems aware of the fact.

I stand facing him and he smiles. His voice boils with the wonderful pattern I spoke of earlier, but behind the boiling is a notable rattle, his lungs struggling for breath against seventy plus years of smoking.

His voice is both impossible to ignore and sad to focus on; an iron bubble knocking against the rusting hull of a sinking ship.

"I wonder if you leave a laptop on your bed when you go out? Because you know it is very dangerous. There could be a fire. Amit leaves his on sometimes when he goes out and so I must have a word with him...Do not be telling Amit I am knowing of this."

A perfect smile flashes across his imperfect face.

Mohammad is probably in his eighties so I've waved away his previous divulgence he enters the rooms of his tenants when they're not in as a man who means well, but doesn't realise he isn't meant to do such things.

His smile tells me Mohammad, my landlord, knows all too well he shouldn't be prying.

"Colossus I am wondering if you are having the sexy time with a girlfriend?"

I smile back at Mohammad but I'm thinking two things. *First* he breaks into his tenant's homes and when I'm out he may enter my studio flat and smell my underwear. *Second* I don't fancy talking to an old man about my sex life.

I tell Mohammad I don't need a girlfriend because Sainsbury's are selling curry sauce for thirteen pence a jar.

He doesn't know how to respond and in his moment's pause I'm able to escape his clutches and leave the house.

I buy the curry sauce in Sainsbury's and grab a bottle of red wine.

The curry sauce is reduced from thirteen to nine pence. I'm so excited by this I consider knocking for Mohammad on the way back to tell him the new price, but naturally this is only a passing crazy thought.

I'm back inside my studio flat without disturbing Mohammad and evening rolls into my home, covering everything in darkness.

I lie on my bed wishing it was a chair and consider putting trip wire across my front door so if Mohammad breaks into my room whilst I'm at work he would be covered in oil and duck feathers.

I search around for anything I can find to make this a reality, but the only oil I have would need to be drained from tins of tuna and the closest I have to duck feathers is the dust settling into every pore of my flat.

I imagine Mohammad covered in natural tuna oil and flat fuzz.

My only other possession is an elastic band.

Perhaps next time I see Mohammad I'll flick the rubber band at his massive earlobe from a well thought out position of cover on behalf of Amit; who I'm sure would be livid if he knew his landlord was letting himself into his flat whilst he was out.

I don't know how it's possible Sainsbury's thirteen pence curry sauce is now only nine pence, because surely nothing can be taken out of thirteen pence sauce worth four pence.

It costs three times more to take a piss at London Bridge train station than it does to buy this curry sauce.

I start drinking red wine and realise I've hit Saturday night television gold as Good Will Hunting is on.

I keep drinking and follow Will's journey with his hairy friend and the more I drink the more absorbed into the plot of Good Will Hunting I become; eventually I'm over connecting with Matt Damon's mental problems and his failures to connect with the opposite sex.

I feel warm with the red wine and at random moments tell myself how great the film is, and consequently what a great time I'm having.

Red wine, a good film and alone in my own place I work every day to just about afford.

All my lights are off, just the light from the television flickers into my warm face, a sun leaving rainbows on my skin.

Heaven is not living on a cloud with millions of other people who share the same beliefs; it's being on your own to get on with being wrong in a million wonderful ways.

Matt Damon is having a fight with his girlfriend because he can't love her and tears fill my eyes.

I love these warm moments sponsored by indulgence, isolation and wine.

My phone on the wall rings; a vibrator drowning in a cold bath bounces off all four walls, ruining my peace.

I freeze and stare at the white machine hanging from the wall.

The phone in my room is connected to the front door buzzer outside the main house, that's all it does. If someone buzzes my flat number from outside, the phone rings in my room.

I stare at the phone for a moment longer, beg for it not to ring again, and turn my attention back to Matt Damon.

The phone buzzes again.

In the darkness my head turns and my focus is no longer on my television but once again on the object or my wall.

The rainbow dancing on my face turns to a thousand grey dashes; rain falls across my skin.

Perhaps someone who lives in the flats above is trying to get in.

I can't leave them outside.

I get up out of my beautiful comfort zone, walk to the wall and lift up the white phone. I hear the sound of passing cars, traffic, the wind, the cold, the city, life and all the mill ons of tiny bits of hectic living outside I was blissfully forgett ng.

A rolling stone gathers no moss, but if enough stones stand still we call that place a city.

A familiar voice speaks loud and clear over the crackli ng background of hectic suburbia.

"Colossus, do you want to be comings out for a drink with me so it is or isn't it so?"

Mohammad. My landlord.

I check the time, gone midnight.

I'm perfectly comfortable; I don't want to babysit an old man.

This is my Saturday night, no, no thank you; going out for a drink is the last thing I want to do. I want to be with Matt Damon, my tears, my alcohol; and why are you buzzing me this late at night, especially on a weekend?

I hear my voice respond to Mohammad; I sound weaker than usual, and a lot dumber.

"What, you mean out for a drink?"

"Yes, this is what the words I am saying to you are meaning."

No.

Go away.

"Sure, why not?"

For reasons beyond me, I tell Mohammad I'll be down in five minutes. Matt Damon looks at me like he can't believe I'm about to walk out in the middle of his greatest performance.

I can't believe it either.

Mohammad has some mystical power over me, part him being my landlord and part me feeling sorry for him.

I grab my coat and twenty minutes later I'm walking towards Mohammad's car wondering what kind of pub a pensioner goes to at one am on a Saturday night.

As I put my hand on his car door, I think I'm going to be lucky to survive the journey.

Mohammad can't hear and his eyes are going but somehow he still has a licence to drive; we get into his car and I look back on the house and wonder if it will be the last house I ever see.

I sit down next to Mohammad and desperately paw at the space where in a real car the place to plug my seatbelt would be; the car is so small when I look back up, I find the end of my nose too close to his flaring nostrils.

As I'm discovering there's no seatbelt Mohammad gets his priorities in order and lights a cigarette.

The car already stinks of smoke and it's hard to breathe. The plastic dashboard in front of me is stained yellow with nicotine and the ceiling of the car has a sickly brown tar stain caked across it.

Mohammad drives away and I try not to cough.

An enthusiastic baby dragon trapped inside the body of a rotting carcass breathes smoke into the car from his face, as deaths icy hands massage my shoulders.

I need to cough as smoke from his mouth engulfs my face but I manage to resist.

I need to wind down the window.

I need air of some kind desperately.

I'm trying to shallow breathe in the hope less smoke gets into my lungs, and I'm trying not to cough because I don't want to offend him.

I can see myself never fully expressing myself to Mohammad until one day I pick up a gun and climb a clock-tower.

It's an odd fit that the word guns is snug backwards.

I stare straight ahead, red eyed, at the Christmas tree air freshener dangling from the rear view mirror. The air freshener was once green, but now it's an unrecognisable black and as I stare into the little trees dark sad figure I'm reminded of dead trees, burnt alive in forests to make way for industry.

I can't stand this any longer.

"Mohammad, do you mind if I wind down the window?"

"Yes. Do not be touching my windows."

I don't even like him. Why am I in this car with a man I don't like going somewhere I don't want to go?

Mohammad reacts like he has heard my thoughts, croak voiced, he blurts out more cracked words:

"I will put on the air conditioning."

Not a second too soon because I'm about to black out, or worse, throw up in his car.

"Thanks Mohammad."

I wait for fresh air and clean oxygen to blow into my face and take the nausea away.

Mohammad turns the air conditioning on and a new wave of old stale smoke that's been sitting in the pipes of his car for years blows into my face; making me feel like a chimney sweep on his first day up one of the large funnels on a cruise liner in the middle of an ocean storm.

The car is so full of smoke all the air vents can do is move the old smoke to the back of the car and the new smoke to the front.

I feel sick.

I'm going to throw up.

I stare out of the closed window through gritted teeth with red burning eyes and tell myself I'll be out of this snuff box in a minute.

Just keep it together until then.

If I could wind a window down none of this would be happening; instead, whilst looking away from Mohammad I throw up in my mouth and swallow again.

Fifteen minutes later, Mohammad and I are standing at a bar in the worst pub in the world, which seems to adhere to the dance like you expect to be shot policy.

The music is so loud I can't hear Mohammad and Mohammad can't hear anything; even the loud music.

He shuffles around the bar in that way really old people do; a walk I call the shumble; the shumble is the half shuffle half bumble judder of old people walking that younger people witness with worried faces but never talk about.

His walk says he might fall over and if he does he'll shatter into four triangles that will never fit back together.

He shumbles slowly, with most of his weight on the bar, around to the dance floor toward girls half my age and a quarter of his, young girls walking around in skirts shorter than the oxygen capacity of his lungs.

We stand and I watch my old landlord stare at the legs of women sixty years younger than he. As he stares fixated on one larger girl he turns to me and shouts:

"I like the wobbly ladies with the big bums that wiggle when they dance. Do you like the big bums or the thin sticky ones that do not be movings?"

To accentuate his meaning, and in case the girls on the dance floor are not aware he's talking about them, Mohammad uses his hands to gesticulate a shapely womanly figure then turns back to continue to stare at the rear end of the lady, like he's in a strip club and has paid fair money to ogle.

I stand awkwardly next to Mohammad as he drools over any bum wobbling close enough for him to tell, with certainty, they're not a man.

A feeling of being used, and stupid, creeps over me.

Mohammad points his long spindly finger at a large woman in a short red dress. His long finger reminds me of a broken rake pawing through dead autumn leaves for a ring never dropped, as his finger reaches full extension he turns and hisses one word, sounding like a boiling kettle thrown in anger at a surprised lady lobster calmly applying make-up to her claws in a mirror:

"Prostitute."

I pray silently if he's going to approach this woman his chat-up line is better than walking up to her and calling her a prostitute.

Even if I wanted to leave, and I do, I can't because Mohammad has the car.

I wonder if I should save the Christmas tree a r-freshener.

I know its dead but after the horrible life it's been subjected to I sense a decent burial is the least it deserves.

Mohammad smiles and rakes dead leaves over another innocent girl.

As his long spindly finger reaches full extension the woman moves forward a little, prodded by some dark invisible force.

Mohammad flashes his devilish grin and spits out the same word but this time with a deeper and more t red hiss; a rattlesnake twitching in its sleep subconsciously reliving the time it was trod on by a blind elephant on a pilgrimage to the fountain of the wailing pervert.

"Prostitute."

How are his teeth so white?

Mohammad is no charmer of women.

It is not until three in the morning I'm finally back in my flat from the weird place politeness had dropped me in via the smallest car with the highest nicotine and tar content in automobile history.

I moved here to indulge in alcohol and reclusiveness, not to hold the glass of an old pervert dribbling on his feet staring at women who have their backs to him.

But, I guess, life exists where expectancy meets disappointment.

"NO SPACE LEFT BETWEEN US"

14th June 2004

I had quit my job in the bank three weeks earlier and still had no idea what I was going to do. Most people wouldn't walk out of their job without some sort of plan; at the time it seemed natural for me to quit, like wearing flippers in the sea; but in the three weeks since leaving nothing had happened.

Working in a bank, for me, had been unnatural and I felt out of synch with the moment.

I was a stranger in my life and a step out of what should have been my own occasion; a bride on her wedding day doing "the worm" down the aisle wearing a sea-lion costume because she thought it would be a laugh.

My highly loose plan was to quit my job and see what happens.

I was expecting the universe would hear I quit my job and lay before me some fantastic opportunity that could never have happened if I was still employed.

I'm not saying I was expecting to find a magic key, or be visited in the night by a gnome with a flashing beard who told me in an Irish accent I had to travel on his back to the land of the Grumplebarks to save the last gnome colony; but, I was expecting *something*.

Nothing happened.

Just when I thought I had the key I looked up to see a thousand doors.

My money was running out and I started drinking, which wasn't helping with the money running out, but at least I knew what I was doing.

That morning I was sitting on my own in the back garden of the place I rented in Greenwich drinking neat vodka and wondering why I hadn't gone out with my friends the night before.

A beautiful house in its own private mews and I shared it with three friends, the house of dreams, but the voice in the back of my head was telling me I was going to have to leave the house, and Greenwich, and become one of those people who hold up signs with arrows on.

I'd make three or four pound an hour and live with a hundred people from all over the world in an underground basement, keep rats as pets and at night we would all get together and sing folk songs to keep warm; like the poor people who eventually all died on the Titanic.

That was what I thought my life was going to be like.

I hadn't completely lost faith though. In the back of my mind I still had this ridiculous concept good things come to good people; I just had to wait it out, my plan of thinking it will work out will work out if I keep thinking it will.

I was sitting cross-legged on the concrete patio in the garden, wondering what I was going to do with my life, spinning a red top from the half consumed vodka bottle leaning against my leg and seeing a white faced clown staring back at me mouthing the word "bang."

My phone beeped and I received a text from my best friend Rob.

Rob looks like a Lego man with short black hair and glasses climbing down a tower on a windy day, half secret agent half library assistant. His parents are from Mauritius and Ireland respectably so he has tanned skin all year round and when he's really drunk he puts his arms in the air and shouts "bendy sticks" like a crazy Lego man on a windy day searching for sticks which bend.

As far as we can both tell, bendy sticks are pipe cleaners.

It's a curious habit, and although he's yet to find his bendy sticks, every drunken bender is a step closer to living the pipe dream.

He's honest, I'd trust him with my life, and he's clever because he owns his own company that builds websites and is likely to go far; as long as he keeps his bendy stick habit secret.

One time he turned up at my home with three cushions he had taken from a bin and he left them on my doorstep with a note saying he thought I might like a new bed.

He has one of the most expressive faces I have seen and if he likes something his eyes light up, but if he doesn't like something he'll disappear and become one single eyebrow.

His voice is what dessert would be if it was a secret robot; light, fast and whips up at the ends but in blocks of sound that, if I close my eyes, makes me see children grabbing at chocolate covered spoons.

Rob's text told me everyone was going to Blackheath common to meet and then out for a bimble around Greenwich. Blackheath was a short walk away and so I spun my vodka bottle top one last time and, with the sun on my back, decided to go.

Life wasn't going to help me if I didn't let it, and so as the bottle top settled I stood and went to meet my friends.

My friends had been out clubbing all Friday night which meant they would be a curious mix of trysting beavers, shabby rainbows and bright brained hugging limpets and as I approached the group on Blackheath common I could hear high pitched squeals of delight; a series of piglets accidentally catching their penises in a series of closing car doors.

I love my friends, over the years the scene has added children and marriages and if you close your eyes when you're in the middle of them and listen to the main sound, the main sound has never changed; and that sound is laughter.

This has always been the case, it was in 2004 and it is today.

I approached the group, chatted to friends, someone gave me some acid and I removed my shirt and the sun was on my back and the acid was having the beautiful effect of switching off all my internal thoughts and placing me in the middle of colour.

The acid pulled apart the jumper the vodka and doubt had knitted in my mind that morning of a decapitated sheep, and replaced it with a knitted jumper with a picture of the same sheep being reintegrated back into his flock after successful surgery and counselling.

A beautiful day, a beautiful place; green fields mind builds.

I found a soft sponge ball and started throwing it to Lee and Wednesday's kid, Pippa.

Wednesday is the food equivalent to a sausage tractor with mash potato wheels and gravy hair and Lee looks so much like Steve Guttenberg I sent him a picture of Steve Guttenberg wearing an all in one leather outfit and Lee's mum found it and questioned her son's weekend sex habits.

Pippa then was six years old with a round pasty face; she still to this day has a laugh that reminds me of the first rain-drop hitting a wind chime on a hot porch in a dehydrated town that has never had rain before. Her laugh is a pinging relief in the air to those around her.

That day Pippa wore her black hair in bunches and ran around giggling as I threw the sponge ball towards her. The ball hit Pippa on the shoulder and sometimes in the face and then she would pick it up and throw it back to me.

I would then retrieved the ball from wherever it landed and repeat the game; the sun at my front, my friends to my back; a large green field, a pond full of ducks completed the scene: the perfect day.

I looked up and saw the shadows of three people walking across the field, late arrivals to the fun.

From the outline of the shadows I could tell I knew two of the people. One was Joe, a man who will eventually figure out before his last day on this planet how to live on as a brain in a jar. I hope he can figure out how to live on as a brain in a jar with legs; because without legs his brain is going to get really tired.

Joe looks like a rock and roll scientist and his hair changes colour, I believe, on the basis of what colour uniform Captain Pickard is wearing on the Starship enterprise that month, though he won't thank me for saying so.

He is the blue mark left by a toy train hitting a freshly painted white surface that inspires the owners of the property to paint the entire room blue because they realise they actually prefer the colour to the white.

His voice is a nervous Speak and Spell crashing an expensive ball at a mansion hosted by a rival toy company.

The other shadow was Max; Max is bald like me and looks like the kinder brother of Ming the Merciless because he has a long goatee.

Max is a man in a bear costume at a hospital ward for sick kids. Always bouncing, always smiling; problems dissolve in front of him like vampires forced out into the sun.

His laugh has a naughty edge and his voice is a cross between a horny dolphin trying to hump the leg off a chuckling sailor and a boy finding out he's going to spend that summer in Disney land.

He is both man and boy, infectious, fun and brilliantly saucy.

Walking between Joe and Max was another, entirely different, shadow.

Hers was a shadow I couldn't take my eyes from.

I could tell the outline was feminine because of her shape and long hair.

The shadows of Max and Joe faced her and her head tipped back in laughter, so I knew she was likely attractive because she was the centre of their attention.

I kept throwing the ball at Pippa but I didn't take my eye from the shadow in the middle.

Moment by moment, step by step, they got closer until I could hear Max's laugh and Joe explaining something; and then, finally, I heard her.

Her laugh sounded like that moment you know your life is changing forever; marbles spilling over angel wings playing harps in the orchestra of a play about a boy who very suddenly wished he was more mature.

Her laugh was high pitched, but not too high pitched. It wasn't self conscious, she laughed like she was finding Joe's Star Trek joke genuinely funny and she sounded like she didn't care what her face looked like when she did.

She walked out of the shadows and into the sun.

I immediately knew why she laughed like she didn't care what she looked like; this woman could never look ugly. If she was thrown out of the top of a bell-tower after losing a three hour fight with Quasimodo her contorted body on the pavement below would still be beautiful.

Sometimes Quasimodo sits up in his bell-tower looking over the beautiful city, with the beautiful people, and he thinks how vain, how ugly.

The ball hit me in the face, followed by the sound of drops of rain hitting wind chimes, and I was reminded I was playing catch with Pippa.

The new girl sat down with my group of friends and at first I ignored her.

I thought I'd play it cool and keep throwing the ball to Pippa; I couldn't ask for a better first impression because there's only one first impression better than playing catch with a laughing child and that's saving a baby penguin with a broken wing from drowning.

I knew I couldn't look away for long and when I turned around I regretted I hadn't turned sooner.

She had uncombed blonde hair like sand on an undiscovered shoreline and it fell from her head and over her shoulders like blonde sun rays reflecting through the eyes of curious manatees.

Pippa threw the ball over my head and it rolled to the feet of the mysterious girl.

I had no choice but to retrieve the ball.

I walked over to the blonde girl sitting cross-legged attempting to tense my average, frankly quite pasty and too hairy body into something akin to what I felt a beautiful woman watching me walk towards her might find attractive.

As I got closer I noticed what she was wearing, a flowery skirt and bright blue top; flower ear rings and flip flops.

I noticed her smile; her front two teeth were a mouse dropping larger than the rest, making her look permanently happy, her skin was tanned; but my search for more attributes ended when I was halted in my tracks by the sky in her eyes looking back.

She held up my ball and she smiled.

She didn't look like she'd been clubbing all night.

I took the ball.

And she noticed the sky in my eyes too.

Our eyes kissed, and from that moment we were inseparable.

She told me her name was Lily and we walked into Greenwich and on the way she picked a yellow flower from a bush and giggled as she put it behind her ear, then we went to a pub with all of our friends and she ate a burger and gave me half.

We had our first kiss two weeks later in a club in Brixton, South East London, called The Fridge; the kind of club you enter at night and come out in daylight.

You go there to dance, to sweat, to roll your eyes into the back of your skull and to be free from ringing phones and broken traffic light systems.

Even though the mantra for dance clubs is rather sensibly dance like no one is watching I was dancing whilst thinking any second the music will turn off and I'll be escorted out of the building for trying to falsely impersonate a person having a good time.

Lily could dance, of course, Lily could dance. Every beautiful woman dances.

With green and purple lasers behind her Lily moved slowly and in time with the music in a way that made me not care about anything but the moment watching her.

She danced like no one was watching but she knew that I was.

Her slim arms moved above her head and when they did she looked to the floor, and then she moved her head back up, and our eyes locked again.

Her eyes.

Pale blue, making Lily look soft, but behind the soft blue flames burned.

Her eyes said protect me, but also place a soft hand around my throat and press me against a wall.

Without breaking eye contact Lily danced closer and her wild calm pale-blue eyes reminded me of a tiger who once mauled its owner and in guilt ran to the Himalayas to shave all his fur off and live as a Buddhist monk; to live in silent contemplation for five years until the fierce wild eyes of the tiger melted into an ocean of peace and pale blue moons.

I wanted to touch but I knew it would be her kiss to take from me, and mine to break free from.

I danced like a pancake flipped from a frying pan that upon re-entry missed the pan and hit the edge of the kitchen side, where it flopped broken over its own body to the floor as Lily edged closer and closer.

The music zoned out to nothing.

The lights turned off.

Lily in her little black dress.

Her skirt stopped just above the knee, a large purple flower pinned to her chest.

I could feel her dancing closer, somehow closer to me.

Just an average guy, applauded by fate for simply being, a poem unwritten, the beginning of hearts feeling.

Her hands moved around my waist and mine around hers.

Still we held our eye contact.

Still for some reason I had the confidence to hold the look of this tiger who felt like a flower.

She bit her lip, her eyes bit mine.

Her blonde hair fell from her shoulders; a few beads of sweat collected on the open part of her chest her black dress allowed me to see.

We moved with each other, or perhaps I moved with her, from the moment her hands touched my waist I no longer cared if someone was watching and I could dance.

Suddenly, I could dance.

A dance track connected club, minds and bodies.

Our noses touched.

I moved my hands to either side of her face, and as we stared into the abyss behind our eyes the lyrics drew us closer until there was no space left between us for the words.

"Every time I see your face ...Sends my senses into space ...Every time I hear your name ...love rushes through my veins ...Every moment I feel like I'm falling in love ...Every time I see your face ...Sends my senses into space ...Every time I hear your name ...love rushes through my veins."

And we kissed; soft lips and wet fingertips.

"HUMAN INTERACTION"

Friday 20th August 2010

I've returned home from work to find I have new curtains hanging on a new curtain rail between my main room and kitchen. These curtains are necessary as they divide the two rooms and give me some privacy (there are no curtains over the two large windows in the kitchen).

Mohammad did not tell me he was putting them in nor did he ask my permission to enter my flat so, I suspect, his version of privacy is not quite the same as mine.

It's an odd feeling standing in a place you're trying to call home to be reminded the person you rent from clearly sees your home as a room in his house and his to use as he pleases.

I imagine walking out of the shower naked to find Mohammad in my kitchen making a cup of tea; without looking up from the tea bag, which he is carefully lifting up and sinking back into the hot water, he tells me to put something on whilst I'm in his house.

I never asked for these curtains and Mohammad has been in my flat without asking me.

How many other times whilst I am at work has Mohammad let himself in?

The end justifies the mean.

I feel like I've been handed a sword and told to go and fight Merlin the Wizard; I may have a weapon I can use against Mohammad, a cause to complain, but I by no means have the power to defeat him because he might just kick me out onto the street; cardboard sword in tow.

I stare at his new curtains and my inner rubber chicken defeats my metaphorical robot shark monkey and, as it does, I justify not complaining about a lack of privacy in my own home by concluding it might be ungrateful to complain; because on this occasion Mohammad has given me something I need.

I will thank Mohammad for the curtains next time I see him.

<u>Saturday 21<u>st</u> August 2010</u>

I've had my ear pressed against the front door of my flat for over an hour listening in tense silence for signs my landlord is at the bottom of the stairs, when I realise my light is on and may have given away my position.

I'm a soldier inside enemy territory caught upside down in a tree, tangled in his parachute, who accidentally fired a flare gun into his own face.

I'm listening from my side of my front door for signs Mohammad is watching my front door from the bottom of the stairs for signs I'm in.

I can't relax inside my own flat like a recluse should be able to. If I try and leave I risk being caught in the process of leaving by Mohammad and his need to make he and I best friends.

To distract my imagination from picturing Mohammad naked with a cup up against my front door listening to me listening to him, I clean.

I clean the dark marks on top of the cooker and around the heating rings, bruises delivered by drunken saucepans.

Mohammad will spend his last days thinking he is Keith Floyd, imagining he is with the rabbit from the film Harvey shouting into a bread-bin for a carrot they both swore they saw run in there.

I reach the point I want to leave my flat and risk the flight of stairs to freedom so I decide to pour myself the last glass of wine from the bottle in the fridge, and, somewhat recklessly, neck the contents in one gulp.

With the bottle of wine empty and the alcohol content of my blood rising steadily I'm a thermometer under the wing of a grouse evading bullets fired at its head by red-faced farmers.

I head towards my front door and pull the handle down.

I look back one last time and see an opposable thumb at a prosthetic limb convention for monkeys injured during moon landings; a single grain of rice standing out on the corner of the rug.

I turn so I'm facing my door, ignoring the single grain of rice, and take a deep breath and walk out of my flat.

I scuttle down the stairs, a crab leaving a nightclub at four in the morning after a long night, edgy, paranoid and twitching nervously.

My back is pressed against the wall and my eyes dart in all directions looking for Mohammad.

My hands are unnecessarily pinched together forming crab-like claw shapes.

I make it to the big heavy black front door and, keys in hand, compose myself and quietly unlock the permanently locked inside bolt on the door.

I jiggle my keys in the lock, draw a breath and look over to the door to Mohammad's flat.

The jingle from my keys hitting lock is high pitched and frustratingly jaunty, a row of young teaspoons nervously chattering as they take their seats in an auditorium moments before witnessing their first ever performance.

The bolt unlocks without incident.

My heart pumps.

I open the main front door and close it behind me.

Outside I relock the door in accordance to Mohammad's anti-Somalian policy.

There are no Somalians, I should make that clear, these are Somalians who live inside Mohammad's brain and every night Mohammad locks and unlocks the front door five times, and checks every window twice, in case they crawl out of his ears and ransack his face.

There is no sign of Mohammad outside either.

I have made it to the Promised Land.

The day is bright but cold. A wind chills the air and holds ice cubes against my face whilst whipping up leaves and spinning them in circles; as the leaves spin like visible puppets on invisible strings, I pull my grey coat closer to my body and fasten its three buttons.

There's a tree outside the property and its roots smear under the twisting driveway and continue into the house. The tree is using the concrete to hide behind whilst reclaiming it's land, a giant octopus sucking out the brains of a sailor through the sailors own ears, then using the sailors body as a coat to lure future sailors into a similar trap.

I walk to the end of the uneven path; fingers pointing outwards from my hands resting down by my sides to increase balance.

I head across the road and walk aimlessly along pavement, a nun who has renounced religion and swapped her bible for a one-way ticket to Amsterdam.

The meaning of the words "god" and "exist" are paradoxical. If the question was "Does God unexist?" we may logically reach the same miracle.

I don't know where to go.

I don't know what people do when they aren't inside wondering what to do outside.

There's a pub around the corner called The Windmill but I'll need some reading material first, to hide behind, should people attempt interaction.

The newspaper is the equivalent of the modern day castle; as long as you have a newspaper in a pub, and you're reading, you're inside your castle and safe.

Once inside the pub, and sitting at your table, looking up over your newspaper and around the room is the equivalent of dropping your drawbridge; locking eye contact with another drawbridge dropper is both high risk and dangerous as every other drawbridge dropper is either a possible knight bearing humorous tales of unknown towns or a peasant carrying the plague.

Enter a pub alone without reading material and, to everyone else in the pub already reading, you are the peasant with the plague; needy and desperate to penetrate the walls of well thought through castles.

I enter a shop thinking I'll buy the Guardian. If I'm in a pub reading the Guardian and drinking a wine I'm a civilised man of the world, but, if I'm in a pub drinking without the Guardian I'm just an alcoholic the people with books will think illiterate.

The flaw in my plan is The Windmill is in Kilburn, South West London; a short walk from Willesden Green.

Whereas in some places the Guardian would get an a l knowing nod of approval from a local gentleman in his Sunday best walking his dog, in Kilburn it's going to suggest I have spare change to give the annoying alcoholic who stands outside the shop asking everybody for a pound.

He doesn't even pretend to be homeless.

When he gets a pound he goes into the shop and buys a can of Stella, sits outside the shop on the floor, drinks it and then goes back to asking people for a pound. That's his whole day.

Occasionally he will cross the road to enter the cafe and shout sexually aggressive verbiage at the two blonde girls trying their best to ignore him and serve customers.

He is always inexplicably covered in dust and looks like he spends his evenings going round and round inside a cement mixer, in an old dusty attic, blowing dead air from the glass surface of old paintings into his hair.

I enter the shop and the shop doesn't sell The Guardian.

I look at my alternate reading options:

 "The Sun" if there is an intelligent girl in the pub there would be no faster way of her judging me.

I'm single and the only reason I leave my flat, on the occasions I do, is in hope the sleeve of my coat will somehow get caught in the hood of a woman as she passes by, both of us laughing and trying to untangle ourselves as we look up and, for a moment, catch each other's eyes.

"The Mirror" strikes me as a stupid name for any non-reflective material.

I'm not sure if I grew when I entered, but now I'm inside the shop it feels small, like I'm stuffed under a toy bed inside a dolls house.

The newspaper rack is too near my face and there's no distance from me to the counter.

I look away from the newspaper rack and towards the sound of a breathing bear and realise the shop feels tiny because of the presence of the shop worker; a man so large he makes the shop feel small and the outside seem far away, unreachable, yet vast and oxygenated.

I'm staring at the shop-keeper equivalent to the giant man inside the smart car.

He's Asian with short black hair.

His head is the size of the average PC monitor and shaped like a Tetris block.

His nose spreads flat against his face, a quick instinctive glance down to witness the space where his knuckles should be on his wild boar-head sized hands tells me this isn't a man I want to upset, but from the direction of his one eyebrow, pointing directly at me, I appear to have succeeded in doing exactly that.

"Are you going to buy something?"

His voice sounds like someone punching a small dog in the face with a big dog; a barking, growling snarl yelping up at the end of his sentence making his question a threat.

He leans towards me and I feel my testicles shrivel in my jeans.

In fairness to the shopkeeper, his question has made me realise how long I've been standing in front of two newspapers, not even reading them; just watching the front pages whilst thinking about how small the world feels sometimes.

I mutter meekly about needing something to read in the pub and grab The Sun.

I hand over my money but already know there's no way I'm reading this paper in the pub. Really I don't want either paper, but this hulk of a shopkeeper has forced my hand and before I know it I'm back out on the sidewalk having spent sixty pence on a newspaper I have no intention of reading.

I walk the few yards from the shop to the pub and pause for a moment before going in.

Knowing I have a newspaper, but one I'm not going to read, essentially means I'm about to enter the pub with no reading material. Despite knowing the rules of the castle I'm about to enter as nothing more than one of the annoying plague bearing peasants.

Anyone with any sense will turn their back the moment they see me coming.

I enter the pub using the door on the left.

The pub has one bar running along the upper left wall and three booths sit to my right.

A cartel of round tables and chairs take up the space between the bar and booths.

I always imagine 1920's gangsters huddling around these tables, smoking from pipes in thin pin-striped suits, with thinner moustaches and fine-lined morals.

In the far right of the main room are the toilets.

The floors, bar and tables are all made from the same dark wood and three large windows take up the entire length of the wall opposite the bar.

These windows are tinted, and the tinted windows combine with the dark wooden floors to make The Windmill feel like a mafia owned illegally licensed strip bar minus the girls, but with the same clientele.

The main room thins into a fireplace where two old light brown leather sofas face each other like two retired American daytime TV show hosts arguing over whose face transplant has been more successful at standing the test of time.

The withering TV hosts are divided from coming to blows by a wobbly pot-marked, scratched table.

An old one-legged unbalanced chicken that once fought cock fights, to this day unable to remove the ashtray on top of its head.

Continue walking past the battered sofas and damaged table and you end up in the garden, The Windmills main feature.

Over hanging plants, bushes, winding concrete paths and lanterns make the outside resemble the Blue Peter garden on acid.

The pub is busy, far busier than usual; I look up behind a sea of heads to see a football match is about to kick off.

I shuffle to the front of the bar where I thumb nervously at the edge of the wood, and wait twice as long as anyone else; I'm swallowed by an environment where the philosophy seems to be oppositional to waiting and is based on pure impulse.

Actual philosophy cannot exist.

If people wait for a bus they line up. If people wait at a cash point, they line up. When people wait at a bar to be served alcohol they barge their way to the front and wave their money around whilst shouting facts about their monthly salary, penis size and how many bedrooms their home has.

I'm eventually served by a young guy with straw hair and an infectious smile.

Whilst the cattle of angry drunk cows moo at him to milk them first he ambles around like he's trying to find the right size shoe at a bowling alley.

I hope in another life cows have wings and get to dance on the face of unarmed wingless flies.

To the background noise of a hundred mooing cows I take grip of my large white wine and, as my fingers touch the base of the glass, the mooing cows become singing angels and I don't mind how they queue.

I glance up to the corner and briefly take in the screen everyone watches.

Between the computer screen at home and work, the television screen at home, and my mobile phone, which carries a screen between my home and work screens, I have a lot of screens.

So I decide today I'm going to avoid people *and* flashing screens.

I shuffle out of the immediate herd and head around the bar, past the retired melting TV hosts and unstable chicken, and into the garden.

There's a television in the garden; naturally.

The television has been mounted underneath a roof so it's protected from rain and underneath the mounted television sits two more battered sofas and several dented coffee tables.

There must be a shelter nearby housing abused sofas.

I look around and take note of the people in the garden watching the television.

In the future people won't go outside to watch the sunrise; they'll watch the sunrise on televisions whilst huddled in dark rooms behind closed curtains.

I take a seat on an empty bench and I'm immediately overwhelmed by the heat coming from the heater above me. The day is not warm, but this heater feels like it's been burning all night long and may have been the inspiration behind the 1983 Lionel Ritchie hit.

If I had a couple of eggs in my pockets I could crack them on the table and have fried eggs and mulled white wine.

The off button for the heater fusing my coat to my skin is directly above me; but it looks complicated because there's more than one button.

There's a strong possibility I could stand and try and turn it off, fail, and be publically humiliated.

The button could embarrass me in the same public fashion as the window that refuses to budge on packed commuter trains.

I look around because I know I can't be the only person suffering in silence and, sure enough, every sweaty red face I glance at screams for someone else to be the first person to stand up and summon the help of someone with the appropriate knowledge to spare us from burning alive in a pub garden in central London.

I can't bring myself to be the person who stands up and says what everyone else is thinking, so I, like them, try and convince myself I can't possibly be as hot as I think I am.

We are all in this lie of pretending the temperature levels of the garden heaters are normal, and we are all in this lie together.

We all look to the door; all hoping the next person who leaves the pub and joins us in the garden of hell will be stronger than us. We need a more expressive, less patient and volatile type.

We need a leader.

The doors to the garden swing open and an older lady in a long pink skirt and flowery shirt makes a hash of walking down the one step and eventually takes a seat under the last empty table in natures garden of man-made heat, electronic screens, and people heavily smoking.

The lady sits directly under a furnace moonlighting as standard outdoor heating equipment, just like me, and just like everyone else.

Circumstances have made her one of us and now the inevitability of time, and the impatience of old people and a good education will set us all free.

She is pale skinned and perhaps in her forties or older; her hair blends from blonde to grey as it's entering the menopausal phase, when women's hair shrinks into t ght curly balls and sits on top of their heads, scrunches of wool blowing in the wind hanging from the mouths of recently shot deer.

Her cheeks are large and wide, her eyes small and her nose too tiny to describe; she very much resembles a puffer fish in an ill-fitting wig tiring from defending herself from an invisible enemy living in her pocket, which might also explain the permanent scowl on her forehead.

Give a man a fish and he'll eat for a day, teach a man to fish and he'll evolve to become so skilled at fishing he destroys the ocean and kills every last fish.

She looks like she's given up on waiting for something exciting to happen in her life; which could very well be good news for the overheating people in the garden because that mindset is the mindset of an activist.

Her drink of choice is a good sign.

She's drinking a coffee, showing she's more than happy to do things her way regardless of her environment.

She doesn't need to fit in; she doesn't require invisibility to sustain comfort.

She is drinking cappuccino, not regular filter coffee, so standard as a standard is not acceptable to her. This is a subtle conflict because the implication is she does, therefore, care at least how some people think of her; but not us. Not the beer drinking, wine guzzling class of Kilburn.

Her face twists into a mystery.

She's found a baby horse in her garden shed.

Her face unfolds into anger.

She looks up into the flames of the heater.

We all know what she's feeling; we all feel the same way.

Complain.

For the love of God complain.

I watch as her lips purse together and, in slow motion, the beautiful sounding tut she makes falls from her lips and spills across the garden like an iron barrel rumbling over a floor of forgotten musical triangles.

This is the start of our revolution. She's going to turn around and tut once more and then say "honestly, it's like a bloody oven out here isn't it?" and everyone will agree.

This woman may not be wearing a kilt, but she is our William Wallace.

We will build signs and find pitchforks and storm into the manager's office and demand for the heaters to be turned off and we'll be led by this woman; this wonderful puffer fish-faced woman and once the dust has settled we'll petition the council and ask nicely for a statue of her to commemorate our finest hour.

The woman stands, picks up her cappuccino, and walks wobble-bottomed away from the heater, through the arches and to the area of the garden without heaters; where she sits down with a smile in relative comfort.

By simply moving to a table without a heater the woman has managed to surprise us all.

Moving is not in the rules; everyone else in the garden knows the British way is to not help yourself as others do, and then complain about not being helped, and about others being helped.

The rest of us briefly glance at each other and return to our slightly charred papers and over-heated conversations, red faced and sweaty palmed, with the understanding we will not be moved.

We have stuck our flags in these overheated tables and we don't care if we burn alive.

Our coffee drinking potential leader has become a symbol of our enemy. We, the garden people, batten down our hatches in the belief soon the winds will change and a storm will come.

The coffee drinking woman will be sitting on the wrong table then, and our stubborn ways will prove correct.

I take a large glug of warm wine in celebration.

Darkness slowly creeps over the day as it fades into early evening.

The top of my head is sore, red and peeling.

From underneath my burning heater I look left as a girl looks right.

I'm not sure if I look at girls as they look away, or if girls never look at me, or if when I look at girls they look away because they were looking at me.

If this was a film that girl would hold eye contact and I'd think of a charming first line to captivate her heart and mind. Instead, I look away at the awkward timing, finish the last of my warm wine, and decide to go home to moisturise my burning scalp.

I make it back into my flat with no signs of Mohammad.

I'm sitting on my bed; the television flashes and the glass of wine in my hand whispers there isn't enough wine in the world.

The front door downstairs (the main door to the house) opens then closes.

A further locking noise, then the door opens again, followed by another locking noise before the noises finally end.

Mohammad is checking the front door is locked for the Somalians living inside his head.

As I close my eyes I wonder what it must be like to be scared in your own home of someone who doesn't exist.

When your enemy is in your head, making the world your enemy, there is nowhere to hide or run.

The only peace to be found is found in sleep, but sleep is an enemy too, because when you're asleep you think you are vulnerable, they can get you.

I don't think Mohammad sleeps.

Not like I do.

"WHISKY EYES CRY TEARS OF POISON"

Saturday 10th September 2010

There was a time when people slept when tired; now we drink coffee.

I've not long been awake; the day is early, too early for my red brain and throbbing eyes.

I'm on a tube on the London underground.

My face is the proud owner of five day stubble, my hands shake, my dirty little secret; the hangover from failing to control the fallout from teenager to adult.

I'm the stereotypical burnt out cop seen in American movies only ahead for me isn't my last chance to be a hero; it's Swiss Cottage tube station.

I'm staring at the underground map opposite me with unconscionable frustration.

My impatience with nothing and everything is paramount.

The lights in the ceiling of the underground train are too low, too bright and the sound is the silence of people uncomfortable in an unnatural environment clunking against the constant churning of comfortable machinery.

Should anybody talk they have to shout, and once they shout everybody looks up, steel eyes and robotic tuts, exchanging looks affirming the talker is not part of the programme.

There's no good place to need a drink and not be able to have one, but stuck on the London underground, when you can look at the diagram in front of you and count how far away you are from natural light is one of the worst.

The tube is empty except for a guy sitting next to me.

The guy sitting next to me is asleep and breathing too heavily. I glance at him to take in his full face. He's a slim man. Pasty white skin, stubble and red blotches around his face defy his potential beauty like road blocks on a formula one racing track. His nose is broken yet feverish and stutters around aimlessly on his face, a lone pigeon recently surrounded by all the bird seed it could ever eat.

Long thin hair falls down from his head then curls upwards and away from his shoulders, grown men avoiding the stare of medusa. His suit is a cheap grey, but more expensive than any suit I will ever own; he completes the professional rebel look with trainers.

He's in his early twenties and either he, or something near us both, smells of dolphin breath.

The train stops and the judder wakes the man up from his bodies attempt to recapture moments taken from him by a life too pressured. His eyes dart left, then right, and he leaps up and escapes through the doors at the last second.

I watch as he runs down the platform, something tells me he'll be moving fast until the next time his body can steal a moment back.

The area still smells of dolphin breath.

A sensation it may be me who smells of tuna washes over me and I am the moment a beached whale accepts it's unable to help itself back into the sea.

Given the current plight of whales we need to start saying we had a "whale of a time" only when backed into a corner and harpooned to death.

I search my coat pockets for a half opened tin of tuna, which is not as implausible at it sounds; I once pulled the remote control for my television out of my coat pocket on a packed train.

I find no tins in my coat pockets and scan the rest of the tube half expecting to see a dolphin sitting at the end of one of the carriages, legs crossed, deeply engrossed in this morning's edition of The Financial Times.

Now the over worked young businessman has left I can see the rest of the empty carriage, only the carriage is not completely empty.

Sitting further along on the same row, to my right, is an ex-girlfriend I dated when I was eighteen.

Just us in the carriage, on the train, underground, in London for all we know.

Just us in the world, for a moment.

Rebecca is a beautiful girl with long dark hair weaving and flowing like she's in a constant shampoo commercial. Her face is smooth, pale in complexion and unwrinkled.

Her nose is a ballerina in the heavy metal band of her face. Which is not to criticise her face, which is stunning, but to highlight the perfection of her nose.

Her smile slants away slightly to one side, which might normally look strange, but on Rebecca it gives her face a character which defines her laugh. Her voice, to me, has always sounded stronger than how I believe she thinks it sounds.

Her eyes are brown and calm. They don't dart around like some eyes and, when I talk to her, they hold their ground, tiny guards to the brain refusing to let me in.

She's a beautiful woman, a model making good money from her work.

I was a young idiot when we dated, eighteen, and inside the man, the last organ to develop a voice is his heart.

The only difference between how she looks today and how she looked when we dated, from my brief glance across the tube, is she no longer wears braces.

I think her brace made Rebecca doubt her beauty at the time we dated; which to me is, and was, a great shame because she was always beautiful.

When she was in a good mood she would run fast and turn her run into a cartwheel just for the fun of it, but only ever on concrete; I always liked that.

I glance over, look away, glance back again.

I hear a familiar voice convincing me there's no need to talk. I might enjoy talking, I maybe even *should* talk; I probably *need* to talk, but I'm not going to.

We met not long ago for a brief coffee and I had a sense the reason she met with me was half curiosity and half wanting my eyes to observe unobtainable beauty.

Darth Vader destroyed the entire universe because of unobtainable love; I picked at the paper edge of my Americano and thought about asking her to part her legs a little for me in public.

After the coffee Rebecca sent me a message then ignored my response a couple of times, so I decided our relationship was less about friendship and perhaps more about an ex girlfriend scoring points.

As a consequence, I blocked her on Facebook, like adults do.

And now here she is, after I blocked her on facebook, sitting nine chairs away on the only empty train carriage in the world.

Life is funny like that.

Life is driving a bus into magicians; apart from the odd rabbit head landing on the bonnet most of the moments you won't see coming.

All Rebecca has to do is look left and she'll see me, any movement will draw her attention.

I look straight ahead, narrow eyed, hoping she doesn't turn her head.

I don't know why I'm like I am these days.

Alcohol has played a part in rotting my brain, and alcohol breeds false confidence, and the natural consequence of relying on false confidence is the longer I've relied on it the greater the damage I've incurred to my own.

I stare straight ahead, hoping not to be seen; feeling relieved I'm getting off at the next stop, Bond street tube station in central London.

The creaking train stops, the doors open, and I move off the train.

Everything about the London underground not only seems old but feels like it was never young.

I enter the every man for himself world of underground human behaviour; hundreds of people spill from tube shaped objects and race to be first out of the dark tunnel, ejaculating sperm running for life through the female womb.

A body to my left bumps into me; forced to bump into me by the body bumping into them.

I glace left and shrink when I see Rebecca.

Our shoulders touch.

This is the kind of bumping into each other when bumper pretends to ignore the bumped and vice versa. Each person hopes to stay invisible, neither party can take their peripheral vision from the other, in case the other person turns around to notice them first.

If one person breaks the stand-off and looks then the game is up and both have to notice each other, and consequently fall around laughing and squealing like a couple of three year olds running away from their first wave.

So we both stand, shoulders touching. Our peripheral visions stare at the sides of each other's faces as we both wait to see if the other will make the first move, both hoping the first move never happens.

Human instinct says you have to make eye contact when apologising about something irrelevant to a complete stranger.

We fight our instinct.

We throw the rule book out of the window and sustain pretending we aren't who the other knows we are.

Another moment people look at each other is the point just before embarking on escalators; who takes the lead, who falls behind, this is all done with terrible politeness.

Everyone wants the stranger they don't know to go first up the escalator.

Yet here, we both have to choose the opposite, one has to fall behind, and we can't embark upon the two second dance of *no you*. We have to be rude.

I move ahead, not looking up, Rebecca falls behind me.

With Rebecca behind me, we exhale collective relief. We've successfully participated in ignoring each other; if we hadn't been so in synch, we could never have done it.

Once I'm up the escalator, outside and walking in natural light, my fears dissimilate through ego and question how Rebecca could not want to say hello.

I text Rebecca with a light hearted comment referencing the situation in the hope we can poke fun at each other, with my intention to apologise for blocking her on Facebook.

I text her, my way of building a bridge:

"I smell of tuna."

I get a text back from Rebecca immediately:

"I don't know what you are talking about."

Either Rebecca hadn't seen me, or that wasn't Rebecca.

I smile.

If Rebecca is telling the truth, and she likely is, I blocked her on Facebook and just sent her a random text message about fish.

Saturday 11th September 2010

I'm on the floor of my flat gulping the remains of a bottle of wine.

I listen to the rain crash against my kitchen windows, a guy living under a bridge on a dark rainy night.

I should get off the floor and head to the pub.

I don't fancy The Windmill so hop on the tube and head a few stops into central London to a pub called The Spread Eagle.

An eagle playing chess with a serious face, but with a flea tapping his bald spot to entertain a lady flea so small he can't feel it.

The Eagle is not a great pub. I would go as far as saying it's a bad pub. The Eagle takes the philosophy *if it ain't broke don't fix it* to new heights by adhering to the policy *if it seems broken turn your back and maybe it will go away.*

Average food, chipped wooden tables and dark red peeling walls are The Eagles hallmark.

The pub is also home to London's smallest toilet for men; one urinal, and a cubical used as a storage cupboard for broken chairs.

What makes The Eagle a good pub are the people who drink in the pub and the staff.

Despite my best efforts to remain alone they have a way of making me feel I'm not.

The manager is a bubbly blonde character who wanders around the pub in the evening drunkenly clutching half empty bottles of white wine to her large breasts, she spends her days complaining the white wine stocks are low and questions her staff on their measurements.

She's in her mid to late thirties and thinks every man who talks to her is trying to chat her up, which means if you're the unfortunate person who happens to catch one of the rare moments she decides to work, you have to wait half an hour for your drink as she attempts to turn the words "white wine please" into a chat up line, which she manages to do, before handing your drink over with a rolling of her eyes like you've just flirted over the line because she's trying to work.

Her skin is tanned from the many holidays she takes in the year and the thin line of permanent black hair on her top lip agitates me, because I question how she can miss it when shaving her beard.

She holds an air of superiority I don't think she warrants, so for the most part I avoid her.

I order a wine from the lady behind the bar who I know to look at but not to talk to, and climb the wide staircase to the small area upstairs, to a usually empty place.

There's a guy and a girl on one table, I sit in the corner as far from them as I can.

I drink from my glass and stare at the dark wooden table, which looks like it would rather be somewhere else.

You and me both; a broader sense.

The guy laughs loudly on the table and the girl laughs along. I listen to their conversation and the man talks, then laughs once he's finished his sentence, the girl laughs along with his laugh.

When he laughs first it's because he knows he's just finished saying something unfunny.

They *seem* to be having a laugh.

The guy is in his forties with short grey hair styled into a side parting. Something about his side parting tells me his mum parted his hair for him when he was ten years old, and he's never thought to change it.

He's hunched over a little and his voice sounds rounded, full and soft at the top but harder than it needs to be at times around the edges. When he's worried about whether she'll laugh his voice clutters and clanks and clashes into a more common tone, a breadbin full of stale bread falling down a staircase in a block of council flats.

The guy talks of money and at the end of his fact about the FTSE he laughs and so does the girl. The girl is younger, in her twenties and blonde. She wears a short skirt and white top, at times her eyes widen and her mouth gawps as she tries to swallow the information she cannot understand, periodically resembling a fish out of water.

The guy ignores her look screaming *I don't understand* and the girl chooses not to explain she isn't following.

I'm alone and sitting with nobody but I wonder, if they were more honest with each other, whether the consequence of that honesty would mean they would be sitting alone too.

He laughs then she laughs then I laugh.

Oops.

They look over at me and I look back; a moment of awkwardness I look away from but still feel.

I finish my wine and enter the worst toilet in London.

The toilet is only one urinal and so small only one person at a time can enter.

The cubicle is to the right, but floor to ceiling high with bits of broken wood, old chairs and upside down tables.

Whenever I enter the toilet I push the cubicle door open to check if the cubicle is still in the condition it's been in for at least the two years I've been coming to the pub.

The toilet does not disappoint. Not only is the cubicle piled high with wood, the toilet is still unflushed and contains the oldest unflushed poo in London.

I'll be sad when the old poo goes because every day the old poo survives it sets a new record.

I close the door of the cubicle and enter the toilet. I shuffle along, with the wall pressed against the end of my nose, and squeeze myself along to the urinal.

As I'm urinating I consider no matter where anyone is in the world. No matter how lovely their surroundings or nice their food, they're probably much closer to an unflushed poo than they would like.

I wash my hands, return to my table, pick up my glass and head to the bar for another drink.

Sveta has flirted with me for two years and has just started her shift.

One time she handed back my change and held onto my hand for a second longer than needed. We held eye contact until we knew at least one of us liked the other.

I've never taken the flirting any further than the looks, jokes and laughter.

Long curly hair falls down to her waist, sprayed into place, reminding me of eighties pop videos. If I close my eyes and think of her the first image I see is her smile, because she smiles a lot, and the second image is her walking down an alleyway with smoke in the background wearing a white suit singing a power ballad.

She has large brown eyes and I like her accent when she says my name, because she makes me sound like I have the answer to the question she is about to ask.

She always asks how I am and waits around until she knows.

Some might say that's because it's her job to ask and the bar is too narrow to put any significant distance between her question and my answer.

She's attractive; guys far better looking than me stand at the bar talking to her, hoping for the same interest she shows in me.

I stand at the bar watching her eyes watch mine as she serves me more wine and my usual strength, or weakness, dissolves through a combination of alcohol and lack of sex, because I'm returning the look and thinking tonight, with the bar lights glowing behind her, Sveta looks like Angelina Jolie before she met Billy Bob Thornton.

I should leave. Instead I ask Sveta when she finishes her shift.

I can't believe the words coming out of my mouth because I'm sounding full of confidence.

Sveta tells me she finishes at midnight and seems excited.

I write down my address and phone number on a chip-grease stained receipt, and she tells me she might not be able to come around until really late.

I don't tell her it's been years since I hugged a girl, because I don't want to sound like a serial killer.

I tell Sveta I'll be awake, I want to see her. We can have some fun.

She nods and smiles.

I leave the pub around eleven, stagger into the dark, wave to Sveta and fall, pushed over by myself.

I stand, Sveta now flaps her arms in my direction, laughing; I wonder who she thinks she sees in me.

On the tube on my way home I get a text message from an old friend, Nicola.

Nicola is no bigger than a thimble but possesses the largest breasts I've never seen. She has long blonde hair, a small round head and a small round nose. Her tongue piercing makes her sound, during specific words, like a broom trying to sweep empty cans from grey pavements.

Her text says she thinks people think something is going on between us, and I respond there isn't so who cares, let people think whatever makes them happy.

My phone vibrates again and through bleary eyes I read she wants me to ask her out.

I can hardly see my phone, so I text her back two words: Burger Costume.

My phone vibrates again and I read her response "arrogant prick."

I put my phone in my pocket and feel my eyes getting heavy.

Sometimes Nicola is a bit like my wife of twenty years I never married; I get problems sometimes I don't understand and at Christmas I get turned down sexually.

I get back to my flat and sit on my bed with a glass of wine in my hand.

I feel my head getting sleepy, but I can't fall asleep because of Sveta.

Don't fall asleep.

Odd turn of phrase, *fall,* because when I close my eyes to sleep I don't *fall* into darkness, I remind myself it's always there.

Even with my eyes open and in daylight, a single blink reminds.

Don't fall asleep.

"THE RE-DOCKING OF PROFESSOR MERRYDINKLE"

Sunday 12th September 2010

I fell asleep.

The day feels too early to be this bright.

Daylight beams through my kitchen window, burning my eyes, showing the cracks on my skin. Showing beneath the surface, I'm aging.

I'm in my soft bed listening to Mohammad ta king to the Polish builder outside my front door.

My front door is so thin I hear everything happening outside my room; I'm living in a dolls house with the roof removed.

Mohammad is talking about me to the builder, believing I can't hear what he's saying because he can't see me.

The builder has ginger curly hair on top of his head resembling a nest owned by a confused hen with OCD who insists on keeping the twigs in perfect symmetry, and a thick moustache giving him the look of a McDonald's manager from 1970 who spends his evenings sitting in the smoky back row of theatres in Soho.

He's tall and muscular with hands the size of shopping baskets and, on the one occasion I did briefly meet him, I stared into his eyes and was shocked by their darkness.

His nose is broken in three places and is the size and shape of a chicken nugget; a deep scar runs the length of his cheek hinting at a violent past.

Old tattoos fade on his arms.

The builder may have killed another human being at some point in his life.

Mohammad has mentioned to me the builder only knows four words in English, those four words Mohammad says he taught the builder. How Mohammad met a builder from Poland and then managed to get the builder to convert his house into studio flats without either party understanding a word the other said is beyond me.

However, somehow the curious relationship of the racist deaf old man and the violent looking Polish builder who cannot understand English seems be working.

Mohammad is telling the builder he wants him to put a blind up in my room. The builder says nothing in response. I know the builder is there, because if he isn't Mohammad is outside my room talking to himself about me.

Mohammad says he thinks I might still be asleep, and I listen with relief as he walks back down the stairs.

I only hear one person walk down the stairs.

Perhaps the builder has work to do elsewhere in the building.

I'm so hung-over Bruce Willis has crawled into my brain and thrown out Alan Rickman. I miss Alan Rickman; he made my brain hurt less and encouraged me to take an interest in German politics.

I sit up and remember last night I took Sveta's phone number and told her to come round, and she said she was going to.

I passed out.

I feel bad, lean over the edge of my bed and pick my phone up from the floor.

Apart from my bed and the chest of drawers my computer is on, I have no furniture; so anything normally on a table is on the floor.

My television, a lamp, my mobile phone, my mobile phone charger and seven books sit on the wooden floor amongst four bottles of white wine, the last I don't remember buying or drinking.

I'm slowly creating my own squat, but instead of breaking in, I pay all of my money over to my landlord, and in return he controls the heating.

I check my phone and have two text messages from Sveta.

I don't like I've not kept my word to Sveta.

The first text message from Sveta arrived at just after midnight, and asks me if I'm still awake and says she's really looking forward to seeing me.

The second text was sent an hour later.

In the second text Sveta explains she can't make it; but I think the second text is probably a reaction to me failing to respond to her first one.

A feeling of sober dread creeps through my floorboards, a grey ghost grips my stomach with invisible claws, I feel bad for Sveta because I fell asleep, and I feel bad for myself because that was the chance I've been waiting for, and running from; the chance to get close to a woman again.

The familiar feeling of the room beginning to slowly spin takes hold in my mind, and my skin starts to sweat despite my flat being cold.

I move slowly out of bed and grab the bottles of wine and move them to the bin, the rest of the clutter I move to the end of my bed so it's less visible.

I shuddle into my kitchen, desperate and helpless, a blind man following the yelp of his guide dog into a cave neither will come back out of.

A "shuddle" is a word I use to describe a shuffle and a huddle. The movement is cautious; a shuffle screaming *safety first and nothing to see here* all in one crouching side step.

Alcohol breeds paranoia and as a consequence my first thoughts are often how I want to be left alone. My phone rings and its Mohammad. My instinct is to not answer, but I know if I don't he'll just knock on my door.

I cannot escape.

Trapped in my own home.

Trapped in a big room in his house.

If I don't answer my door he'll just let himself n.

Mohammad *tells* me he's putting the blind I've been waiting for up in my room.

I don't tell Mohammad now is not a good time for me, nor do I tell him I haven't been waiting for a blind.

Instead I tell Mohammad the timing is good because I was about to go out.

I want a hot shower but the only two temperatures my shower emits are freezing cold or skin boiling hot. Whenever I have a shower I have to hold the showerhead away from my body until the exact fifteen second window between the water temperature moving from freezing cold to boiling hot.

During this fifteen second window I wash myself as fast as possible with my right hand whilst my left hand twists the heat button.

I'm an astronaut desperately trying to get a response from his crashing spaceship.

The fifteen seconds of useable temperature is reached by flicking the switches, then waiting three to five minutes with the water pointing away from me.

I have to repeat this process all over again to get another fifteen seconds of usable water.

On more than one occasion during the fifteen second window the water pressure has dropped to practically nothing, so I'm just standing naked, cold, angry and shivering.

The shower is not an enjoyable experience.

I put on some clothes and elect to not take a shower. The only thing worse than having to have a cold shower is having to get out of a cold shower into a colder flat.

This morning my flat is cold because it's cold outside.

I pour myself a strong coffee.

My tongue has been replaced with a nun crying alone on a step, so I feel heat on my tongue but taste only nothingness.

There's a knock at my door, not the type of knock from someone asking to come in, but the type of knock from someone who has already broken in.

I walk up the little step from my cold kitchen into my cold all in one front room and bedroom.

Mohammad is standing hump backed and whale eyed in the middle of the main room.

Not even by the door.

The builder is taller and silent, like his assassin, and stands behind him.

Mohammad shows me the blinds he wants to put up in my kitchen. I know I don't have a choice. He wants to put them up in what he sees as his window.

Mohammad will buy whatever is cheapest, thinking he's saving money; but everything he gets from the pound shop disintegrates and infects its environment.

What he's showing me are not blinds; but I nod by head because I don't want to get into a conversation with him about the difference between a blind and a set of rolled up paper.

They're a horrid lime green colour.

Two rolled up bits of paper not thick enough to keep out the sun, thin enough to turn the colour of the light entering my flat pale lime green; making my entire flat lock seasick.

I watch and marvel as Mohammad explains in complex, fast English to the builder what he wants the builder to do.

The builder does not respond.

They walk past me and into the kitchen, Mohammad picks his nose as he moves, samples what he discovers, and flicks the contents down into the corner by my bed.

I follow them into the kitchen, biting my tongue, wanting to explain etiquette, and breaking and entering.

Mohammad finishes explaining and the builder blankly blinks at Mohammad.

Mohammad points to the green rolled up piece of paper on the side of my kitchen and points to the window. As he points to the window Mohammad grunts from the back of his throat, which I don't think is intentional.

The builder stares at Mohammad.

He's not an idiot and has made the connection between the rolled up paper and the massive window he's looking out of.

The builder's arms are folded; he waits for the child to finish explaining what they learnt at school that day.

Mohammad points to the rolled up paper again, and once more to the window.

"Understand."

The first time I have heard the builder speak.

His one word is delivered from a mouth that's been hit with more fists than its kissed woman's lips. There's no love to it, no rounding of his words. He couldn't care less to be liked.

The builder said one of his words; I wonder what his other three are.

I've taken a step back, perhaps wary of his confidence.

If I were in his shoes I'd be nodding my head and laughing unnecessarily, a clown at his first job interview for a city job.

This guy doesn't even nod his head.

He just stares.

No smiles, nothing.

Having a repair guy in my flat makes me an idiot in my own home because he's fixing something I can't.

I tell Mohammad I'm going out and go for a walk with a loose plan to visit the local Sainsbury's.

I would much rather be in bed to get on with my hangover in peace, but walking alone in the bitter London cold is a better option than hanging out with Mohammad and the builder in the comparative warm.

I walk down Melrose Avenue, the road one over from mine, hung-over; all thinking reduced to fitting surfboards in toasters.

A policeman stands outside a house on guard with a serious face, neighbours peer over walls trying to take in the seriousness of it all.

Police tape across the front door of the property indicates someone has been murdered inside, possibly a wife whistling to herself mid laundry.

Nobody is whistling now. No sound comes from the house.

At the end of the road is a church. I watch a pregnant bride and her groom exit the church to the sounds of laughter; happy tears drop on beaming faces as confetti falls from tightly gripped, numb yet gleeful fingertips.

Two different ends of the same road, two different stages of life; one paid back and one still using time borrowed.

I'm standing in a queue in Sainsbury's and in front of me a girl, no older than six or seven, asks her dad what a hen night is.

The little girl has blonde hair worn in pigtails and the wide expressive face children have when they have a world in front of them and are full of questions, before their adult face narrows and becomes a face beaten back by the realisation adults, though implausible to think when a child, don't know any of the answers.

The dad wears a long black coat and glasses. He has short, receding grey hair and a narrow face.

He explains to his daughter, in a playful voice, a hen night is a night when ladies go out to parks around London and chase hens. I hear this and smile because I think this guy thinks it's okay to lie to his child if he puts on a silly voice; but the kids not buying it.

The dad, misreading the thought behind my smile, asks her daughter to ask me.

I feel a tug on my sleeve and look down at a little wide-faced fact searcher on a mission from her brain.

I smile at the girl and look up at the dad. The dad winks. He glances down and looks into my shopping basket and notices the contents are three bottles of wine. He involuntarily swallows, but it's too late, his daughter is already tugging on my sleeve based on his advice.

The daughter asks her question.

A hen night is a woman's last chance to legally drain fluid from random men's balls using their mouths.

I tell the girl her dad is correct and one of my friends went out on a hen night once to a local park and came back with four hens.

The daughter is surprised, and now completely believes the story as two adults have confirmed it.

I've lied to a six year old.

My choice was please the dad at the expense of letting the girl know adults are liars, or accuse the dad of lying to his own daughter in the middle of Sainsbury's.

Nicola calls me and asks me out for a drink with some of her friends. I've said no to Nicola a few times and I try again to explain I'm not sociable, and at my age additional friends are going to be burdens to bury in a few years but she insists, and like Mohammad before Nicola, I hear myself saying yes and hate myself a little bit for it.

*

Nicola is already impressively pissed. I am by no means sober after heading back to my new lime green flat and drinking a bottle of wine by myself, but Nicola's words are slurring and her basic cognitive functions (the ability to grip her glass and not spill most of her drink over her toes) are failing.

Nicola stops every fifteen minutes or so to look at her toes poking out of her shoes. Her open toes are painted purple but appear to have been painted purple not by a woman using a small brush in close proximity to them, but by a painter and decorator using a paint brush on a broom handle from across the room.

As Nicola stares at her toes her face screws up in puzzlement, in her head someone has just thrown a canoe at her and screamed the Jet Ski she sold them doesn't work.

She looks up at each of her friends with a look saying she knows someone is spilling wine on her shoes, and she'll catch them in a minute.

Her friends all seem friendly enough and quite normal, there's a guy in a suit with black hair. His cheeks are a little chubby and his eyes dart to the corners of the room.

The other two friends are girls; one is blonde and sharp with her mind and says what she thinks. The other is a brunette, softer, keeps her ideas to herself and could sit on a busy table and not be noticed.

Ideas have no chance of sticking to the walls of minds if you don't throw them first into the world of eyes.

I like them all.

Nicola starts boasting to her friends about me and it dawns on me I've never seen Nicola this drunk.

What she is saying would be borderline funny if she was sober, but because she doesn't know what she's saying it's a massive lie to her friends.

Through slurred words Nicola tells her friends I'm a published author of a book but Nicola doesn't stop there...She tells them they can buy the book from Waterstone's and she has a copy and it's amazing.

I know she's never read anything I've ever written and I know my book is not available in Waterstone's.

I know I have a book, but there's no way Nicola knows I have a book because I've never told anyone.

I'm faced with a dilemma just by standing still; correct Nicola on every single point she's saying about me and let all her friends know she's capable of being a massive liar when drunk, or go along with the fantasy, and when they all try and buy this book let them discover I'm a liar because I never corrected Nicola.

I don't know her friends, or Nicola seemingly, and I don't really know what to do.

I consider *they* say for evil to succeed all good needs to do is nothing; and say nothing.

I hope Nicola diverts her attentions and stories away from me before she tells her friends I'm a fully qualified pilot once responsible for saving America from alien invasion and the film Independence Day was based on my diary of actual events, long since kept under wraps by the American government.

We're sitting upstairs around a table in the pub with the exception of the guy, who is in the toilet. Nicola nods her head to the brunette in the desperate hope she'll be liked, but I'm disagreeing with everything the brunette is saying.

The more detailed the brunette gets in her point the more flawed points I see.

The brunette is talking about foreign policy, war and terrorism. Us versus *them* and *they* are evil and *not really people*. Her words sound informed, but if I close my eyes all I can hear is one side of the story, and not surprisingly, the side of the story our government feeds us.

If you take those three words, war on terror, the mind does not look at war it's drawn to terror; an incredibly clever piece of marketing.

Nobody should kill anybody and any sentence, no matter where you're from or your history, any sentence starting with "I don't believe in war *but*..." is a sentence beginning with human instinct and ending in programming.

But that doesn't excuse what I do.

I stand up from the table, too drunk to think logically, I remove the glass of wine from the brunette and proclaim I think she's had too much to drink.

And just like that, in one moment, everyone hates me.

Nicola immediately takes the stance of defending her friend, because she panders from one person to the next craving attention and love.

The blonde tells me she finds my actions offensive and as I'm trying to explain I'm sorry the guy returns to the table and Nicola is immediately all over him telling him she can't believe what I've just done; managing to make the moment of bad judgement on my part sound like I've taken a chainsaw to her friends face whilst screaming "For the trees!"

One by one I watch as they turn on me.

There is nowhere to run.

The brunette saves me by telling everyone it's okay, she's pretty drunk and was ranting on about war for a long time, and she's tired and going home.

Everyone else leaves as well.

Except Nicola.

Nicola goes downstairs to see them out of the pub, crawling up their legs, hoping somebody will pat her views on the head.

When Nicola returns ten minutes later clutching two half glasses of wine because she's spilt most of it on the stairs, and somehow over her shoulder, she's completely forgotten her reasons for being annoyed with me.

We're drinking the wine, her face screws up and she tells me she can't find her wallet.

She asks behind the bar and the woman says she's sorry but hasn't seen any wallets and Nicola accuses the woman of stealing.

I'm generally appalled and tell Nicola I'm sure her wallet is fine, I apologise on her behalf and we walk away; the woman tells me Nicola is nearing the point we will be asked to leave.

Nicola is insistent; ranting about how you can't trust "them" as if being a paranoid drunk and imagining your wallet has been stolen put's her in a higher class than the sober people working behind the bar who know where their personal possessions are.

I find her wallet in her bag.

Nicola doesn't thank me and instead heads to the toilet muttering ramblings about she knows it wasn't in her bag earlier. She offers no apology to the member of staff she falsely accused.

I'm left with my head in my hands.

This is why I never go out, why I don't need to know people.

I could be at home, on the internet or watching television drunk in my own bliss without any of the issues of the world, or the issues of other people.

Tonight is making watching Mohammad watch young girls wiggle their bottoms seem almost harmless.

Nicola returns from the toilet, fortunately without toilet roll trailing behind her, clutching her phone and informing me she's staying the night at mine.

Nicola is so drunk if I leave her to try and get home on her own she's going to fall into a skip, call the police and yell Pac-man is trying to eat her.

We get back to mine.

I only have one bed so Nicola and I have to share it.

Nicola tries to say hello to a little guy with a big heart called Professor Merrydinkle.

She takes her top off and her face flops into the side of my face.

She dribbles over my neck.

I'm scared.

She groans, her breath wraps my body in stale alcohol and homeless soup kitchens.

Tell her to stop.

I need to tell her to stop, but don't want to offend her.

She bites my chest, hard, and I want to cry.

I'm being raped.

She sits above me and removes her bra, her massive breasts dangle in front of my face and I turn my head away.

I could take her nipples, like moons, into my mouth, but instead I look to the wall.

Happy thoughts, think happy thoughts.

She grabs my throat.

I can't breathe.

I'm going to die.

She leans into me and a wet tongue licks at my chest hair, she slurps down my body, leaving wet trails, her grip loosens around my throat.

I can breathe.

I just want to be clean.

She reaches my jeans and I find my voice.

I might be desperate for sex, but I don't want this.

I tell Nicola to stop, and she looks up from my waist, slurs something I don't understand, speaks words from a language unknown to man.

I tell her I'm serious.

She looks through empty glass bottle eyes, the ships inside long since sailed, she climbs back up my body and rolls next to me, accidentally butting me with her head, breast and elbow on the way.

She swears, calls me violent names; I wonder who she thinks I am too.

She closes her eyes, I was right to speak out, Nicola had no idea what she was doing. Even though she was on top, and raping me, I don't think she wanted to.

I would have been raped, but also, she was using me to rape herself.

I can't know for sure, better to stop whatever was happening, that's for certain.

Besides, sex with her would have been like trying to wrestle a plunger from the face of an alligator.

She is flat out on her back and snoring at the ceiling.

Her half eaten burger sprawls across the floor, her lips are covered in some kind of sauce.

A piece of frightened lettuce rests on her belly.

I fall asleep thinking years.

Years it's been since I've had sex and twice in the space of one weekend it could have happened; but the first time I was too drunk and fell asleep and the second time the woman was too drunk.

I hear sex is just like riding a bike so tomorrow I might fall into a bush and cry for my dad and see if that makes me ejaculate; it would be easier.

Monday 13th September 2010

I open my eyes and stare at the ceiling.

Morning thoughts mix with last night's booze, making me feel adventurous and confident.

There's a half naked girl next to me and I haven't had sex for a long time, and I know this girl wants to have sex with me.

It's been so long my wet dreams consist of asking a girl's father if I can take her out on a picnic and he always says no; then the dream ends with me buying a microwave meal for one, a bottle of wine and a DVD of The Notebook.

I review last night's decision and decide I was correct not to have sex with her then, but *then* is ages ago and, most importantly, this morning Nicola is sober.

I decide to put Professor Merrydinkle back in his ship and sail him towards the uncharted waters of Nicola.

I roll over so I'm facing Nicola.

She's on her back and facing the ceiling.

She doesn't move.

I can't work out if she's asleep or pretending.

I'm not sure if I should try and kiss her face.

In a film this stuff would just happen.

My lips are only a foot away from the side of her face.

I could just lean over and kiss her cheek.

I glance down and notice her breasts cascade over everything, such are their size, and I can just about see the top of one of her nipples.

I notice now sober a tattoo of a lion above her breast.

Classy.

She's in my bed, half naked and last night tried to have sex with me; *and* she has a tattoo of a lion on her boob.

She surely must welcome a kiss on the side of her cheek.

Then again, if she is asleep, perhaps it's a bit of a liberty to kiss the side of her face because she hasn't given me permission to try and kiss her.

Try and think less.

Do people give other people permission to kiss them, or am I meant to just give this a shot?

I stare at her face.

She isn't unattractive.

I think, based on last night, Nicola would most likely want to have sex with me now just because well, she's indicated she fancies me and it's convenient.

I know this isn't romantic, but after so many years perhaps I can work myself towards romance.

Perhaps if she didn't want sex she might give me a wank.

I'd settle for that. I'm sure she would at least give me one of those.

First though, I need to kiss her.

No easy options; just lean in and go for it.

She tried to rape you last night, so must be interested, just be confidant.

I move my face slowly towards the side of hers.

My lips slightly advance ahead of me, bumpers on fairground bumper cars.

I inch along slowly, some sort of lip-sex ninja.

I'm suddenly acutely aware of my breathing.

I can't possibly usually breathe this loudly; if I did I would never be able to hear what people are saying.

My breathing doesn't sound romantic, it sounds laboured and heavy, a panting dog driving out of control bumper car lips into a sleeping girls face.

I inch closer still.

One more forward move and my lips will be attached to the side of her face.

Like that creature from Alien, only probably not as painful.

I move forward.

At the moment my lips are about to touch her skin Nicola makes a groaning sound and rolls over, so her back is to me.

I'm not sure if Nicola rolling over is a sign for me to kiss her neck, if it's a sign she wants to sleep more, or if she is denying me and knew I was trying to kiss her.

I stare at the back of her neck.

Unless I have a concrete no I'm not going to be certain of the answer.

If she does want to have sex with me but is asleep then I'd be a fool for not trying a little harder to wake her up.

I move so I'm behind Nicola, the front of my body against the back of hers.

This is a brave move.

I've not been this brave in years. This could be the start of a new me.

I put my arm around Nicola's waist and move my hand slowly up to the beginning of her massive breasts.

She makes a noise, I think it's a groan, and she pushes back against my body.

This is the best moment of my life.

My right hand approaches the cusp of her right breast, she turns around, fully awake, and asks me what the hell I think I'm doing; and she asks me in a voice screaming sexual assault.

This is the worst moment of my life.

I thought last night was bad; I thought the week before with Mohammad at the bar was bad. I thought passing out when I could have been potentially having sex with Sveta was bad.

But none of those things are bad compared to this moment.

I explain last night she wanted to have sex with me but I didn't because she was so wasted, and we're two single adults in a bed and stranger things have happened.

Nicola doesn't admit to it but her face changes as, I believe, she recalls hazy images from last night. As her face relaxes she starts to sound less rape alarm and more lost child being returned to her parents.

She laughs heartily three inches from my face whilst, through tears of joy, assuring me there is no way she would never want to have sex with me.

I'm waiting for her to say if I was the last guy on Earth, because that would be the best thought she could leave me with, but thankfully she doesn't say anything else because she's too busy laughing.

I remind Nicola about some of the events of last night, about losing her wallet, about coming back to mine being her idea; about her trying it on with me when we got back.

She accuses me of lying to her and inventing stories.

Nicola turns gets this wild look in her eye like she thinks I'm trying to put things in her mind.

In my head I see a cuckoo clock hitting noon and bursting out of its little wooden home, bouncing around sporadically on a spring barking "cuckoo" "cuckoo" "cuckoo" over and over as it dawns on me in my bed, right next to me, is a crazy person.

Nicola hops out of bed, grabs her bag and clothes and leaves without finishing her burger or removing the last piece of last night's lettuce still stuck to her belly button.

I call in work sick.

The silence in my flat sounds louder than before.

I shuffle to the kitchen, open my fridge and stare at two bottles of wine.

I remove one and pour a glass.

This morning I don't fancy coffee.

Sometimes in life you can do the right thing and nobody will ever know about it. I guess those are the only right things.

People act kindly when observed by others, but those same people can be cruel in private.

That's the weakness of kindness; it needs an audience for us to know it exists.

I take a swig of wine too early in the morning; a bat in daytime, a glove in a hand.

Because of alcohol I let Sveta down and thought it best not to have sex with Nicola, so it's lost me two opportunities. When

I say opportunities I don't mean sex, I mean the chance to be close to someone; to kiss and to hold.

Then again, without alcohol, I would never have asked for Sveta's number or ended up back at my flat with Nicola.

I have a glass of wine and exhaustion hits and I fall back to sleep.

When I wake up, sometime around four in the afternoon, I head to The Windmill to try and shake the smell of half eaten burgers and rejection from my bald head.

There's a new girl working behind the bar and I've had a few glasses of wine and find her quite attractive, and I'm drunk enough to *almost* tell her this.

She has a shock of straight ginger hair falling down to her waist which crops along the top of her forehead in a fringe, revealing a pale circular face, a mouse with a lion's mane.

She's quiet and humble; takes the small things lightly because she's survived the big things.

She is at work, but walks like she's strolling through a park on a hot day enjoying her first lick of ice cream, and when she talks her words are soft and sprite, they could put false eye lashes on butterflies in the dark, in a forest away from moonlight.

Nobody ever sees dead butterflies.

She has a smile she only allows herself to flash occasionally; as if there's a line she doesn't allow herself to enjoy life beyond.

That's why when I make her laugh, we both notice; I notice because it's the first time I've heard her laugh and she covers her mouth and looks away, like she's breaching some kind of personal code.

She reaches to pour me another wine. Her shock of red hair warns me away, but her eyes plead with me to stay.

This is the moment I'm meant to say something witty and captivating; but if I say something too witty she won't take me seriously, and if I say something too captivating she'll think I do this all the time.

I could tell her I haven't had sex for years.

That would make me sound like a pervert.

I could tell her sometimes the sounds of the city remind me of the sounds of the ocean.

That would make me sound broken.

I could tell her merely hours ago I was being accused of being a sexual pest by a crazy woman who tried to rape me last night.

Probably best to remove that from public record.

I could tell her there's a specific beer that takes me back to the island. An island is land.

That would make me sound bitter.

I could tell her about blonde hair, blue eyes, the moments we turn our back on that grow in size behind us.

I need to say something, because I'm just staring at her.

I tell the girl she has the straightest hair I've ever seen on any head.

She tells me she likes my t-shirt.

My t-shirt says "So far...this is the oldest I have ever been" the message is structurally sound.

I take my glass of wine and sit down, inside now, keeping the girl with the straight hair in eye sight in case something amazing happens, like she accidentally spills hot coffee on my top and lives across the road and I have to go over the road to her place, so she can wash my top. She takes a glimpse of my body in the right light; eyes squinted, ignoring my extra bit of fat, man tits and back hair.

It's the same reason I prefer sitting near a girl on the train or on the tube, because you never know where love could come from.

The concept is weak at best and the film industry has a lot to answer for.

I take a glug of wine.

When I'm next at the bar we chat, I almost ask if she thought saying *you have the straightest hair I've ever seen* made me sound like a serial killer.

Thankfully I don't ask because being drunk and mumbling about serial killers to a girl I've never met before can't be the way to chat up a woman.

I'm not sure what way is the way to chat up a woman, but something tells me it has nothing to do with serial killers.

Eventually I'm so drunk I have to leave and say goodbye.

I arrive home at about midnight and fall into bed in a drunken stupor knowing my alarm clock is going to wake me up, and when it does I'm going to feel like deaths minion.

I stare up at my ceiling and lock my fingers behind my bed.

I breathe out and feel happy.

Her name is Julia.

I never remember people's names when I first meet them, but I remember hers; impossibly straight haired Julia.

The main heavy door downstairs unlocks and opens.

Then closes again and locks.

Then unlocks and opens again.

Why am I living here?

When the door opens I can hear the cars outside passing the house.

When the cars pass, they pass with a rhythm and a sound.

That rhythm and sound is the ocean.

And I remember.

"MAX'S VAN"

12th February 2006

Lily was back in London from Hawaii. She'd been away for three months to see her family and friends so our main contact due to the time difference had been phone calls at peculiar times or e-mails.

The beautiful girl I met after quitting my job had family in Hawaii, in paradise.

Our plan was to move to the island.

I had taken another job in a bank but this time it was okay; I was working for a purpose, I was working towards escaping.

We were so in love to put it onto paper and try and describe it using only words feels like giving Beethoven a set of bagpipes and asking him to prove his genius.

I remember walking over Blackheath Common as the sun came up one morning hand in hand on our way to a friend's house, we walked past a police car parked on the side of the road.

As we walked past the female officer inside the car looked at her male work colleague and pulled the type of face usually reserved for trying to get the approval of babies.

Lily and I were also lucky to have the amazing group of friends we had.

It was a moment in time when people will look back at the photos and say what an amazing moment in their lives it was. How lucky they were to be part of that group, to be part of such laughter and love.

We will look back at the photos and say with envy we were so blissfully unaware of the freedom in joy.

We walked hand in hand talking about nothing in beautiful tones and excited gestures and met up with our friends.

I remember I spent most of the day feeling the energy coming from Lily, making electrical noises whilst holding my hand only an inch away from her face; I would make the noise and she would make a face like she could feel my hand on her skin, then I would repeat the noise and she would laugh and her eyes would widen as we caught the invisible sparks igniting our hearts.

Our hands were always on each other.

We left the party and walked up the drive to the road because we wanted to get something from Max's van; parked directly outside the house.

Lily was in the van and I stood by the door. Lily leant away from me looking for something and the sight of Lily leaning away from me made me forget everything except one thing; I needed to get in the van with her.

So I did.

The middle of a sunny and beautiful day.

We closed the doors of the van and made love; young hands moving in old ways.

We temporarily lost our environment because we began to only exist in each other's eyes, but we were brought back to earth by a large and heavy bang on the side of Max's van.

We froze, and immediately realised the van had been rocking back and forth.

The banging was followed by a violent woman shouting at the top of her voice:

"There are kids out here you animals! In broad daylight! What the hell do you think you're doing?"

Suddenly we could hear children; *they were everywhere.*

Children laughed and played in the street outside and close to the van.

We looked boggle faced and goggle eyed at each other because we felt we were about to be attacked.

The banging on the side of the van and the screaming continued.

We held each other, unsure what to do.

The situation was not helped by the consumption of enough acid to kill a cow.

The screaming, angry woman left the van and stormed down the driveway of our friend's house and banged loudly on the front door. We could hear her shouting at Phoebe about her dirty friends in the white van parked outside her house whilst her kids were playing.

The screaming woman became silent. I remember thinking I didn't like it when she was screaming, but the silence was worse, because we had no idea where she was.

She could have been anywhere.

Lily and I scrambled quietly for our clothes.

We tried the back doors to the van but they didn't work and we couldn't open the front doors of the van either.

We were locked inside the van, high on hallucinogens, with a woman in the road that wanted us dead.

There was only one way out of the van, through the window in the driver's seat.

Like the last scene in the film The Last of the Mohicans I held Lily's face close to mine and told her that no matter what happened she had to stay alive.

That no matter what happened to me she should stay in the van and somebody would leave the house and find her eventually.

And to stay alive, just stay alive.

She told me to be careful.

I told her we had no other choice.

One of us had to try and escape because otherwise we might both die of hunger.

We kiss and I jumped off the waterfall in my mind.

I pulled myself into the front of the van, wound the window fully down, and crawled out of the window, head first.

My landing was far from graceful, I put my hands on the concrete first and pushed my legs out of the window and fell to the side and managed, somehow, to flop over my own head like a discarded banana peel caught inside a Slinky.

Twisted on the concrete, I looked around, eyes hopping from object to object, sparrows aware somewhere a fat cat sits.

Everything was a little too quiet; wasting no time I jumped to my knees.

No sign of the woman or any children.

I ran to the back of the van and tried the door from the outside.

I called Lily's name and she asked me what was taking me so long and I told her I couldn't get the doors open from the outside either.

Lily's response captured the essence of the moment:

"You idiot."

My voice was a hushed shush and as I spoke into the van I looked back over my shoulders and across the road, looking for signs of the incoming woman who wanted to kill us to set the right example for her children.

"Lily, you're going to have to climb through the window too. I can't open it from here."

Her silence meant she wasn't happy.

Lily crawled through the window too and, with the sun beating down on our backs, we made a silent crouching run towards the house. The woman appeared at the end of the driveway as entered the house; just in time to call us *dirty cunts* in front of the children she was protecting from bad influences.

I told Lily I would love her forever, and she responded by saying forever and ever.

I had a T-shirt with the slogan "Love is a girl called Lily" and wore it in clubs. People threw up and I collected the sick and made heart shapes with the carrots.

Lily taught me *I love you* and *I love you forever* in sign language.

I love you is two fingers to my chest, arms folded across my chest, finger pointed at her; I love you forever is the same but with a big circle at the end.

If we were on different sides of the same room Lily would look over at me and sign *I love you* and I would sign back *I love you forever*.

We looked at each other from across the rooms at parties.

Neither would turn away.

She pointed two fingers to her chest.

Folded her arms across her body.

Pointed a finger at me.

A sunny field near Greenwich, her name is Lily.

I pointed two fingers to my chest.

Dancing in a club, our first kiss, fireworks exploding above us.

I folded my arms across my body.

Pointed a finger back.

Made a large circle in the air with my hands above me.

Forever.

"AHEAD OF US BEHIND US WASN'T"

July 21st 2006

Every year a large group of friends would go to a festival. Every hot summer was spent with Lily and friends in a field surrounded by laughter, music, flags floating in warm breeze, fun in tents, losing drugs, finding drugs, watching sunsets, suns rising, being hypnotised by feet dancing, naked people dressed in purple, set up bars selling booze which have no place in fields cows usually use.

We had been to Glade, a psytrance festival, for the last two summers and this summer we were going to The Secret Garden Party then flying straight from The Secret Garden Party to Hawaii.

We had saved up the money. Our plan was happening. Our dream was coming true.

Lily passed her occupational therapy exam in England and she was going to become an occupational therapist in Hawaii and was taking me with her.

I would write a book to make people laugh and Lily would help the disabled children of Hawaii integrate into regular life.

We were on a chocolate plane with toffee pudding landing gear and soon we would be landing in the mouth of a fat man chewing skittles.

Everything was perfect.

My life was incomparable to the grey vodka induced lonely existence it had been the day I stood up from my job in the bank, fired off *that* email, and walked out of the office.

Lily and I were going to party like we had never partied before, and end up living on an island in paradise.

The Secret Garden Party takes place in July and is a festival in Cambridgeshire, England.

That year it was set to the backdrop of a burning sun, lush green grass and a clear blue lake. It was one of those rare summers people write about in books, the type when the wind blows it plants small kisses on your eyeballs so gentle your eyelids don't know it's happening.

Our group of friends was, and still is to this day, too large to mention all by name.

Adrian Seale is a friend I have known for many years, as I have all of them. He looks like the milky bar kid on steroids and if I phone him I'm not allowed to swear in case the government are listening.

He works for the government but nobody knows what he does because if he told us he would have to kill us. He sleeps sometimes at work, but it's a secret spy sleep that's a rest break for exploratory thought.

He tells the worst jokes, and often the best jokes; but the best joke of all is his worst jokes are his best.

Jim ran away from home when he was twelve and the entire police force and UK TV media searched for him as he peddled south, helicopters circling above. He looks like Thor chiselled him out of his own penis and sent him down from heaven with a Scottish accent and a granite chin to see how successful he would be with the ladies.

He's always a laugh and sometimes a hectic lunatic.

If we were Teenage Mutant Ninja Turtles Danny would be Donatello. Only, Danny doesn't do machines he does music. He's a tall guy with a skinhead and has the heart of a hamster who wouldn't fall asleep in wool without asking the wools permission first. He's brilliantly funny and when he laughs it's a baritone cacophony of sound that's as infectious and delirious as the music he makes.

As my friends Rob, Scottish Jim, Max, Adrian, Danny, Joe and Lily bumbled along with acid smiles along winding paths under the cool shadow of slow dancing trees; we became the gentle breeze planting small kisses on eyeballs.

The world stopped blinking back tears for a moment in time, as rather than crash through life covered in oil, chasing cash and armed with guns, we people graced its presence dressed like fairies in search of fun.

Around the festival were hundreds of random rides, instalments, objects and art works. Some we could interact with and others we could not. There was a door leading nowhere, cups on either side of a large wall making people talk to others they couldn't see, a giant Ferris wheel, silly mirrors, random mud wrestling, treasure hunts and even a pirate ship dance floor we could row to, floating in the middle of a lake until the last night where it was set on fire.

The pathway we walked along took us through trees covered in fluorescent leaves and past people sitting in mushroom chairs and tables made from frog's derrieres.

The festival was somewhere down the rabbit hole.

We reached a clearing and gathered around an art instalment.

The computer printed sign was a clear warning this wasn't like some of the other attractions:

"Please do not touch or play on the artwork."

We were not meant to climb on, fall into, or try to smoke this piece of art.

The artwork didn't seem special, but we took the sign and artwork most seriously.

The artwork itself was a collection of car tyres stacked on top of each other, each car tyre painted a different colour and each set of tyres reached up to the sky stopping at different heights.

The instinct was to climb the tall stacks, and sit on the short stacks, but we stared boggle-brained at the words and reached the conclusion the sign must be for good reason and the right thing to do would be to leave the artwork untouched and unharmed.

We turned to walk away unhappy, suddenly we had rules to follow as we walked through the unwritten parts of Alice in Wonderland, on acid, at a festival.

We questioned the purpose of putting art that couldn't be touched in the middle of a festival all about exploration.

A white Jack Russell with a brown face appeared from a floral archway that led into trees; his tongue hung from his happy face and his tail wagged left and right at a pace of knots suggesting either the dog knew he was at a festival, or he had taken speed.

We watched the dog walk straight up to a large blue tyre and sniff it with his black dribbling nose.

We all stopped.

The dog walked up to a yellow tyre and sniffed that tyre too.

We were all thinking the same thing.

We wanted the little dog to urinate on the tyres.

Screw them and their rules in the middle of our festival.

Go on, go on little dog, piss on their rules.

Piss on their sign.

Good boy.

The little dog completed a full circle around the biggest set of tyres, smelt the ground once more, then cocked his leg.

We drew a collective breath.

Dog urine gushed from the little dog's penis and covered the biggest part of the collection, and as the wee hit the tyres we all cheered at the universe for restoring balance.

*

Later that night I had to use the dreaded festival toilet; one of the few places on earth which reminds us we're all just monkeys bashing coconuts into our own faces because we like the feeling.

A festival toilet is so far removed from the beauty of man learning to fly, or landing on the moon, the distance between the two is nothing short of a miracle.

How can mankind reach the moon whilst some people, instead of aiming poo into a toilet, spray faeces all over the ceiling and walls, and seemingly everywhere else *but* the direction they should have been aiming; when the aiming part should be taken care of?

Those thoughts went through my mind as I urinated into the festival toilet whilst trying not to breathe in.

Nobody wants to use them, but you simply have to.

The toilets add to the experience in their own way, hence why you're reading about my experience in one; which speaks volumes about their impact on the human psyche.

After I had finished urinating I turned around and was immediately struck by how dark the toilet was.

This was no common darkness like the type you might find in moonlight, whilst talking to a girl under a tree, as you steal the last minutes before she has to leave.

This was creepy and intense dark.

This was a human being doesn't belong in this environment dark.

I went to push the door but it didn't move.

I moved my hands around the door but I couldn't find a handle.

I turned left thinking I must have the wrong side of the cubicle, and that movement completely and utterly disorientated me.

I was lost in the most shit-covered festival toilet to ever exist.

I turned around and tried what had to be the door, but I pushed, and it wouldn't move.

I stopped panicking and thought logically.

I had to exercise some caution because I only had three sides to choose from and if I tried to push the fourth, the side of the actual toilet, I could end up falling in, landing amongst all the horrors of man.

In my pocket I had a glow stick, I removed and cracked it open, with the idea being it would act like a ridiculously happy torch.

I waved it around for a moment, saw nothing helpful, and promptly dropped it.

I looked down to see the pink glowing stick covered in black stained toilet tissue.

For the glow stick, this festival was over.

As well could mine be.

Was I going to be the person who needed rescuing from a festival toilet?

I've been a lot of things in my life but this was one accolade I was hoping to avoid.

Life is funny; sometimes you get a bang on the side of the place you're in and it's someone screaming obscenities at you because you're probably breaking a law.

Other times you get a bang on the side of the place you're in and you're probably still breaking several laws but the bang is helpful and not frightening.

A hand wrapped against one side of the toilet and a voice asked if I was okay.

That voice was Lily, and when I heard her voice I knew that I was.

I followed the banging and her voice to the panel to my left and once I knew I had the correct door I moved my hands slowly around until I found the lock in the dark.

I unlocked the door and threw myself out into the night sky of festival, sound, fun and Lily.

Lily had saved me and was also readily at hand to supply me with hand sanitizers, body wipes and an assortment of freshening up condiments she had in her bag.

Like everything else the festival had to come to an end.

Before we knew it Lily and I were saying goodbye to our friends at Heathrow airport as we prepared to board our flight to America.

After a weekend of partying I was a sweating, shaking mess and as I handed my passport over I was certain I wouldn't be allowed to board.

I was still trying to control my jaw from performing its own version of the teacup ride and to border control was surely a confused pelican chewing a Turkish Delight.

Somehow, as always, Lily floated through unfazed; she looked like she had just arrived at the airport from staying in a five star hotel where she'd woken up after a full night's sleep to a hot shower, good sex and breakfast in bed.

The guy at the passport desk stared at me for so long I threw up in my mouth a little, but I was able to swallow it without him noticing.

Somehow, he let me through.

An hour later our plane took off.

As we soared up into the skies I looked out of the window and back at what I was leaving. I watched as England, friends, family, work and my whole life I had led for twenty five years became smaller and smaller, until I could no longer see land, and everything that was before faded to clouds and memories.

I looked away from the window and clouds and into Lily's eyes and everything that was going to be weighed far greater than everything that was.

Lily squeezed my hand and rested her head on my chest and I smiled at the thought *this is me becoming a man*.

I closed my heavy eyes with Lily asleep on my shoulder and listened to the humming of the plane engine and thought about the other side of the coin. Yes, I was leaving London and friends and family behind but I was also leaving behind banks, the daily commute, mind numbing television, advertisements, Prêt D Manger, grey skies, smoke, pigeons, stressed faces, Wednesday night drinks with work colleagues, repetitive football seasons clacking with cliché blinded fans, coin-eyed people heads dropped floating on the tube network to work with their burnt out minds failing to reignite, buses breaking hard to avoid those people, coffee fuelled idiots, innumerate digits fading into endless emails sent from faceless two-necked no fingered spineless washed up future parents, or parents too soon, cash points, fruit machines, long queues, that feeling there has to be more to life matched with the realisation richer people want their slice and your slice too, isolation, kids carrying knives, briefcases, bitter cold gripping bones and not letting go, night buses, daily rushes, headphones on to ignore conversations, children being told they have to go outside but there's nothing to do except keep off the grass, or face prosecution for playing ball games in front of signs set by people who stop the fun; but are the first to complain when the bored kids do wrong.

Ahead of Lily and I was everything behind us wasn't.

Lily had given me a new life and she was making it happen with a head strong determination I could never possibly match.

I knew wherever I was, as long as we were together, I would be okay.

And Lily knew that too.

Forever.

"FIGHTING DOG EYES"

Saturday 25th September 2010

My coat wraps tightly around me, my warm hat grips my head, but neither stop the cold wind from biting into my face with every step I take as I drunkenly lurch on auto pilot towards The Windmill, the one extra in Cheers who never knew he was in a television show because he was such a drunk he thought he was at a real bar.

Daylight has gone and my fingers ache with the night cold and I can't tell if my hands shake because I need a drink or because of the temperature.

Either way the gloves I have chosen to wear are not stopping the cold.

I walk into the dark oak-drenched warmth of The Windmill feeling weak, cold and with thoughts crazier than a pencil with a rubber at both ends.

Julia the girl with impossibly straight hair has cut her ginger hair short just past her ears, leaving a new gap between her hair and her shoulder, a deforested area of rainforest.

From the gap I hear the sounds of chainsaws and screaming monkeys running from birds-eye view eyesores.

I put my hands on the bar and she takes a second glance at the over-sized blue gloves covering my hands.

"Getting something out of the oven?"

"I don't have glove gloves."

She stares at my hands and smiles broadly.

I notice for the first time Julia has one grey upper incisor on the right hand side of her mouth, making the rest of her teeth look whiter.

I think it odd I've never seen her teeth, yet the image in my head when I think of Julia is her smiling. Perhaps this is because whenever she smiles she looks away or covers her mouth like she's just told me a secret she meant to keep to herself.

She asks how I am as she pours a beer for a tall man with a face too red for his age, and I tell her I'm fine but I think myself and others, I whisper, have been taking walking too seriously.

I want to tell her I've noticed her hair is shorter yet still impossibly straight but before she can serve me the manager is asking me if I want to leave my oven gloves in the kitchen, and would I like a glass of red or white.

The manager is a new guy and looks remarkably like a Greek statue minus the shield, or horse.

He has a neatly trimmed beard, short curly ginger-brown hair and is dressed like an American in a basketball shirt and black New York Yankees cap, and, although I can't place his accent to me he sounds less American and more like an over worked French postman frustrated at the freshness of his morning baguette, and disappointed by the discovery he is smoking his last cigarette.

I leave the bar to drink my red wine and sit inside so Julia is in my eye-line.

Only a fool would go outside to the garden in these temperatures, with those heaters and without oven gloves.

My red wine is over too soon and I go up for my second.

As I get up Julia is the only person serving, but by the time I reach the bar I'm served by the manager.

The manager's name is Tom and he's not from France but from New Zealand, I return to my table in the middle of the pub and hope next time I'll talk to Julia.

As I sit down Julia walks out of the kitchen, through the bar and says goodbye to Tom.

I watch her walk towards me with her impossibly short hair hanging straight from her head like straws on fire in a bowl.

I never got to let her know I remembered her name.

As Julia reaches the door to leave, she stops and pauses, as if remembering she could have used the phone behind the bar for free rather than wasting her minutes on calling her mum to pick her up at the bus stop. Holding onto the door handle she turns around and looks straight at me.

She smiles and gives me a big wave.

She turns and walks out of the pub and into the bitter cold night and she's gone...short-bob-impossibly-straight-haired-she-doesn't-know-I-have-remembered-her-name-but-she-waved-at-me Julia.

I respect her so much my eyes don't even glance down to check out her arse as she leaves.

There seems little reason for me to be in The Windmill now, as the only other person in the bar other than Tom is the tall man in the suit and glasses with the face too red too soon, and I don't think he would appreciate me interrupting the conversation he's having with his umbrella.

Outside The Windmill my memories are rearranged and my common sense is scattered by the strong winds pushing invisible crazy up into my face, a sailor alone in his kitchen wearing a lifejacket, making a tugboat noise shouting "prepare to be boarded!" through a megaphone and shining a torch into his own face.

I wrap my coat closer then pull my eyes tighter and walk into the wind as headlights from cars drive by like iron sharks cruising along dark coral, needing to move to breathe.

A short woman with grey hair, so dirty she must wash it with cabbage and discarded tampons, wheezes towards me and grabs my arm with chubby, yellow hands.

She's wearing a purple tracksuit stained in the stains of a thousand weeks, and from the size of her I deduce the stains are kebab grease and dried chip fat oil. Her face is wide, wrinkled and her brow crinkly; a bawled up fist with hairy knuckles.

This woman has had a hard life, I think.

Her eyes are desperate, fighting dog eyes, they blink.

She opens her mouth to speak and reveals an abyss of decay and bad health choices; one yellow tooth hangs nervously onto a diseased gum like a five year old girl half-way across monkey bars who knows she isn't going to make it to the other side, but is too scared to let go.

She clings onto my arm and asks me for fifty pence.

Spit from her lips falls onto her purple sleeves and screams as it dissolves into a million invisible germs carrying unconfirmed types of microscopic disease.

The words she barks at me are tired, full of frustration and a little aggression, her breath is heavy with poisons from a heavy nicotine habit; if her words were people they would be old people, waiting in an angry line for a bus that never came, on a Monday morning outside Argos.

I'm intrigued by the amount the mad woman holding onto my arm is asking for.

She isn't asking for one pound or for "any spare change" but for fifty pence exactly.

The woman claws tightly onto me and slowly climbs up my arm as she speaks, a cat smelling a dog; she tells me she dropped her last fifty pence and it rolled down the drain.

I don't know what to do but fearful if I don't say yes she'll end up sitting on my shoulder, and spitting into my ear lobe, I pull some lose change from my pocket and hand her fifty pence.

In my life I'll never see fifty pence make someone so happy or remove their hand from my arm so quickly.

The woman removes her hand from my sleeve and turns slowly, a drunk taking a tight corner at speed in a trolley wearing a hat stolen from Primark.

She ambles back into the darkness, clutching between her thumb and forefinger a single silver coin reflecting the warm light pouring out of the nearby launderette.

I continue walking through the bitter cold and my phone rings.

Mohammad's voice pops weakly at me, two turtles pulling a Christmas cracker with teeth; he tells me he's in my flat checking my radiators.

I note he isn't calling to ask my permission if he *can* go inside my flat to check the radiators.

Knowing if I return home now I'll be trapped in a conversation with Mohammad about radiators for three hours I head to the pub opposite my house called The Queensbury.

This pub is opposite Willesden Green tube station in London and in comparison to The Windmill I've always found it a tad more desperate to be loved.

The drinks are expensive, the staff supermodels with chiselled jaws, thick hair, perfect smiles and not much to say.

The manager marches around with a permanent scarf wrapped around his neck, he wears a beret and has a tiny triangular piece of hair under his bottom lip like an artist, and perhaps he is; in his spare time when he's not running a pub.

There are no small problems in The Queensbury. A dropped glass is a reason to call the police, a refused credit card a reason to move daddy's inheritance from one bank account to another.

There's nothing wrong with any of this; it just takes time to cultivate, whereas I prefer the slap dash brutal honesty of The Windmill; there's no great need to attempt sophistication when in a building selling poison to the dying.

The Windmill is feet on ground; The Queensbury is head in illusionary gold clouds.

The Queensbury isn't large meaning often I walk in, look around, see there's nowhere to sit, and walk back out.

On those times I've been able to get a seat, the bar itself can be beautiful.

When you walk in to the left is a large fire, a cube of comfortable sofas and dark wooden floors.

The warm lighting is never too dark or too bright, making everyone look better than the sum of their parts.

Each time I go into the pub the restaurant seems to get larger and the bar smaller and these days the bar is so small it's almost just a waiting area for the restaurant.

The worst part about the pub is no matter what you order at the bar your change is handed back on a silver platter. I don't mind tipping, in fact I rather enjoy it, but if you're bar staff and I'm walking up to the bar and asking for my drink and walking back to my chair with my drink, then I fail to see how the concept of tipping has even entered the spectrum.

Because there's a social pressure to tip by the bar staff I'm embarrassed by their lack of self respect.

However my problem is not the change handed back on a silver platter; my problem is I fold every time and end up leaving my change because I feel my change on their property is already theirs.

I don't like myself for my weakness in failing to take my change, and wish I could proclaim loudly my offence at the suggestion they think they deserve a tip in the first place.

Let me buy you a drink if I want to, I should say, but don't offend me; you may look pretty but you've asked me how I am.

I've been in twice and paid with a ten pound note for a large glass of red wine and when the tray has come back covered in coins supported by a look; half prostitute half puppy with a broken jaw, I've folded and walked away leaving my change.

Consequently I've become the biggest tipper, creating an environment where they think I have money and so expect me to tip.

I order a large red wine and run away from my change.

The bar is quiet tonight and I look at the magazine rack and pick out a magazine I've never heard of, there's an interview with the lead singer of Travis advertised on the front cover.

I take a seat at one of the wooden tables and look up and notice there are a couple of guys sitting next to me who appear around father and son age, but they sit a little closer than father and son would normally sit.

The older guy has a narrow face with a small beard and tiny eyes but his sausage roll forehead is large and dumpy. Grey hair falls unkempt from the sides of his head and over his ears making him resemble a battered peacock crawling out of a vat of wrong sized nappies.

He leans in close but his smile is too broad, menacing even.

The younger guy, probably early twenties to the other guys late sixties, has a baby face with haunted eyes and although his dark hair is undeniably beautiful it doesn't quite cover the rings under his eyes, or the red marks around his nose.

As the older guy leans in the younger guy looks down at his drink; I wonder if they're arguing, or getting on, and if they're father and son or more.

I open the magazine randomly and I land straight on the page with the Travis interview.

My feet tap under the table to music.

The old fox and the young rabbit get up and leave the pub holding hands; I wonder if what haunts the rabbit's eyes is the very thing he holds onto.

Two more guys walk in and take the seat next to me. I don't notice them at first because I'm distracted by the small dog with them, somebody has put gizmo through a washing machine, used 'Bounce' and dried each hair individually using the warm breath of a virgin mermaid's new leather purse.

Give a horny hungry man a fish and he'll eat for a day, give that man a mermaid and he'll have to make some pretty tough decisions.

I stroke the dog, look up at the guys, compliment their dog and look back down to continue reading the article; Travis is asked what he thinks about his massive gay following.

I look up from the magazine at the guys on the table next to me.

They're in their thirties or possibly forties.

The guy on the left has long black curly hair touching his shoulders. His small nose points up and his two eyes are wide on his face, the nose a parent looking up at the eyes of children, forever stopping what they were just doing, for fear of getting caught.

He looks a serious man and my eyes dart to his friend.

His friend has a soft and kind face. He's a black guy with bright eyes and a broad smile. He's wearing glasses and his clothes; a brown jacket and hat, with impossibly expensive looking brown leather shoes, inform he's a man of taste and expense.

I look back down at my magazine and a thought dawns on me.

I flick to another page of the magazine, and another, and I realise the magazine I'm reading is a gay porn magazine with a random interview with Travis between the pages.

The fox and the rabbit, Kylie Minogue playing over the speakers, the immaculate men dressed in clothes with thought behind them, the cutest dog in the world, the pub called The Queensbury, the beautiful staff, the scarf and beret wearing manager, regardless of the weather, and now a magazine packed with man penis.

Sherlock Holmes has nothing to worry about.

I smile I hadn't noticed before; the male toilets always being so clean and forever smelling of lemon makes complete sense.

I already have the magazine, so I finish reading the article.

I look up from the magazine and a guy sitting over by the fireplace is staring straight at me. I look to my left and the guy with the nose pointing upwards also appears to be checking me out.

Well, I am reading gay porn in a gay bar.

Why isn't it this easy to find love in a straight pub or venue?

Straight people are doing something very wrong.

Mohammad calls me to tell me he's left my room and is no longer looking at my radiator so I finish my drink and, for a moment, I stare at the empty glass sitting on the table.

Whenever Mohammad talks about my flat he uses the word room so I know, in his head, I'm renting a room out in his house.

I have no idea how many glasses of wine I've drunk today.

My glass is half fool.

"THE SMALLNESS OF I"

August 24th 2006

Our shoulders touched, our toes touched; my foot was in-between hers and hers in-between mine.

The hot sun tumbled down us like a bucket of cold water thrown into the face of an exhausted man; spreading itself across every exposed piece of skin and bringing the mind and surface it kissed to life.

Lily and I sat on the bonnet of the red beetle car we bought once we landed on the island of Hawaii. Lily had wanted that car, and it had to be shipped to the island from mainland America because there wasn't a single one like it on any of the Hawaiian Islands.

Lily stuck flower stickers all over the poor thing, making it look permanently trying to escape a pop-up Floriculturists fact book.

We had both doors to the car open and had parked on the edge of the ocean, on a cliff, looking out to the sea.

I passed a spliff to Lily who smiled, and her eyes directed the sunlight inside me.

We had the radio playing in the car and KT Tunstall sung about being on the other side of the world to her. I didn't know where in the world KT was in that moment, but despite her fame and success there was no way she was happier than Lily or I.

Sunsets are different in Hawaii. Everything about nature is different in Hawaii.

We were staying on the big island for a few weeks whilst Lily waited for the results of her occupational therapy exam. Lily needed to pass the American exam in order to practice in the United States, if she passed we could live on whatever island we wanted, and she would work full time in her dream job, and I would work from home writing my first book.

The big island of Hawaii is the island the tourist board thought most people would visit because of its size, so a lot of money has been spent on infrastructure, like making sure the roads are safe. However the tourist board were surprised when most visitors to the islands preferred to go to the smaller islands for nature, or the capital for life, leaving the large volcanic island easy to drive around and, for its size, sparsely populated.

Lily and I would drive for hours sometimes and not see another car.

Lily took a drag on our spliff, we sat next to each other on the bonnet of our flower covered red car, and we looked out at the ocean and into the fading sun.

Behind us a long road led to more amazing places, we were just taking life in.

What we had achieved, how far we'd come.

Our knees touched and I moved my hand to her lower back and gently placed finger tips to the skin at the base of her spine.

So more of our skin was touching.

The sun set slowly in front of us, spreading colours across the ocean and sky; two kaleidoscopes exploding into each other and falling into the sea, which glittered the light back up and onto our faces, making us look like children holding their first disco ball in amazement.

The sky peeled back and behind blue the real colour of heaven, or the universe, was revealed; dark purples, oranges, reds, pinks, and then Lily put her head in my chest, and listened as my heart did my thinking.

From behind my sunglasses, so stunned was I by the beauty and perfection of our moment, I wiped a tear from my eye she never saw.

The CD playing KT Tunstall ended and Lily and I were left watching the kaleidoscopic sun drop into the disco ball sea to the sound of waves gently hitting the cliff face somewhere below us.

We had made it.

We sat on our bonnet clinging onto each other until the sky was dark, and the stars came out and covered the night; shining so brightly our skin illuminated.

Lily looked at me and asked me if I wanted to see something cool.

I told her I did and she went to the boot and threw me a jumper; she told me I was going to need it and, with a smile, told me to get my cute arse in the car.

*

We reached the end of the road high up the mountain and parked our car, got out, and continued our march to the summit on foot, which took a further hour.

After three hours of travelling, and one of walking up a steep mountain, I wasn't sure if I still wanted to see something cool, or if anything could still be cool after walking up a mountain for an hour.

We approached the summit, the ground evened out, and we walked to the edge of the mountain and took in the view.

I was mistaken; there was no walk on this planet steep enough that could make this view not cool.

I looked up into the sky and down below and I wasn't sure what to focus on first. The night view was so amazing, so perfect, so awe inspiring it was like somebody had stuck love hearts to my brain and thrown it at a wall of sticky toffee pudding.

We were standing above the clouds and beneath the stars.

The hot sun had long set and given way to a cold night; cold at this altitude. The largest moon I have ever seen beamed across the night sky like God was using a lighthouse as a torch to search the stars for someone he had lost who was close to his heart.

There was no way he was going to find who he was looking for, not amongst billions upon billions of stars.

There was no way anyone could find anything.

Someone could lose themselves in those stars if they didn't constantly remind themselves they exist, and as I stared up in disbelief at the information my eyes fed my brain, for a moment, that's what I did.

I stared up into the stars, more of them than any person could comprehend; for the first time in my life I had a greater idea of how infinitesimally small our planet really is and, furthermore, how tiny and insignificant I was in the grand scheme of the vast universe and still far larger than I planet.

I took a seat on a rock next to Lily and took in the moment to comprehend the vastness of everything and the smallness of I.

The smallness of I.

I could look down and see the tops of other mountains surrounded by cloud or I could look up and see the moon surrounded by the galaxy, and there wasn't a cloud in the sky because we sat above them.

We sat between the best view of everything and the best view of nothing at all.

I held Lily's hand and thanked her for giving me the jumper because it was cold, and she laughed and pulled from her bag my warm hat; exactly what I needed.

Lily and I sat side by side on our rock and watched those stars for two hours, we laughed, held each other, kissed; we shared moments when even though the universe seemed just a few feet from our heads, even though the stars felt touchable, even though we sat above the clouds with the whole planet beneath us, there were moments when we looked into each other's eyes, kissed, and forgot where we were completely.

And it was in those moments of thinking on our rock, as we left our embrace, and we sat looking up at the moon and the universe my love deepened further for Lily, if possible, and I wondered if there had ever been a luckier man alive than insignificant I.

Love is a bath of beans with a pig dressed as a clown and a naked farm girl.

Pretty much amazing, once you get over the shock.

That night we slept in the car; a curious mix of Lily's feet in my mouth and gearstick in ear, and a haunting feeling in the morning we would run out of petrol and be eaten by wolves.

In the morning we kept on driving, after all, we had a flowery tent in the boot behind us, and an island in paradise to drive around ahead of us.

We drove with the ocean on our left and the jungle to our right.

The beaches changed from white sand to black sand and even to glass; all magnificent.

Small beaches hid behind large trees like shy children hiding behind the leg of their mother; large beaches with smaller trees unable to hide because of their size stretched out for miles in plain sight, shy mothers trying to hide beneath the legs of small children.

Where the sand ended the ocean began, and the sky was so clear and the ocean so flat, I couldn't tell where the blue ocean stopped and the blue sky began.

The city smell of smoke fumes from cars, cigarettes being smoked outside bars, dog faeces, tramp urine, stale beer and emotionless tears had been replaced by the smell of green grass, flowers, flowing water from waterfalls and cleansing salt thrown into the air by waves breathing out solar fireballs.

I rested my head against the red edge of the passenger seat door with my window down and, for a moment, I simply listened.

The sounds of the city had gone.

No longer could I hear stressed voices screaming above other stressed voices clambering to be heard, brakes of vehicles long since tested slamming down hard to prevent the death of too rushing pedestrians, beeps from automatic machines in supermarkets set impossibly high so blood drips when it shouts through my eye; no longer could I hear the clanking of till machines taking money from people for items the television made them think they need, printed receipts juddering out from similar tills that go on for hours merely to confirm I purchased a coffee at a time when I would rather be in bed, so I can sleep off all the negative thoughts in my head.

As I rested my head on the side of our car there was so much *less* to hear.

Think and you'll miss it.

The city sticks a dirty rag into the mouth of nature, suffocates and muffles its voice until nature is blacked out on a chair and too spooked to sound.

All I could hear with my head against the car driving under the sun with the sea to my left and jungle to my right was nature; the ocean breathing in and out in perfect synchronicity with the gentle warm breeze passing over the car and into me.

A thought popped into my head I couldn't shake.

A dark cloud shook me in its cold embrace and the more I struggled with the thought the more the thought told me it was right to have.

I turned quiet in the car and hoped Lily wouldn't notice.

I thought I could try and pretend to be asleep but, of course, she knew immediately.

I wanted the thought out of my head, I wanted the thought to leave so I could return to who I really am, but the thought wouldn't go.

The devil is only ever a whisper; he doesn't need to shout to be heard. He speaks so quietly nobody else hears him but me.

Having an imagination which sometimes leads me can be great when it leads my thoughts to dancing biscuits in Japanese coffee shops being eaten by robots enjoying their programmed break from serving humans in a restaurant called Life Knocks, but, when my imagination goes the other way and I don't know how to control it I end up in a place I don't want to be in, and don't know how to escape from.

And it happens, like life, in the blink of a thought.

Who had Lily seen the view with before?

Who had Lily climbed the mountain with and sat under the stars with before?

I knew the thoughts didn't matter, shouldn't matter, but the thoughts had other ideas.

A watched pot never boils but if I took my eyes from these negative thoughts for a second they would spill over the edges of my lips, and boil the beautiful moment alive as we lived it.

Lily squeezed my hand because she sensed something was up and I pretended to be okay but she knew I wasn't.

Lily stopped the car with a confidant smile, but her pupils wobbled in subtle denial, she took my hand and led me down a jungle path, over rocks and streams and around bends, and I felt Lily's hand and tried to focus on the warm feeling of simply being held.

I wanted to think of the warm feeling of her hand and forget my silly thoughts. I was in paradise, with a beautiful woman who loved me, all I had to do was hold onto her hand and not open my mouth and let my fears out.

The path opened up and we were at the place Lily wanted to show me.

A beautiful and extremely secluded waterfall surrounded by rocks with a large pool of water at the base.

Lily sensed something was wrong, we were too connected for her not to, and she walked over to me and suggested we made love under the waterfall.

Every man's dream; making love to a beautiful woman under a waterfall in Hawaii.

My brain had other ideas; instead of saying yes, I withdrew from her and backed away. Lily asked me what was wrong and I said not to worry, then she asked me if I wanted to go back to the car, and I said yes.

We walked back to the car in silence and, even though I was trying not to affect our perfect memories, I already was.

My brain was an ocean storm and my face was a small boat being smashed against rocks for Lily to plainly see.

Who had she made love to at the waterfall?

Lily was trying to show me her favourite places on planet earth and all I could think about was me.

If you're standing on the shoulder of giants expect to be crushed by dandruff.

We sat in the car facing outwards. Eyes fixed ahead, heads not turning.

I knew Lily would break the silence first because I didn't want to tell her what was wrong.

Our car was parked on the edge of a large beach.

The beach stretched away from us to the left and curved into a small bay.

Waves slowly rolled in and back out of the bay and in the distance children and adults surfed and laughed at play.

A group of campers started to cook on a barbeque as they drank beers and sat around benches expressing positive emotions, oblivious to the two English lovers sitting in their car full of hopelessness.

The sun's rays beat down in front of us, streaking golden lines through palm trees swaying in the gentle summer breeze, and the cliffs above us stared down onto perfect sandy shores compounding the irrationality of my ridiculous thoughts.

In the car paradise breathed down my neck pushing me up against the windscreen, making me feel like I couldn't breathe, and my thoughts screamed at me I should be hurt Lily would take us somewhere she'd been before with another love.

Lily asked me what was wrong and I didn't answer and the silence became claustrophobic.

I stared straight ahead, unable to look at her; she started to cry and sob gently into her hands.

Outside the car was Hawaii, the ideology of nature crafted perfection; inside the car I was creating my own version of hell.

If you jump to a conclusion be prepared to fall between your thoughts.

Two pink fluffy dice dangled slowly under the rear-view mirror and I couldn't understand how they were moving.

I told Lily I was angry she was taking me to places she had been with other men and Lily told me the places were the best places in the world; she wanted to share them with me because they meant so much to her, I called her cheap and she cried. I looked out of the window because I knew I was wrong; my words sounded like they were no longer mine.

The tiny things biting my mind are so tiny I can't see or feel them bite, and they leave no marks on my skin.

Through tears Lily screamed I was ruining this and I was.

You are ruining this.

I couldn't stop the pictures in my mind, the invented, ridiculous, made up pictures in my mind.

We both stared ahead out of the window of the car.

Only last night we were looking up at the stars like two separate pillars supporting the same structure; two people joined by one experience, but now I was throwing a hand grenade at us.

Lily asked me to look at her.

Look at me Colossus, look at me, turn your head and look at me.

Turning my head took a lot of effort, partly through anger, frustration at my weakness and shame, but I turned my head and stared at Lily's beautiful face and her eyes were puffy, and her nose was running, and I thought what a bastard I was, because my words had caused this.

I looked up from her nose and into her eyes and we paused for a moment as our gaze gathered strength, I felt my anger subside then Lily smiled and when she did I smiled back, and she nodded her head to the side, as if to say she knew I wasn't really being me, and she squeezed my hand and I told her sorry.

Lily told me I needed to grow up and stop bringing her past into the present because it had no place and I told her I would try.

But I didn't know how.

And I knew I didn't know how.

I knew Lily deserved better; I looked out of the car window at the ocean whilst throwing mental punches at my brain hoping to change its pattern, or in the hope an answer would reveal itself so I could understand myself and explain.

Possession is nine tenths of the flaw.

Lily looked at me looking out the window and wondered what she'd done, but, she wasn't questioning her stance on the argument; she was questioning the calibre of the man she had travelled to Hawaii with.

She wondered who I really was inside, and so did I.

The fluffy dice stopped moving, and I thought good; die fluffy dice, fucking stop moving, snap off, and die.

I watched the waves breathe in and out, and thought sometimes moments that should be amazing, are just a reminder of our failings.

"MENTAL INEQUALITIES"

Friday 2nd October 2010

My hands are so cold I feel like I've been giving a hand-job to an abominable snowman.

The world is too in focus.

I enter The Windmill hoping Julia is working but the place is empty and Julia is not behind the bar.

I panic because the guy behind the bar looks up at me; a young guy with long blonde hair grouped together into a single dreadlock sticking out of the side of his head, the tail of a golden retriever.

He cleans a glass and smiles.

I've already digested the pub is empty, meaning if I go to the bar to order a drink then sit down on an empty table t would be an obvious slight on the barman, who from his smile seems sociable and wanting to chat.

The idea of talking to someone I don't know at length about the cold weather and *have I heard they say it's going to snow* makes my blood run cold and my palms clammy, and I think I'm going to have a seizure.

I need evasive action so instinctively I smile back at the friendly looking barman and make a hand gesture, my phone is ringing and I'll be right with him.

I pull my phone from my pocket and pretend to talk to somebody.

Why I can't just turn and walk out I don't know.

The conversation I'm having with nobody, to the ears of the barman, appears to be a conversation I'm having with a friend who has decided he wants to meet me somewhere else, and this friend is asking me if I can go and meet him.

I have a go at my made up friend for letting me down, again, and tell him he should come and meet me at The Windmill because it's a better pub.

I nod to the barman and he nods back at me grateful for the business I'm trying to get him.

What am I doing? Am I about to lose an argument with myself to stay and drink in a pub I don't want to drink in?

I tell nobody on the phone if they want to see me I will be in The Windmill.

I hang up and look to the heavens pulling the *some people* expression knowing full well the barman is watching.

I look at the barman and the barman looks back; his dreadlock wags expectantly on the side of his face.

I take a step forwards; frustrated I'm going to drink in The Windmill when I don't want to.

I tell the barman I'm just going to the toilet; he smiles and tells me no worries, he'll still be there when I get back.

I return his smile.

In the toilet I panic.

White fear grips me at the thought of being having to talk to someone I don't know, or having to talk; I sweat, I'm colder than I was before.

The toilet starts to spin; my breathing shallows and I grip the side of the sink.

This is no time for a panic attack.

I need to call the friend I made up on the phone and tell him to call an ambulance.

If I freak out now, my only hope is the guy behind the bar.

We would become friends.

I rest my head against the wall and get a grip of my breathing.

My heart race slows down, I feel weak, but my strength starts returning.

I drink some water from under the tap.

I need to leave this toilet or he's going to come in after me to find out if I'm okay.

I could just run out of the toilet, burst out of the toilet doors, sprint straight past him and out of the pub, but that would make me look crazy.

Think.

I might use the urinal, might as well.

My breathing returns to normal.

I'm urinating and read the poster on the wall asking for people to sign up to the Thursday quiz night.

Think.

I wash my hands.

Think.

I dry my hands.

Think.

I'm about to leave the toilet when an idea hits me.

I note the phone number of the pub on the quiz night poster and store it on my mobile phone.

I can't risk walking out and calling him, because he might ignore the phone for the customer.

The pub phone is in the kitchen, so to answer it he would have to enter another room and have his back to me.

I leave the toilet, and wait in the corridor, just off the main pub floor.

I hold my phone in my hand, put my back to the wall, like James Bond, but a crap one who has panic attacks and suffers anxiety.

I call the number.

The phone rings.

Horrible slow moments drag, he doesn't answer the phone, I wonder where he is.

The phone stops ringing, and goes to the pub answerphone.

Maybe he's cleaning tables; maybe he's on the way to the toilets.

My heart starts beating faster.

Sweat creeps back over my skin.

My hands shake, I hit redial in panic.

I close my eyes, try and control my breathing.

The phone rings.

Answer the fucking phone please!

This time the phone is answered straight away.

I relax.

My plan is to make a run for it, while the barman has his back turned, distracted by my phone.

Julia's voice says hello.

I panic, unable to take being trapped any longer by these mad people.

Plan B.

I run out of the toilets, down the length of the pub, narrowly avoiding the blonde guy with the dog tail hair, I hear him say *easy man* as I brush his shoulders with mine.

I need to get out before Julia puts the phone down and walks out into the bar.

I look to my right and she's still saying hello into the phone with a puzzled look on her face, and I burst through the exit doors and out into the cold winds of London with the desperation of a civil war soldier scurrying up a muddy bank with a bullet in his stomach, and a photograph of his family in his bloodied right hand.

Saturday 3<u>rd</u> October 2010

The sky is grey and overcast and the sun sits behind a wall of fog giving the day a depressing feel of loss before it's even began.

A cowboy's harmonica, not played in years, waddles down a deserted town towards the wind; hoping to be reminded of musical things.

I place my cold hands on the door to The Windmill with the intention of going in this time and, unlike yesterday, sitting down and having a drink.

I feel calmer now, which is easy to think when I'm outside, and if the guy is working then I'll have to explain I had an emergency.

I've never seen him before, so he is likely part time.

I try the door to the pub but it's locked.

I'm sure it must be noon so I pull the door towards me and push it away one more time; again the door doesn't open.

Why do people always try locked doors twice? Perhaps we are either, by instinct, more optimistic than our nature leads us to think or more stupid than nature intended us to be.

I'm not a fan of trying a door to find it closed because whenever any human is faced with an unexpected locked door the law of sod states someone sees, but, when you turn around to face the shame everyone looks the other way, hiding secret smiles.

I move away from the door as quickly as possible, almost certain somebody somewhere is chuckling.

Unsure where to wait until the pub opens I find myself taking a seat at the bus stop a few feet from the entrance to the pub.

From here I'm able to keep an eye on the door whilst using other people to check whether it's still locked or finally open.

An older gentleman whose face is hard to see because he's wearing a warm and colourful scarf, grey coat and matching warm hat tries the door with gloved hands.

He pulls the door toward him then away, waves his hands in the air and shakes his head in grand gesture so if he turns around, and someone is watching, he won't feel stupid for being foiled by a door.

Some are born stupid others achieve stupid and some have stupid thrust upon them.

I look down at my feet and smile secretly.

There's an old man sitting at the bus stop with me and I can tell from the corner of my eye he's looking at me and wanting a conversation.

I look straight ahead, screaming in my head *please universe I don't want this*.

He begins with a tut.

Then sighs loudly.

We burn youth away until we look back on it through just our bones.

Unhappy his subtle noises have failed to engross me he finally speaks, as if to himself, but yet somehow not:

"I don't know eh?"

I stare at my shoes but prepare myself for imminent conversation about the running times of buses.

Then it happens:

"These buses, I don't know. I've been waiting here for twenty farcking minutes."

His voice is deep, rough, his vowels stretch for longer than his consonants and the spaces between his words are punched away, making him sound like someone trying to pull a pineapple from the throat of a scared elephant.

I have no choice now so I look to my right, meet his eye and get an immediate feel for the way this old man, probably in his seventies, has lived his life.

A boxer's nose resting violently across his cheek and his old bald head is littered with dents and divots, he rubs his face with a cheese grater then burns away the grazes with hot irons.

Old men in their seventies who used to fight and still think they're in their twenties are more intimidating to me than guys in their twenties who fight.

There is unpredictability about the old boxer whose one defeat is to age; they're angry their body has given up on them and they can't hurt people like they could.

They have an eagerness to prove they can still take on a young man.

I have stumbled across the type twice in pubs and both times each man stood inside my personal space demanding me to reclaim it.

Perhaps I'm wrong. Perhaps this old man just sounds angry because of the bus; perhaps his nose isn't squished because fifty years ago he was a bare knuckle boxer.

I look into his eyes and find them menacing, he is sitting down but I know even at his age he's twice my size and processing half of my patience.

The guy stares at me waiting for a response, so I tell him I know, I speak in a voice mimicking his, and I tell him buses are unbelievable, and I use the word *bloody*, to let him know I'm comfortable with swearing.

He balls his knuckles in his lap, breathes in deeply and I prepare for his life story, which will probably be he used to be a boxer and worked for the Krays.

He breathes out, and catches me off guard by asking me what bus I'm waiting for.

I look up at the bus stop and pick a number, hoping he doesn't ask me any further bus related questions because I'm not waiting for a bus, I'm waiting for the pub to open behind us.

I tell him I'm waiting for the 332.

I have no idea where it goes.

An awkward silence falls between us, I look forward and he looks at me looking forward.

The 332 bus comes around the corner and stops right in front of us.

I don't want to get on the bus, I have no intention of getting on a bus, but the old man stares at me and is curious to know why I'm not moving.

"That's your bus."

"Thanks."

I get on and pay for a fare I don't need and wave to the helpful old bastard who made sure I didn't miss my bus.

The bus pulls away from the bus stop and takes me away from the pub.

I get off the bus at the next stop and walk back up the road ten minutes in the freezing cold and thankfully the old bruiser has gone, no doubt barracking the bus driver a little too close to his window about his wait in the cold.

I try the door to The Windmill for a second time and the pub is still closed.

I stare through the window half in excitement and half in fear, a bit like a stalker up a tree outside someone's house looking through binoculars in the knowledge he's left his book of birds at home, so if caught his excuse is going to look weak.

The girl setting up the bar isn't Julia.

I don't really fancy drinking anywhere else and the only reason I wanted to try The Windmill was because of Julia, so I turn away from the window of the pub and, with cold London wind blowing straight into my face I tuck my chin in, keep my head down, and head back home.

Sunday 4th October 2010

I place a shaking hand on the door of The Windmill for the third time this weekend feeling like someone has thrown me into a cement mixer with Celine Dion, on her period, and left me with the responsibility of getting us out.

I've tried to have a drink in this pub twice already this weekend and failed on each occasion.

Going into a pub is only walking forward with intent so how I keep ending up outside on the pavement, flipping around like a gasping salmon, puzzles me.

I enter the pub and Julia is working, finally.

My mental inequalities have finally worked in my favour because entering the pub now on a Sunday afternoon makes me look a lot more responsible than peering through the pub window waiting for it to open first thing on a Saturday like an alcoholic stalker.

I imagine if Julia had been setting up the bar yesterday, if she had looked up and seen me with my hands over my eyes watching her, well, I'm not sure how well that would have gone down.

I order a large red wine and she smiles at me and I smile back.

I compliment her new short hair but leave out the part about hearing homeless monkeys crying from beneath her bob, and Julia tells me she had a pretty crazy weekend in Brighton.

I could sit at the bar but instead I walk outside and take a seat in the garden.

I don't know why I don't sit at the bar because if I sat at the bar I could talk to Julia, the reason I've been trying to drink in the pub for three days, but now I have the opportunity to finally sit and chat with her, I instead sit as far away from her as possible.

I don't want to crowd her or make her feel pressured like she has to talk to me, but perhaps that's just a coward's excuse for fearing having nothing to say.

Julia comes to the garden. She is collecting ashtrays and cleaning them but I notice all of the ashtrays are already clean and have probably only just been put out that morning, so I wonder if, perhaps, she's finding an excuse to strike up conversation with me.

And then she is standing above me, with a strong smile and the weak London sun behind her.

The pale sun lightens the edges of her hair making Julia look as if she's been cut out from somewhere better and stuck here, in this London pub garden, to help people by being lovely.

I tell Julia I had a massive daddy longlegs in my kitchen recently.

Julia tells me I told her this last week, but I know I didn't, so I tell Julia I don't think I did and Julia's smile weakens a little but she insists.

The week before whilst at the bar I told Julia about a massive spider in my flat, not a daddy longlegs, and if Julia had let me explain further I would have been able to make it clear to her I wasn't repeating a spider story; but informing her I now have two spider stories completely independent of each other.

However Julia's weakening smile is enough for me to start apologising for repeating myself, even though she should be apologising for making assumptions about my spider stories, and not knowing the difference between Tipulidae and Tegenaria domestica.

Julia says she must get back to the bar, but says it as if she's just decided I'm one of those drunks already repeating themselves and therefore not who she thought I could become; as she walks away the confusion with the spider story leaves me wondering if she's ever listened to me.

Confusion is part con and part fusion.

I go back to the bar and order another large wine, Julia charges me less than she should, and her large glass is a generous serving. As she passes my change back to me she smiles and I have an unusual feeling that, for once, maybe everything isn't in my head and she likes me.

I stay at the bar and move my concentration from the wine in my glass, to listening to the sound of heavy rain pelting the roof of the bar then back to memorising the odd moments when I catch Julia's eyes.

I tell Julia my Brighton story when I smoked a drag on a spliff Adrian handed to me, and, because I was so drunk, I felt immediately sick and had to lie down on the floor of the restaurant.

We were sitting outside, not far from the beach, and all I knew was to save my life I had to get to the ocean.

I managed to stand up and stagger like a man carrying an invisible fish tank across the road to the pebble beach, where I placed my face on the cold stones and prepared to wait for the feeling of being a tea cup in a storm of coffee beans to pass.

Adrian helpfully followed me across to the beach where, during my state of vulnerability, he buried me in stones with the help of Lily.

Julia laughs at my story.

I think she might like me.

All I have to do is ask her out.

That's all.

Never has a simple thing been so complicated.

"LIFE THROUGH THE MEDIUM OF RAINBOW"

September 07th 2006

Lily passed the American occupational exam and had been offered a job on one of the smaller Hawaiian Islands called Kauai.

Lily had never been to this island before so it was a fresh challenge, a new page and a new adventure for both of us.

Passing the exam wasn't easy, Lily had a lot of pressure on her for a while but her hard work paid off.

Impossible boulders roll out of our path and for every heavy boulder gone with the wind we knew, whatever happened, we would love each other just as we did then until we died.

The first sign living the island life on Kauai was going to differ from London life was our plane to the smaller island from the Big Island was no bigger than a canoe.

As we took our seats on the plane the pilot joked he'd only drank five beers that morning so there was a better chance of us landing than the time he crashed after drinking six.

His words divided the twelve people on the plane, those native to the island laughed, the tourists whispered feverishly to partners and made sure their seatbelts fastened.

Lily and I smiled into each other's eyes knowing if we died what we felt for each other was universal, love had been felt by people before us and love would be felt by people after us; love didn't need us to be alive for love to exist, and so, perhaps we didn't need to be alive to feel love.

As the small plane flew over our new island I looked out of the window and the wild view took my breath away fast; punched in the stomach by a beautiful lady wearing an oxygen mask and being attacked by an out of control vacuum cleaner.

From my tiny plane window I looked down on mountains, different types of green surrounded by sandy beaches, waterfalls cascading down mountains.

Not a tall concrete building in sight.

The doors opened, warm air rushed into our faces, burning nose hairs. The air normally reserved for holidays. Air that hits you in the face, immerses you immediately, demands you breathe in; and the moment I did my lips curled into a smile because it warmed my entire insides, like starting the day in a sauna eating porridge with an attractive girl sitting next to you.

Only this was better, because the sauna was my new home, and the attractive girl next to me was my girlfriend.

We booked a night in a hotel whilst looking for somewhere to live, but somehow Lily was able to talk to the people at the hotel desk and we were shown to a cleaning lady, and the cleaning lady let us stay in an empty room for a couple of extra nights at a cheaper rate, just because Lily smiled and asked nicely.

That was the thing about Lily; she had this way of bringing out the best in people. The staff at the hotel didn't have to help us, but not only did they help us, they took a risk in doing so.

The hotel room had large bay windows with cream curtains when parted revealed our view: the ocean, miles and miles of ocean, and clear blue sky.

The bay windows opened out onto sand.

A sofa looked out of those two windows and at the sun; and in the evening the moon.

On the first night, with the bay windows open, we sat on the couch with a glass of wine looking up at the stars and listening to the ocean lap at the shore and I remember thinking, what did I ever do so right, what did I do to deserve this?

I was nobody special with somebody special, in a place I would always remember in the land time forgot.

The next day Lily and I found a place to rent. An American couple had converted the back of their house, it was only small but had new wooden floors, a kitchen, a front room, a bedroom and a bathroom complete with Jacuzzi.

We had our own driveway, our own entrance and our little place backed onto a real jungle; we had a small lawn between our place and the jungle where giant trees dropped giant leaves the size of dinosaur feet.

We packed our new place with furniture from various stores and in each store made new friends, a beautiful American actress called Sherilyn Wolter, beautiful outside and in, sold us our sofa and TV cabinet and became a close friend.

Pierce Bronson lived on the island and gave the local school twelve donkeys.

I was in K-Mart and rather than put my shopping blindly through the till and asking for the money in a depressed voice, like a doctor delivering bad news to a patient, the member of staff talked to me for ten minutes about how my day had been.

People would take any job and be thankful for it because work kept them on the island; they would sell their feet for more hands to cling onto the sides of Kauai with.

In London we're replacing people with machines in our shops so there's no longer any need for human interaction...but in this shop, in this town, with these people, I was reminded of something machines will never be able to replace; human contact.

My walk to the local shop was a pleasant stroll past white houses with green lawns and, on the corner at the end of the road, lived the largest pig I've ever seen.

The pig was larger than the plane that flew us to the island and, judging by the beer cans scattered across the grass around him, the pig was twice as drunk as the pilot by most afternoons.

I walked down the road with the sun beating down on me, and at the end of the street I crossed a main road to enter the local store.

If I looked right the main road cleared the path to the most magnificent view of a huge mountain. I would stop every day, before I entered the shop, and stare at this massive mountain split down the middle by one of the largest waterfalls on the planet.

Always sunny outside that shop, but at the top of the mountain, always thunderstorms and rainclouds.

This was not just any mountain, this was a mountain covered in a million types of green. King Kong, the television series Lost and Jurassic Park were all filmed on Hawaii so when I say mountain, I mean paradise, but not just any kind of paradise, the kind of paradise film studios have sold back to us as the stereotype of what we believe paradise is.

The mountain reminded me we are standing on the most amazing experience we could possibly have; Planet Earth, and to speak of a Heaven is to sell short what we already have.

To be standing in one weather condition and witness another before buying a loaf of bread was as surreal as it sounds.

Lily started her job helping disabled children; she was one of only three occupational therapists on the island.

The school system was a little backwards in how it cared for disabled children, so Lily had her work cut out; but she knew in her heart her actions directly helped the disabled children living on the island.

During the days Lily would work and I would stay at home, I started writing.

We were happy.

In the evenings we shared a glass of wine and watched a film, or would go down to the beach and breathe paradise in.

With each passing day the home we rented became more our home; bean bags, penguin pencils, flower cups, coasters and colourful bowls were purchased and pictures of us at festivals with friends, and on holiday in Egypt and Spain made their way into frames sitting beneath the ledges of flower-stickered window panes.

We could drive around *most* of the island in only three hours, but it was impossible to drive around the entire island because one end led to a huge crater, looking like a meteor the size of Darlington had struck the earth, and the other end was a road leading to, and ending at, one of the most beautiful beaches in the world.

The most beautiful beach in the world is a stretch of beach which rolls around the corner at the end of the island, where no car can drive because of a series of cliffs juddering out from the land, ending somewhere deep under the surface of the ocean.

The sea itself is surrounded by an underwater coral reef the naked eye can't see. The reef keeps the surrounding blue waters completely still; like the tight-skinned face of papa smurf after plastic surgery.

At end of the world the sunset is like a child smashing a pack of crayons into Gods face.

As the sun disappears under the horizon every colour of the spectrum is thrown all over the Hawaiian blue sky; and this sunset happens *every* night.

On Kauai once in a lifetime moments are everyday occurrences.

One early evening at the end of the world, as a child smashed crayons into Gods face above, Lily and I watched two monk seals have sex on the beach in front of us.

Lily wasn't sure if we should be watching, I regretted leaving our camera in the car.

We took a helicopter ride over the island; the beautiful island at eye level did not disappoint from above. In fact, from the helicopter we witnessed even greater marvels of planet Earth.

We flew over lush green mountains and dipped to fly closer to gigantic waterfalls impossible to get to by foot.

One giant waterfall cascaded down the middle of the island and crashed into a huge pool below and, further down this large mountain, scores of other smaller waterfalls broke out and made a run for it toward dry land.

I was expecting to see a rainbow, because on Kauai they are as common as tins of beans on supermarket shelves, but I wasn't expecting to see two together.

We flew above two rainbows, looked down through them, and our eyes witnessed Kauai through rainbow lenses.

A double rainbow moment on the breeze, my heart gone with the wind.

Everything so perfect, so beautiful, except for us in our flying machine, spilling fumes and burning gasoline; hurting what our hearts love to see through the way humans being.

Sometimes there was tension between Lily and I because I forgot to perform a household chore, or couldn't find the time to, like raking the dinosaur feet leaves that fell to the ground outside our house, or cleaning the bathroom taps properly.

We were both frustrated at times because I was limited to what I could do because I couldn't drive which meant I relied on Lily; which at times made her feel she had less of a boyfriend and more of a child.

And at times she did.

These small quarrels and tensions were expected because of our new environment and every relationship has them; and each quarrel was soon forgotten and floated away on the waves.

And then sometimes, on our silly days, the arguments returned on the waves too; but the wave returned was taller, a Tsunami, and neither of us knew where to run or what to do.

"MAYBE THE DRINK'S TALKING"

Friday 10th October 2010

The Cock & Lion is the pub opposite where I work, I've spent many a lunch time hour staring out of the window pondering how much I'm lost in the life of my erroneous job, working me in several roles yet choosing to pay me for the role costing them the least.

The Cock & Lion, or Man Bit and Big Cat, is a small pub with nothing going for it except the staff and people who drink inside.

How a good pub should be.

The opposite kind of pub to the Cock & Lion are massive bars with loud music creating an environment nobody can talk, so people stand around feeling like single woolly gloves left alone overnight on winter ice rinks by children who have forgotten them.

The Cock & Lion is small, really small, no music plays.

The pub squashes you next to someone so you have to say hello.

Familiarity breeds contemplation; I ask for a coke and Dionne thinks about it for a moment, laughs and asks me again what I'm having.

Dionne is built like a pack of Benson & Hedges and so short when she wears her hair fastened tightly behind her head conversations are chats to a moving forehead.

I tell Dionne I have no money and she says not to worry, I can pay next time.

Her voice is East End London and cracks with jellied eels, apples and pears, market stalls and old buildings bombed during two World Wars.

The army put the weapon in cantankerous.

I tell Dionne I'm not drinking today but before I finish my sentence a large white wine is on the bar in front of me.

I asked for a coke.

I told Dionne I wasn't drinking.

This isn't my fault.

I take my wine to the single table in the corner and look out of the window and think about how sometimes my life feels like it's slipping away from me.

I remember a laugh, and curse my memory for remembering only good times through hindsight. When living the good moments, I could only remember the bad.

The curse of being a man, or the punishment for not developing properly into one.

Raindrops splash against grey glass, streaking down the window in front of my eyes.

Tears run easier down empty glass faces.

I finish my wine and return my glass to the bar.

Dionne already has another large glass waiting for me.

I'll pay her next week, she knows, but I wasn't drinking today.

I really wasn't; now I'm faced with my second large glass of white wine, and it's not yet two in the afternoon.

Only when the music stops, and the lights turn off, does the dance with the devil begin.

I walk back into work fifteen minutes late, completely drunk, one hour and fifteen minutes after deciding I was going to quit drinking.

I'm in no fit state to work.

My first thought is the Microsoft paper clip guy who pops up and offers advice is quite a lovely once you get to know him.

Dionne, well intended, has derailed my sober brain and sent me crashing through glass into an old Wild West saloon mid bar fight.

I drunkenly wander around Google, lost, hitting random searches as my mind tries to focus and stand up straight, a silhouette in an alleyway outside a jazz club in Tennessee with hands on knees throwing up lunch contents into oversized bins.

*

On the way home from work I take a detour into The Windmill and order a coke.

If I go home, I'll stay home all weekend and see no people. Likely have to hide from Mohammad at least three times, calling me, knocking on my door, asking if I'm in, asking what I'm doing, telling me he'd like to see me more, letting me know via notes pushed under my door he hopes I'm okay, if I want to talk to him I just have to go downstairs and knock on his door.

Because he's always in.

Always waiting for me.

Maybe, if I go home, I'll have a panic attack.

At least outside, if in somewhere, I can imagine talking to someone, to someone with impossibly straight hair.

She is working.

A person I can talk to, a familiar face amongst all the strangers.

A warm smile; natural kindness, no built up distrust, ro fear built walls.

Real strength, a quality to be admired.

My friend, Julia.

Maybe the drink is talking, but as she turns and catches my eye with her ginger hair and pale face she is a phoenix rising from flames, so much more than a mysterious barmaid.

The universe is challenging my attempt to stay sober, because the bar staff are offering free shots of vodka as part of a brand promotion.

I've been in The Windmill forty times, and this is the first time they've ever given free drinks.

Free shots and free wine; I should stay sober on more Fridays.

I thank Julia, take my coke with the free shot and sit down in the garden to be alone with my thoughts.

I drink a coke, down a shot, drink a coke and down a shot.

The evening flashes past in a hollow blur, a china doll on an out of control merry-go-round.

I drink another large wine.

The drink I shouldn't have, the liquid on the other side of the line.

As too much wine hits too easily suggestible blood, my slow burning mission to make Julia my girlfriend crosses the path of my own mission to be, at times, a drunken tit.

My sober day has turned into drinking all day from one o clock and alternating between wine and neat vodka.

I'm disappointed with myself; and finally have the confidence to talk to Julia.

Julia seems receptive.

We chat, I tell her I write and Julia tells me she likes music, and writes down on a piece of paper the name of two bands I should listen to.

Her handwriting is perfect, considered; instead of dotting the letter 'i' she draws a circle above, so she's creative, or bored of our conversation, and she puts a full stop at the end of her band suggestions; she doesn't like loose ends, and is confident when she talks people should listen.

Even though it's a Friday night I'm the only person sitting at the bar.

Julia turns away from me and, as she does, I decide to give her my phone number.

Try and give Julia your phone number in a humorous way.

Think, think, what's a funny way to give a girl your phone number?

A way she'll remember you for.

Write down your phone number on toilet roll.

I ask Julia if she has a pen and she hands me a black b ro. I tell her I'll be back in a minute, a big grin spreads across my face, I'm convinced I have the best way to hand a girl a phone number ever conceived by man.

I am legend.

I get to the toilet and I'm lucky, the last piece of toilet paper hangs from the roll, a message from the universe.

I'm on the right track.

Doing the right thing.

I write a message on the toilet roll and it's funny and self deprecating; about the class of a man who writes down his phone number on a piece of toilet paper, and how lucky she is to have that type of man liking her.

I look in my hands at my note and phone number scrawled across the small square of toilet paper, flapping slightly in my hand; going to a better place than his friends.

This is brilliant; Julia is going to be swept off her feet by this broom of funny.

At our wedding people will ask how did you meet, and she'll laugh and tell the story of the infamous toilet roll. Everyone will laugh, and I'll say something witty about it being fortunate she enjoys toilet humour.

I turn to leave the toilet but something stops me.

That little musician guy who sits on my brain; usually sounding like two toothless old people kissing with wet tongues after drinking sherry, suddenly sounds like Schumann and I hear him clearly.

Everyone's a writer; write something beautiful, show her you're a great one.

Of course!

Thank you little musician in my brain, I'll write something deep, something meaningful, something with a hint of philosophy.

Something beautiful on toilet roll; a juxtaposition of irresistible comedy.

I exit the toilet and give Julia my revised note with a wink and leave The Windmill laughing.

Julia is probably laughing too and I walk into the cold I cannot feel.

I disappear into the darkness of night; everything illuminated by the lights of my happy thoughts.

By the time I get home, or by tomorrow morning at the latest, Julia will text me.

I'm excited.

This feels like the moment I find the tracks to the rest of my life.

Saturday 11th October 2010

I'm trying to tell someone something really important but I'm chewing gum, the more I try and talk the bigger the chewing gum grows; I'm chewing and chewing but can't take the gum out of my mouth or swallow.

I open my eyes.

My entire flat vibrates lime green from the blinds Mohammad put in, and I stare up at my ceiling with a familiar uneasy feeling.

Every drunk knows the feeling.

What did I do last night?

Pieces of memory shuffle back into my brain, rain reverses up grey window panes and falls backwards through the sky, the drops land on clouds, like the one in my mind.

Shit.

My behaviour last night *could* have been worse.

My behaviour and actions were completely well intended, my heart in the right place.

You gave Julia your phone number on toilet paper.

What were you thinking?

Handing a phone number to a girl on toilet paper is never going to impress.

Shit.

I told Julia I'm a writer.

I recall the words I wrote down for her.

So utterly pretentious and full of crap a sixteen year old would get a better reaction if he ran into the pub and knocked all her teeth out with a fire extinguisher.

I want the world to swallow me up so I don't have to remember, but I know what I wrote:

I could write ten thousand words but all I need is eleven numbers: 079** 5** **5.

Julia would have read my words and thought the same thing I'm thinking now.

What a massive cock.

That passage, if written many years ago, would have been accused of witchcraft, chased through lamp lit towns and burnt alive to the joy of the able to read who feared crap literature.

Another image falls back into my cloudy mind.

Shit.

This gets worse.

This is not just about *what* I said; it's about *how* I said it.

I didn't give Julia my message on toilet paper.

I cringe in my bed, as I remember.

My hands are clammy.

My heart beats faster, the world is swallowing me from the feet upwards, and I want it to.

I wrote my first note on the last piece of toilet paper, so in order to impress Julia with my philosophical depth, I had to be creative.

I wrote my brilliant ten thousand word message of cheese on the only thing left in the toilet.

The toilet roll.

I fucking hate alcohol.

And toilets.

I imagine what Julia must have thought as I handed her a toilet roll covered in the illegible scrawl of a drunk mess of a person.

Julia watching me as I leave, watching me laugh at my self-perceived brilliance, deciding in that moment I'm a man losing his mind, or with a mind already lost; the man with the unfindable mind.

I see her looking down at the toilet roll in her hands, unable to read any of it.

She thinks about calling the police, but instead throws the toilet roll in the bin and questions the sanity of my masterpiece.

I've moved from humorous boyfriend material to creepy guy she suffers at work.

I've lost the person I spoke to, the person who had no choice but to put up with me.

And I realise, suddenly, I've been to her who Mohammad has been to me. She's put up with me, probably tried to avoid me, and has had no choice but to smile at me as I ramble on about my life.

I am Mohammad.

I am who I hate.

I hate myself.

I pull the bed covers over my head and want to be somebody else.

Maybe I should give in, go and knock on Mohammad's front door and give him the friendship he wants.

Maybe we need each other.

My phone rings, I lean over my bed and pick it up from the floor.

I look down at the number through blurry eyes.

I don't know the number.

I don't want to answer.

What if it's Julia?

What if she found me cute, in a creepy way?

What if she thinks I'm funny?

What if she's calling to take the piss out of you, to tell you she's never been asked out like that before, but if you leave the toilet roll at home, you can take her out.

What if she's laughing about the situation?

She sees me.

The wedding is back on.

I answer the call.

A female voice says hello, and I smile, my biggest smile in ages, because the voice belongs to Julia.

I can't believe it.

Julia has called me.

She thinks I'm hilarious.

I haven't lost my friend.

I try and apologise for the toilet roll, but she tells me to listen, says she's sorry, she always thought I was a little odd, but my heart was in the right place.

She says I *was* funny.

She says my behaviour has been too weird, tells me one of the barmen said I almost shoved him to the floor last week.

I try and explain, I want to say I have a social anxiety disorder, I want to open up to her and tell her things about me no-one else knows, but she doesn't let me.

Her voice is harsher than any time before.

She doesn't want to hear what I have to say.

From my bed I look around my room for a moment, my television is in front of me, my computer over by the wall.

I have nothing.

I don't even have heating.

I have no money.

Give me a break.

She says sorry, but I'm barred, no longer welcome in the pub.

Julia you are my only friend, and I don't even know you yet.

I tell her I'm sorry for running, and the toilet roll incident was a stupid joke, I'm a good person, I say.

A joke gone wrong, nothing to worry about.

Don't barr me from the only place in the world I go, the one place that feels like home.

The place that feels more like home than home.

Don't take away your friendly face, just because I gave you a toilet roll by mistake.

Her voice drops down a tone, now more serious than before, anger in her voice, and so I don't share my thoughts or my pleas, I don't tell Julia how much coming to The Windmill means.

I don't say anything, because she's already upset, and I don't want to upset her further.

A half drunk bottle of white wine stands tall by my computer.

Fuck off wine; you got me here.

You snake, you poison, you bastard.

Julia tells me my phone number matches the number of a prank call she had last week.

She says last week when she was at work she answered the phone to heavy breathing, she found out the number, to report the number to the police if it happened again, says she wrote the number above the phone in the pub.

Says the phone number is my phone number.

Angry, she says I called her last week, to scare her, to breathe heavily down the phone at her, that I ignored her when she asked me to stop, ignored her when she told me the joke wasn't funny anymore.

She says I'm dark.

Tells me her mother picked her up from work that night because she was worried.

Tells me I should get help, before I hurt someone.

How can I explain I called the pub to escape from the barman, and when I called the pub I had no idea she was even working.

How can I say when I got outside the pub I had a full b own panic attack, and had no idea she was listening, I had no idea I hadn't hung up.

My phone was the last thing on my mind.

Not dying was the first.

I had a panic attack and she listened, from the pub, to the phone in my pocket.

Anything I tell her now comes from a sick fantasist.

The more I say, the more I confirm who she sees in me.

So I say I'm sorry, I understand.

She tells me never to come back to the pub, she tells me Tom agrees.

I feel my breath shortening, and hope she hangs up soon because otherwise this phone call is going to end with what she thinks is me masturbating over her voice again.

Julia hangs up, taking the girl I fancied and my favourite pub away in a click.

I've lost my friend, eye contact.

Pushing me closer to Mohammad.

Driving me to drink.

I control my breathing, look around my room.

More alone than before.

I grab a pillow, and turn so I'm facing the wall.

I think of sad thoughts, I think of loss, of being alone, of the life I had and where I am now.

I grip my pillow and curl up into a ball.

I want to cry.

I want to cry, but I can't.

I want to feel but I don't.

"A RED CAR SITTING TOO LONG IN A CAR PARK"

February 09th 2007

Lily and I heard the coastline along on the beach we called the end of the world could be hiked.

We read a few short miles into the hike was a stunning waterfall tumbling into a lake flowing into a river peop e could follow all the way to an isolated beach; heaven on Earth, a secret place away from tourists.

The road less travelled on an island few see.

Two miles further along the coast-line from the isolated beach was a second beach we could camp on overnight.

The idea of walking along the edge of the world appea ed.

The idea was romantic, the journey a challenge.

The views soul affirming; self validating.

The coastline ran along the edge of paradise to two isolated beaches, separated only by a waterfall so powerful if you placed a coconut beneath the falling water the coconut would be cracked in half, and your hands ripped from your arms.

What could go wrong?

Lily and I had never hiked in our lives so we didn't know what to expect, we never exercised and enjoyed the occasional spliff.

We shared some minor doubts drinking alcohol, smoking weed and eating pizza is not the best way to prepare for a hike, but we'd seen the movie Jurassic Park and that jungle looked manageable; and this hike was guaranteed dinosaur free.

We parked our red Vauxhall Beetle under the blazing heat of the midday sun in the car park at the beginning of the Napali coastline; as close as we could park to the end of the world.

We planned on staying overnight on the beach two miles along the coast, so I had to carry a tent on my back, in a rucksack, along with the food and water.

The first two miles of the hike were a struggle enough.

The sun boiled and pickled our skin; Lily and I agreed we felt like a pair of lobsters boiling in a pot, placed inside a sauna and hurled into the sun to celebrate national chilli month.

This wasn't fun.

The first cliff face was steep and unforgiving; there was no protection from the sun because for the most part we were walking above any shade.

The path we walked was only a few feet wide, so we walked in single file.

Rocks tumbled off the path and fell down the cliff, we learnt not to look down because over the edge was a sheer drop falling thousands of feet below us, down through jungle and into darkness.

The potential to fall off the side of the path followed us with every step we took, whilst above us the sun drained all bodily fluid.

Sweat poured from us and we made little progress.

Two dried prunes waiting to be fed to a pack of unfussy lizards.

After two hours of walking we finally reached the edge of the first cliff; the hike had been uphill, so when we reached the peek the view was startling.

We could see down the entire coast-line.

We stood on the edge of first cliff and ahead of us cliffs continued to edge out into the ocean as far as the eye could see; hundreds of them.

This was the coastline used in the opening sequence to Jurassic Park; when the helicopter flies over inspirational music.

I bet the coastline looked more beautiful inside an air conditioned helicopter, eating a sandwich, pointing at waves mistaken for whales.

The rickety path we stood on would take us back down around the cliff and then eventually up to the next cliff face, and then from that cliff we would repeat the walk to the next and so on.

We guessed from the next cliff we would look down and see the beautiful beaches we'd heard about, because our view was only more cliffs.

We knew it was going to be exhausting because it already was, as well as dangerous, but we thought one more cliff and we can rest for the night; eat some food, set up camp, then in the morning head back.

At the time it made sense to continue to the next cliff because we'd just realised how much we hated hiking, so we knew we would never be doing it again; making this our best, and last, opportunity of seeing the amazing waterfall and beach.

The blue ocean stretched out as far as we could see and ahead of us green cliffs, covered in jungle and trees, dared us to continue walking through in search of perfect memories.

We continued hiking, following the narrow path back down, around, and then back up again towards the second cliff face; we walked under trees, through thick shrubbery, and at other times we found no shade, and were pounded mercilessly by direct sun rays.

We drank plenty of water in a desperate attempt to rehydrate; content in the knowledge when we finally made it to the top of the new cliff face we'd be rewarded with the view of a beautiful beach, that would stretch out before us, revealing tents full of other hikers and couples like us; all seeking the world's most beautiful sunset.

The path cleared as we reached the second summit of our exhausting day so far, and then we stood, on the second summit looking out to the sea again.

No wind hit our face, draining sunrays sprayed over our skin, and we looked down for the beach but found nothing.

The exact view we had about an hour and a half ago.

Ahead of us stretched rows and rows of identical looking cliffs with no sign of any beach or accessible shoreline beneath.

We turned to look behind us; only cliff faces behind us too.

If a helicopter passed over we would appear no bigger than germs on a carcass, such was the size of our surrounding environment.

We needed to decide whether to go back or not.

Going back meant we'd walked along the coast for three hours just to walk back again; a total of six hours hiking to get back where we started.

The beach we looked for *could* be only an hour away, at the bottom of the next cliff, but if we continued and found no beach we would have a four hour hike back along dangerous cliffs, more exhausted than if we left now, with less water and we would have to hike the last part in diminishing light.

Time was against us.

Everything was against us, nothing here, was designed for man.

Looking out along the coast, I had never felt further away from flat pack furniture and fast food culture.

Anyone walking these cliffs at night would die.

We had limited time to make a decision because each wasted minute could, in a few hours, equate to an extra minute of hiking in the dark.

We decided to keep going; people wouldn't say there was a beach along this coastline if there wasn't, and we must be nearer than further away because otherwise everybody who tried to reach the beach would die, and nobody would be alive to talk about it on websites or the bars of Kauai.

We walked down the face of the second cliff hiked that day and Lily and I both shared the same sinking feeling.

There wasn't going to be a beach when we reached the top of summit three and we faced a serious and potentially life threatening situation.

The jungle at the base of cliff three grew thicker than the jungle before; the terrain was rougher and we dragged ourselves through large brambles, jumped over streams and navigated boulders blocking our path by hanging onto exposed tree roots for balance; if those roots snapped the fall would have killed us.

Mosquitoes landed, took their pound of flesh, and left before we knew what caused the damage.

Our hearts sank and we looked at each other with genuine fear when we found a red backpack on the path, and nobody around.

We called out but received no call back.

We told ourselves if someone fell from the path, they would fall with their backpack on.

The lone backpack was creepy and out of place; isolated, yet so close to civilisation; an empty flare gun washed onto a city shoreline.

We decided it was probably a good sign; somebody had gone to the toilet, or had put their pack down to run ahead and find out how far the beach was, so they could come and get their bag later.

We kept walking and the path widened.

As soon as there was space to walk beside each other we did, and either I put mine in hers or Lily put her hand in mine.

We found a wooden sign; someone etched an arrow pointing away from walking to the summit of cliff three. The arrow pointed to the left, along a rocky bank, we felt sure the sign must point to the waterfall and beach.

We followed the direction of the arrow until the rocky bank turned into a small river, we kept walking along the river until, step by step, the river widened and we noticed between the stones golden grains appearing; tiny genies screaming rub us for wishes.

There's no place like home, there's no place like home.

More grains of sand appeared until the stones completely immersed; and soon we walked on a memory we could never forget.

We took our first steps onto beach as the sun sank over the horizon.

We dropped our backpacks into sand and fell with them; leant into each other, bodies heavy, hand in hand, and drew a collective breath as the sun that had spent the day trying to kill us left.

And it was beautiful.

Fear and doubt disintegrate when staring into a sunset, and our darkest thoughts are engulfed by a glow; even if the thoughts running through a person's mind before and after are terrible, when faced with momentary sunrays even the worst of us feel the lightness of being unbearable.

Two other tents sat on the beach and Lily laughed with relief because we found other people and would be safe, but I worried, because if people were in the tents they would be watching the sunset.

If they aren't watching the sunset they're probably dead somewhere, killed by the mountain.

I chose not to share my thoughts with Lily and we watched, arm in arm, the sun melt into the sea, spreading entire spectrums of colours across oceans and skies through the medium of a million beautiful beams.

The sun disappeared, stars appeared; the moon was so full, and close, it didn't matter I had left the torch in the car because we could set up our tent under the light of the moon.

We collapsed inside our tent, bodies completely exhausted, minds racing; closed eye's seeing cliff faces, barren landscapes and thick jungle flashbacks.

A little red backpack.

We listened as the waves of the sea gently crashed against the shore outside our tent and matched the rhythm of breathing naturally.

Two empty tents.

Lily opened her eyes and said our food had been in the same bag as the torch, along with the rest of our water.

We checked our water supplies and were completely out, we checked how much food we had and, to our horror, we only had seven ready salted flavoured Pringles.

I can't stand ready salted flavoured Pringles.

That night we talked in the tent about whether we should go back or forward.

A four hour hike back with no food or water, in the sun, would kill us.

The hike would be even harder in the morning without proper food and we were hungry now.

With no water our hike felt like a suicide mission.

Two backpacks on a path.

Three tents on a beach.

There was another beach along the coast, the second beach; if we could find people on that beach we would find food, water and help; but we didn't know how long the hike to the next beach was.

We knew it was four hours back out to the car and felt there was no way it could be more than four hours to the next beach.

We thought if we hiked a couple of hours to the next beach we could meet up with other hikers and travel back with them; with food and water.

Or we could hike back four hours with no water and seven ready salted flavoured Pringles.

The next morning, with the beach still haunted by unmanned tents, dehydrated and with three and a half Pringles inside us each, we made our decision: to hike to the next beach.

The beautiful sun became our enemy again, water poured from us we couldn't replace, and as we ventured further and further away from the beach the jungle grew thicker and the terrain more dangerous.

The pathway was so thin and unstable we considered going back, but we knew going back led to nothing and no help, so we continued in false hope for change.

A flaming sugar cube; an old bees last wheezing thoughts of toffee, ahead a broken window and a bucket of old fishing floats to use at sea.

We hiked up the next cliff-face and broke above the tree-line again and, as we reached the peak, we looked down desperately hoping we would see the next beach along the coastline.

We stood on the edge of the peak, with the view of the coast-line below us, sun blazing down on dry skin.

Our hearts leapt to our mouths.

Miles and miles of coast and again, no visible beach, no break in the harsh cliffs, no hope for us.

No hope as far as we could see, just lots of beautiful scenery.

We turned around to see behind us and felt the cold stomach blow of death as we looked, again, at miles and miles of nothing but cliff.

We weren't even arguing.

That's how serious this was, a child fallen from a height turned silent.

There was no point in blaming and not much to say that could help; we both felt the remote possibility of dying becoming not such a remote possibility.

I told Lily we would be okay, around the next cliff would be people who would help us, but as I spoke my words felt like spin and the sun shone them back into my face, so I could see they were as empty as our ready salted Pringle tin.

We kept going because we had no other choice, we walked back down the cliff face and along to the next, and after a further two hours or walking in the blazing heat; we reached breaking point.

We realised if we turned back to the beach we left that morning, because we had been walking for three hours, there was a chance we wouldn't make it back before nightfall.

We had walked too far to go back; the further we walked along the Napali coastline the more we thought around the next corner had to be the waterfall, or the second beach; people, water, food and help.

The jungle path broadened again, we heard in the distance the sound of running water and knew *finally* we were about to stumble upon the massive waterfall we had read and heard so much about reading on-line forums.

The waterfall would be surrounded by hikers; washing, laughing, splashing and jumping. The fall would be over two hundred feet tall; we would throw coconuts under it's torrent and make jokes about how, if we'd been holding onto the coconut, our arms would be no longer be part of us.

Our hopes rose to the sound of water falling.

The path turned, we turned the corner with the path, and paused for a moment.

Looking up at this vision, natures water source.

The waterfall in full glory.

The waterfall we might die for; I've washed my hands in bigger sinks.

A trickle of water dribbled down rock, the fall from rock to pool beneath, no more than five feet.

A small pool collected the water, shallow, no wider than I; a bathtub in unusual setting.

We took our backpacks off and looked at each other, deciding to rest for a few minutes by the stream whilst we contemplated drinking the water.

Sweat dripped from our faces and blood from our legs, covered in grazes.

We held each other.

We knew we couldn't rest for long because we had to be somewhere by nightfall; we *had* to be because a night in this wilderness would mean spending the night with poisonous spiders, scorpions and centipedes.

Facing the other way to fall asleep after a nightmare is the adult version of running to your parent's bedroom as a child.

The hike had snapped us.

The immaculate American family appeared; two adults, one little boy and girl.

They *all* had side partings, even the wife, white flashing smiles and clothes still ironed.

Not sweating, not breathless, and not a single side-parted hair out of place.

They stopped and spoke to us, full of encouragement, we asked how far it was to the beach, and they said just over the ridge and *we were practically there.*

This was important news.

First these were the first people we had seen in two days, second, they were coming back from where we were heading looking refreshed and joyful, and third they had a couple of ten year olds with them, and if the children could make it we simply had to.

Lily and I waited for a break in the initial meet and greet conversation to ask for some water.

We could see the water, in a large bottle, swinging by the husband's leg in slow motion as he spoke; splashing against the inside of his plastic container, sounding like rain hitting sand.

I joked this was the last place on Earth two people from England who occasionally smoked weed should be.

As soon as the words left my mouth I regretted them.

The parents stood in front of their children like I had just pulled a gun and, offended, they mumbled their urgent need to keep pushing on and dragged their kids across the pond, onto a ridge, up and around Lily and I, then back into the jungle; all with the speed and efficiency of a divorced traffic warden sticking parking fines to car windscreens on a cold Christmas morning.

They left as if they had reached the pond and stumbled upon the devil washing himself with salty fish and dead beaver heads.

There was no time to beg for water.

Lily and I both watched the water leave; attached to the side of the man's waist.

Wet drops of life around the top of the container screamed goodbye in slow motion, leaving our lips stained with dry memories of what could have been.

Lily shot me a new look.

The new *'you've killed us with a mountain'* look.

From now on Lily would do the talking to any strangers we met, of that I was sure.

Lily could get us beautiful hotel rooms for days at half price just by asking; I couldn't even get us some water from the perfect family miles into one of the hardest hikes in the world, when it was clear if we didn't get water soon we would die.

I dunked myself in the base of the waterfall, to cool off, and to give Lily a moment without me; to ease the tension between us caused by my mouth running faster than I could catch it.

I removed my shirt and shorts and lowered myself in; I knew the humidity would dry me in minutes and the cool water felt good on my skin.

I kept my mouth closed to make sure I didn't swallow any water, because the last thing we needed was for one of us to contract dysentery.

I was in the pool for a minute, maybe two; I stood up and walked to Lily and watched her as she watched me.

Her expression changed as I walked to her, from a face contemplating how many different ways she could kill me to one of concern.

I asked her what was wrong and she told me to look down.

So I did, and on my penis, about an inch long but expanding, was a leech.

I had no idea what to do and neither did Lily.

I tried to think back to films I had seen and was pretty sure you could pick them off from the skin, and because they had anaesthetic in their bite I wouldn't feel a thing.

Lily thought if you pulled them off they threw up a poison that enters the wound and kills the host within twenty four hours.

This was stressful, and also a little bit funny because I could die from poisoned penis.

If Lily was right, there was no chance of being in hospital in twenty four hours.

Whilst we stood panicking, the leech drained more blood and expanded.

Soon the leech would be bigger than my penis, even more embarrassing.

Maybe, I thought, the leech would get full and drop off. The thing only looked small at first, though was now larger; I wondered how much it could expand and whether it was worth ignoring.

I explained to Lily I remembered in the movie Predator they picked them off like peaches from trees and nobody cried, and they seemed like real leeches.

Lily said she couldn't remember why she thought what she did, but she felt it was common knowledge.

We looked into each other's eyes for answers we hoped the other would have and Lily's eyes welled up because a leech sucking my blood, whilst lost up a mountain, was not part of our plan.

"I'm going to pull it off."

"We don't know what to do!"

"Wait until when? The sun won't stay in the sky forever, our phones have no signal, we can't ask Google, and I really don't want a leech attached to my penis!"

I moved my finger along my penis to the leech's face and pushed it away with my nail, but it didn't move.

Lily told me not to, told me she didn't want me to, but I didn't fancy passing out from blood loss; because then the only alternative would be for Lily to try and get back on her own whilst my skin turned green.

The other option, I thought, was wait until the leech had drank all of my blood and was the size of a person; then Lily could ride out of the jungle on a slow moving, slimy horse.

I tried again, digging my nails in with more force, anticipated pain; but the leech's head came free from my penis, and the process was painless.

Lily screamed when she saw my blood and I panicked too because no man wants to see blood flowing fast from a leech bite on his penis; the leech was somehow still attached and dangled off my body from what looked like it's arse.

I panicked, Lily screamed.

The fat face of the leech tried to re-attach itself to my skin, dangling off my penis, wiggling and waggling around; a panicking bird trapped underground.

I screamed and ran in a circle with my hands waving, in a moment akin to when someone tries to put a spider down the back of your neck and you can feel eight legs crawling along your skin.

Lily shouted my name.

I looked down, still running, hopping up and down, not thinking, panicking, screaming out loud, Lily screamed louder, my body rushed with adrenaline I couldn't afford to use, and I grabbed the base of the dark slimy thing, tugged hard, and looked away as its bum came away in my hand.

I threw the leach back into the waterfall, hopped up and down from one foot to the other, looked down at my bleeding penis.

I shuddered, my body trying to shake off the feeling of being wrapped in creepy crawlies.

Lily came to me and sobbed into my shoulder she didn't want me to die; I assured her I wouldn't have pulled the leech off if I thought her story was factually accurate, whilst I wondered what the chances were of me dying within twenty four hours of an unexplained seizure.

She asked me if it hurt, and I told her I couldn't feel a thing. Which was true.

We looked at each other.

I dropped a smile; relieved I no longer had a leech sucking my cock.

Lily caught my smile before it hit the ground, scooped it up and placed it over her mouth.

And we laughed.

We laughed until we had no laughter left inside us; a moment of ecstasy trapped on a journey towards double homicide.

I put my clothes back on and blood soaked through my shorts covering my groin area; if we did meet anyone, I would have some explaining to do.

We put our backpacks on, breathed out, moved again.

We could still die, that hadn't changed.

The good news was according to the family we were *practically there*.

In a few short minutes we would be on the second beach surrounded by people cooking fish on a barbeque, swimming in the ocean, children running along the sand lofting briefcases above their heads, and parents telling them to hold the briefcases up to their ears, so they can hear the sound of a place called the city.

The children would ask what a city is, and the parents would explain about a land where people congregate to take and profit, and oh look children, here come two folk from the city now; you can tell because they're only visiting us to find a way out for themselves.

And the man has no penis.

They will stop when they see us; run to us, feed us fish and water us like dying plants escaping wrong conditions.

We will tell them our leech story, they'll laugh and we'll be saved.

A wild boar on a spit, someone playing guitar and everyone knowing the same songs.

We'll sing together; all just around the next corner.

So we walked.

We walked around the next corner.

Nothing.

We walked around the corner after that.

Nothing.

We reached the place the American family had been talking about, but there must have been some mistake.

There was no beach.

There was no great gathering of people.

There was no food or water or singing.

There was no rescue.

The family had been *super* positive and entered have-a-nice-day-mode.

Not a problem and quite positive to be around for us miserable anti-social Brits, just rather misplaced on this particular occasion.

We looked at a derelict, jungle obliterated, wooden shack with a rusting tin roof and rotten bench.

This was it.

This might have been a nice place to sit fifty years earlier, but it died long ago; green jungle branches climbed out of the windows and snaked over the roof.

The tin roof had been attacked by a pack of ransacking bears; covered in holes and three quarters of the roof touched the ground.

The glass was smashed out from the windows so long ago the base of the hut was littered with sand; if there were ever windows in this hellish wonderland.

This wasn't a place for people.

This couldn't be the eight mile point.

The eight mile point was the place we'd read about; the beach, the waterfall.

Full of people, some getting boats back to the start of the coastline.

This.can.not.be.the.fucking.eight.mile.point.

My brain drowned in the reality of my formerly positive outlook, my eyes wandered to a thick wooden slab hammered into the ground.

Crudely etched into the wood by knife:

"8 miles"

We are here.

This really is it.

This was what we spent two days walking to.

Our holy grail turned into a plastic cup from TESCOs.

A balloon sword pulled from plastic stone.

We took our backpacks off and let silence do our talking.

Without water Lily was right; I *had* killed us with a mountain.

I was sorry for my part and Lily was sorry for hers but we were now four miles away from the beach we left that morning and four miles worse off.

If that morning we had gone the other way we would've been getting back to the car about now.

I didn't need to tell Lily this.

Instead we were now eight miles away from the car, twice as worse off and twice as likely to die.

Mosquitoes the size of American football helmets buzzed around our heads.

I picked up my backpack and a centipede as thick as my arm and twice as hairy crawled out slowly from underneath; it didn't move fast because it wasn't afraid.

We were in the centipede's jungle and the centipede had tactical advantage.

If we didn't get back to some kind of civilisation before dark there was a real chance one of us could get bitten, or simply slip off the mountain.

No help for miles around.

No mobile phone signal.

Two people who went out for a hike nobody knew who never came back.

Our lives reduced to mail piling up behind a front door, dinosaur leaves collecting on our lawn.

Somebody we didn't know would take down photographs of us smiling at festivals from inside our home.

Our red car would sit in the car park too long towed away; years from now it would be sold to someone who would never know what went wrong.

The flower stickers would be removed.

The pink dice thrown away.

We had to turn around and go back to the beach we left that morning and risk being caught up a mountain, on a thin path, in complete darkness, without a torch and surrounded by the type of bugs that, if bitten, we wouldn't wake up from.

Then stay overnight at the beach of haunted tents and tomorrow morning hike back, past the lonely red backpack, out to the start of what had become the journey from hell.

Without food.

Without water.

And with a leech bite on my penis.

A fast moving, excessively muscular American guy appeared from the path ahead and didn't stop moving but said hi as he moved, we told him it was our first hike and as he moved through the trees his words, although in jest, were chilling;

"No way! You crazy Brits - Oh Jeez. Oh man, you're botn gonna die."

I guess, being Brits, he must have thought we were jok ng about it being our first hike.

He was gone as quickly as he appeared, but before he completely vanished he second glanced my bloodstained groin area.

That would give him something to think about.

We started the hike back to the first beach we left that morning.

At least we knew where it was.

Our morale was at an all time low and both of us were hungry; I had a headache from needing to drink and Lily had the same.

Lily got blisters, and then I got blisters. Lily got angry, and then I got angry; but we didn't have the energy to fight.

We just wanted it to be over.

Blood seeped from my leech bite.

Daydreams of food and being safe at home took our thoughts away from crumbling paths, but the odd slip, followed by the sound of falling cliff was enough to shake us back to reality.

We climbed back up and back down cliff after cliff, and retraced our steps under blazing heat.

We approached the beach we were at that morning just as night was falling; four hours after reaching the eight mile point.

We walked the last thin, winding path down to the beach in darkness.

Putting one foot in front of the other, mostly guessing the next place we planted our weight wouldn't be space.

We put the tent up in the dark again after the longest day; a day we were both thankful for surviving.

In the morning we would be weaker, a concern for tomorrow.

The stars shone brighter still, and the ocean was calmer than the night before.

We fell into the tent, exhausted.

My penis stopped bleeding, some good news at last.

We had somehow managed to hike eight miles, four miles away from the beach and four miles back to it, in one day without food or water...and still had another four to go in the morning.

In the tent I looked up at the ceiling.

We might be the first people to hike ten miles and end up four miles further away from where they wanted to be.

I closed my heavy eyes to sleep and all I could see was jungle.

In the morning I rolled out the tent and next to the two haunted tents was a third tent.

If this tent was empty we died yesterday and God made a mistake and sent us to the tent afterlife instead of the human one.

The zip to the new tent moved, and I fell weakly into our tent to tell Lily the news.

As suspected Lily went and introduced herse f to the owners of the blue tent and returned with a bottle of water and a sandwich for us to share.

We drank, ate and, although it wasn't much, an invisible pressure immediately lifted.

We knew we would have the strength to hike the beginning again backwards.

The hike wasn't going to be fun, in fact we knew exactly how much fun the hike wasn't going to be, but we weren't going to die either.

Setting off for the last four miles back to the car was depressing, four hours of hiking ahead of us on blistered, weary feet and exhausted bodies.

The mood changed when just after the first hour of hiking I slipped and ripped the entire front of my shorts exposing my bloody penis and ball sack.

I'd been wearing light material because of the heat and had no replacement trousers.

Lily laughed hard and so did I.

My trousers covered in dry blood no longer seemed so bad.

The leech already a distant memory to laugh about, because I was still alive and didn't feel poisoned.

I didn't want to finish the hike naked from the waist down, but it was a welcome break from spending two days thinking about dying.

The only spare piece of clothing we had was one of Lily's pink sarongs so I wrapped it around me, but rather than hide my penis and balls as intended, it served only to highlight them in glorious flamingo pink.

The last hike back was *only* the original four miles from the beach to civilisation, so it was a far more popular hike. and on the way out we crossed the path of regular decent folk.

Fresh faced tourists and energetic families past us, and I can imagine what we must have looked like; two creatures emerging from jungle, looking like we'd been living in the mountains for years, caked in sweat, one wearing a pink sarong highlighting a weary bloodstained penis, balls dangling through material.

We turned the last corner, our real life scene from Robinson Crusoe.

Lily's little red car was our rescue plane; it would take us away from the evil mountain we could have died on.

We hobbled on our blisters and boils down the last winding stretch of mountain to the car, and when we finally touched its cool metallic surface we screamed for joy and hugged.

We threw our backpacks in the boot; turned, laughed, kissed, got in the car, shook like crazy and promised each other we would never ever go hiking again.

Not in a million years.

"A MILLION CONSEQUENCES COLLIDING INTO A MILLION COINCIDENCES"

Saturday 17th October 2010

I'm walking home, even though my route home isn't near where I am, and the manager of the pub is smoking outside, he tells me long time no see.

I tell him work is keeping me busy.

He asks me if I want a drink.

I know he knows what I've been accused of, but at no point have I spoken to him.

We could both pretend not to know anything, if he wanted us not to know.

He tells me Julia has left, and I desperately want him to elaborate but he doesn't.

He tells me my first drink is on the house.

He offers me a cigarette, I say no thanks, I don't smoke.

On the other side of the road laughter bellows from the Wetherspoon pub, the sound of lots of people in one place, people milling about, talking, the sound of what pubs used to be like.

Business must be bad if he's prepared to wipe the slate clean, act like I haven't been accused of being a pervert.

Turn a blind eye, like he doesn't know anything.

I say yes, and thank Tom.

I walk into the pub and Tom pours my free glass of wine, before he hands me the glass, he moves to the wall connecting the bar and kitchen.

To the phone.

He peels a piece of paper from the top of the phone, rolls it up into a ball, and throws the ball into the bin.

He hands me my glass, with a wink.

Either he sacked Julia because he didn't believe her story, or Julia left for her own reasons, and he's decided to let me back in because he needs the money.

I look around at the empty pub.

I look back at Tom, nod, so he knows I understand.

The piece of paper in the bin has my number on, probably with "pervert" drawn above in Julia's handwriting.

I turn, and sit alone away from the bar to nurse my thoughts.

I have a feeling Tom is relieved by my choice of seat.

They say you can tell who you are by the company you keep.

The only other person in the pub is a bearded guy, old and way too thin. He's bobbing out of time to music that isn't playing and his lips move up and down as he mumbles to himself; remembering a time when his words mattered to others.

I walk into the garden to avoid the possible scenario of the old guy looking up and catching my eye and to get away from any more of Tom's winks and nods.

The garden is cold; the heaters are on but not set to an obscene temperature.

I miss the roaring heat, in a way, because they remind me of Julia.

All fire, red hair.

Julia must have been setting the heaters too high.

Now she's gone, the garden is just a garden again.

The television sets are off, the lantern lights on.

As I take a seat the garden looks quite beautiful, romantic even.

Sitting with their back to me and two benches in front is a couple who didn't hear me enter the garden.

They're kissing.

The woman is in her fifties; short dark hair and a long blue skirt.

I can't see much else because attached to her is a man in a pin striped suit.

I can't see much of him because he's attached to her.

From the side of his face he looks older, but I can't tell how old; maybe in his sixties.

Two bottles of wine sit on their bench, one empty, they're pretty drunk.

Caught up in a moment becoming a world.

They kiss passionately, not coming up for air.

They are rapidly becoming quite sexual in front of me.

The woman groans.

The man groans back.

The man groans "oh baby" as he rests his palm on the side of her face.

I've never been one to turn their nose up at affection in public. It's a great shame people slow down to look in the wreckage of a car crash, but look away in horror at two people showing the natural conclusions of being so in love they've lost touch with their surroundings.

That said, the old man's hand is on her bare ankle and I watch as his hand goes under her long skirt and she spreads her legs a little wider and moans into his ear as he tries to, no doubt, figure out how to manoeuvre through the type of underwear a fifty year old woman wears.

I'm not really sure if I should be watching this, but there's nothing else to watch in the garden, and I'm pleasantly warm.

The woman reaches for the old man's trousers and strokes his crotch.

I really don't know where to look.

Yet at the same time I can't look away.

I'm discovering sometimes watching a car crash and two people becoming sexual in public can be similar.

The woman pulls his penis out from his trousers and wanks his erection, his hand makes a familiar circular pattern beneath her skirt.

This is all happening seven feet from me.

Shit!

If they notice I'm in a lot of trouble, and there's no way Tom is going to believe anything I say.

The woman masturbates him faster and the guy speeds up his circular motions.

Popcorn would be nice.

In all seriousness, if I move, I risk making a sound. If I make a sound they're going to look up and see me. If they see me, I'm going to be accused of being a pervert, again.

And it's too late to cough politely to let them know I'm behind them because they're in advanced stages.

By not committing I'm now fully committed.

The woman folds in half and the man grunts into her ear, a pig swallowing a whole cabbage.

The man just ejaculated onto the pub bench and the woman, almost, reached an orgasm.

Any second now they're going to remember where they are, turn their heads and see me. Then I'm going to get in trouble because *they* decided to take a risk by wanking each other off in public.

The man rests his head on her shoulder as pleasure blends with guilt; because the impression I'm getting is they're work colleagues and married; but not to each other.

He pulls his head off her shoulder and takes his hand from under her skirt and moans in a drunken slur they should go back to his place.

He's so drunk his words slur and slop out of his mouth, they flubber all over her without any control or grace, lipless Jellyfish playing trumpets.

She laughs loudly like she's crying, and her joyful yelp is a sigh; she sounds like an excruciating mix of boiling hyena and screaming kettle on the side of a kitchen on fire.

The two drunken lovers stand and fall into each other. The woman laughs into his neck and I feel an emotion deep inside I've been trying to bury for a long time.

The anchoring sense of loss.

I want a girl to laugh into my neck.

I want to not care about the world because the girl laughing into my neck is the universe.

I think.

I drink my wine.

The woman grabs the second bottle of wine from the bucket, it's still half full and the two of them swing around and for the first time notice me.

If I was expecting an awkward moment I was wrong.

They don't care; instead of reacting in shock or anger they laugh loudly, walk around me, and out of the garden without a worry in the world.

I drink my wine alone and stare up at the fairy lights in the bushes, witnessing flashes of stars from memories born from wishes.

The old mumbling man from inside the bar walks into the garden.

He has a choice between one of seven empty benches.

Each bench seats six people.

In total there are forty-two possible options for him to sit down on.

Only one out of those forty-two chairs is covered in semen.

I consider telling him not to sit on the bench in front of me because it has sperm on it, but that would make me sound like some weird garden bench sex pervert because it's only me sitting in the garden so he's bound to question, and quite reasonably, why I have been masturbating over pub benches; so I can't say anything.

Because of a million consequences colliding into a million coincidences the old man sits on the one bench (possibly in the world) partly covered in fresh male sperm.

I try and ponder what the chances are of this happening, and on top of that what the chances of me witnessing it happening are, and the odds are so impossible to calculate the only conclusion I can reach is odds of one in a billion are infinitesimally smaller than they appear to be if you are the one.

I leave the pub, brave the London wind back to my home, put my key wearily into the front door and enter the reception of the house.

I turn the light on to see what I'm doing and Mohammad stands in front of me.

A serial killer pondering his next victim.

Mohammad tells me his phone has been stolen by Somalians. His voice is cracked crazy paving; his eyes burn into me from behind his glasses, two round devils waiting for his words to draw me close enough to slit my throat.

His grey hair slicks back against his head and his ear lobes stretch as far as they can away from his head as if they believe their only means of escape is reaching the floor.

I wonder how long Mohammad has been standing in the dark, alone, staring at the front door and listening to the cars drive past outside.

A chill floods my spine.

There's no way his phone has been stolen by Somalians.

He's losing his mind.

I know the only time Mohammad leaves his house is to walk up the road to get cigarettes because he doesn't eat.

He smokes when he's hungry, and if he gets really hungry he chews and swallows cigarettes covered in dusty butter.

In the few weeks I've been living here I've found out, through unavoidable conversations, Mohammad was born in South Africa, travelled to India and from India he moved to the UK.

I don't know what they taught South African children who moved to India seventy years ago but I'm guessing it was to hate everything.

I know Mohammad is losing his memory and so when he tells me he was robbed by a Somalian the truth is his phone is probably in his pocket and he can't remember what pockets are.

Mohammad asks me for my phone number.

He could have just waited until a reasonable hour, or knocked on my door at some point.

I write down my number on a piece of paper for him, and
hope in days to come the piece of paper I hard him doesn't
end up in his bin with the word "pervert" scrawled above.

"AMERICA – LAND OF THE LEAVE"

September 5th 2007

Lily and I were applying for a visa so I could legally stay in America. The application forms were the size of War and Peace and written in hieroglyphics and I mostly left them for Lily to fill out, a bizarre decision on my part.

The visa would mean I could apply for work and I wouldn't have to keep leaving the country.

As it was, every six months I legally had to leave America for three months due to the immigration laws.

My six month period was up, my visa had run out and I had to leave for three months.

I had to leave my love and my life, and all because of an invisible force would crush us and destroy our lives if we didn't do what it wanted.

I don't think any government can understand, or justify, the pain it puts people through or the hoops it makes us jump through. The divide governments create between hearts is often replaced with resentment which means, sometimes, it's difficult to resist becoming the sum of a government's parts; or parts no longer governed by us alone.

I travelled to Thailand, Cambodia and Vietnam for an adventure I barely remember.

I had to leave for three months alone and then Lily would meet me in Thailand.

Lily planned on flying over so we would be together for New Years Eve.

This three month break unravelled me, and when I tried to put myself back together I was missing a piece.

I was alone and away from the girl I loved and hadn't realised how much Lily kept me on the straight and narrow.

I was away from everyone I knew.

Away from routine; thrown into the world to lose myself.

"THE CAMBODIAN MAFIA"

November 30th 2007

I woke in The Cambodian capital of Phnom Penh; not opening my eyes from sleep, but from the failure to remember the moment before I was staring up at the ceiling.

I thought I could feel Lily behind me in the bed, holding me close.

I was confused because the room I was in was not my home.

Another month until I saw Lily, my anchor and life; by then I might have drunk myself dead.

I had survived, as had Lily, being separated by invisible rules; I was meeting her at Bangkok airport in a month and the nightmare would be over and we could get on with being us again, just like we were before.

I would stop drinking.

She would make me smile.

I grabbed the hose and sprayed it over my face and body, the Cambodian shower, before walking out of the building and into the dusty courtyard.

There was a lot of dust in Cambodia, it whipped up in the wind and stuck to my clothes like clay.

I put a hand between my face and the sun and blinked dust from tired eyes.

One idea, to drink, beamed tubes of light in all directions across my dark consciousness; the torch on a miner's hat worn underground by a mole having an epileptic seizure.

"British man very funny, very funny!"

I looked over in the direction of the high pitched voice pumping out words faster than a man with a hangover needed to hear them.

A lady walked towards me with a big smile, her left hand rested on her waggling hips and her right hand raised above her head, limp-wristed, like she'd just shot a ball towards a basket and was leaving her hand in the shot position for the screaming fans and flashing bulbs from watching media cameras.

Being unable to remember the night before was a theme. The definition of a living ghost is an entity that can only look back and recall events with disassociation, and I felt like a ghost; waking up each day one step out of kilter within an environment familiar, yet somehow beyond my emotional range.

The lady walking towards me was a man; at least that much was clear; but the nature or our relationship was still a fog to me. She wore blue jeans and a white top accentuating her breasts, but her Adam's apple and cow sized hands revealed more in daylight than she could hide at night.

He was too thin for a man but not for a lady-man; she had a feminine face, long dark hair and I felt most likely in the evenings she made money from services offered to drunken tourists, under the guise of being a female prostitute.

I would never cheat on Lily, yet at the same time I couldn't remember what I did the night before and there was, naturally, some mild concern the first person running towards me like an old lover was a Cambodian lady-man gushing with excitement.

She stood in front of me and I stared into her dark face; tanned skin, thin body.

I could see how after several beers in a dark room she could look less like a man and more like a female.

"I take you last night to bar. You pay well. You good man. You meet little Madame G. You very drunk. You alive!"

The feeling of being squeezed into a cannon ball and fired at an army of clowns sank into me and the feeling wasn't nearly as funny as it sounds; I panicked, little Madame must be her pet name for his penis.

My sense of relief was brief, tapered by a reality only slightly better than my imagination, because it became clear Little Madame was not the name for her penis, but the name of the head of the Cambodian mafia.

Last night begun like the day had continued from the night before and the night before that; drinking cheap Cambodian whisky in my room whilst staring out the door at the dust covered courtyard; but it ended with me stumbling into a bar at two in the morning, after taking a lift into town with my new lady-man friend.

I held my cheap whisky and stood in the dark because the bar had no lights, so sitting at the bar was only possible if I wanted to look like a silhouette of a witch on the front cover of a book for kids.

The only other lights, three in total, sat on one table at the back; the only table with people on.

The walls were littered with reminders of how disrespectful people can be; scrawled messages from tourists offering fake phone numbers for free sex acts crammed between photographs of soldiers, whose names on the wall made ghosts of them.

With my cheap whisky in one hand sloshing over the edges of my stained glass I stumbled towards the only lights in the bar, and the group of people sitting on the table at the back.

Two fingertips against a smooth surface leave the same mirage as two lips on stained glass.

I stood by the table for a moment completely ignored and took in, all too briefly, the blurred faces and outlines of strangers.

Three candles, two at each end and one in the middle, provided the light.

I had no idea what card game they played, but it wasn't poker.

Twelve men stood around the table playing the game, but my focus was on the woman sitting at the head of the table.

I shuffled to the end of the table and took one step forward into the light.

The only true awkward silence is had with yourself. I break mine by shouting "Dionysus lives!" and jumping through the nearest glass window.

A strong hand wrapped around my wrist and I looked up at a square, pickled face staring down at me, a rock with eyes.

There was nothing funny about the strength of the grip, or the nature of the man's face, but such was my state of inebriation I looked away from the cold eyes of the man with the pickled rock for a head, and asked the woman why she was sitting at the head of the table.

The woman was in her forties and had a plump face and dark skin. Her eyes flicked up, dark, but had more kindness and patience in them than those belonging to the man gripping my wrist.

Her lips naturally arched downwards and her eyes sunk a little, giving me the impression most of her thoughts, for a long time, had influenced states of depression.

Her large fists gripped cards and sprouted broken knuckles which, I guessed, had spent a fair amount of time carrying out the instructions of a sometimes violent mind.

The woman told me in a deep voice, echoing with money made from nightmares, she was the captain of the Cambodian mafia.

With no friends at the bar and a tightening grip around my wrist I should have apologised and made a sharp exit, but instead I heard myself telling the woman I was the captain of the world mafia, and she was sitting in my seat.

Bodies I couldn't see stood just outside of the candle light but moved closer; there was nobody touching me, but I was pushed up against the wall.

Big gangster people making the world very tiny.

The woman looked beyond my shoulders and smiled at the man holding my wrist and waved her hand.

The grip disappeared.

The world felt bigger.

Expand.

Evidently the captain of the Cambodian mafia didn't see me as a threat.

In moments so deeply gripped by alcohol there's a fleeting madness that doesn't care what happens to t's carrier.

I told the woman she should put her Cambodian mafia status on the line and I would put my world mafia status on the line in a one off, best of three paper-scissors- stone match.

The mafia woman smiled at me then looked at the men around the table holding cards and said something in Cambodian, the silence of smoke and flickering flame was broken by the sound of laughter.

A flame alone is temporary, the wind alone unseen. A flame dances because of what we cannot see; universal idiosyncrasy.

The mafia woman waved her hand one more time and nodded her head at a shape behind my shoulder, I was picked up by someone like he was picking up a marble and carried out of the bar.

The hulk of a man put me down outside the bar, waiting outside was my lady man friend.

The hulk spoke in Cambodian to my lady man friend and she looked frightened.

The hulks voice was deep and booming with a stuttering quality attached to every word caused from being punched in the face too many times, he sounded like somebody firing a nail gun into the head of a sheep.

His tongue made jiggidy bumpidy noises against his teeth when he ended words, reminding me of the sound grandmas breasts made whenever grandpa thought about pomegranates or complained about too warm lemonade.

My lady man friend laughed nervously and handed the hulk some money; the man walked back into the bar leaving a very drunk me with a very poor lady man.

My lady man friend fluttered around me for a moment with the nervous disposition of a butterfly trying to ignore its need for heroin by plying itself with several cups of coffee.

I asked her to take me to the ocean because I hadn't seen it yet and she was only too glad to start her little Tuk Tuk and drive into the night; leaving the bar and organised crime behind us.

On the way she informed me the woman in the bar was the daughter of the head of the Cambodian mafia and I shouldn't have spoken to her or approached the table.

But I didn't care.

I was so drunk I leant over the side of the Tuk Tuk and laughed at the road.

The secret in being that smashed was in drinking this illegal concentrated red bull and Samsung whisky. The red bull is illegal in America, the UK and most of Europe and is served in buckets.

The red bull was keeping me awake and the whisky was balancing it; the perfect system to keep tourists awake for ridiculous periods to enhance their alcohol spending.

The upside to this red bull and whisky concoction was great; I could keep drinking.

The downside was even greater; I could keep drinking.

I wasn't sleeping, so drinking was no longer separated by sleep, my life was a continuous consumption into blackness.

Perhaps, no different to all life.

To those around me I looked like some strung out junkie but in my head I was flying high enough to not care about what was happening.

Nobody pointed out my wings were on fire.

The most dangerous aspect to being so drunk yet so alert was over a period of time all fear and caution evaporates.

The rational voice in my head generally there to keep me away from fire and heroin disappeared.

I was free from myself.

I was sitting on the shoreline of a beach at four in the morning with no clear memory of the Tuk Tuk driver bringing me to the beach, or leaving because of the storm.

I was sitting too close to massive waves crashing on the beach, waves sounding like heavy vans full of old arcade machines crashing through shop windows made of glass.

The darkness made it hard to tell how tall the waves were, but the wind swirling up the beach was powerful enough to knock a man from his feet.

One big wave and I would be plucked from the beach and thrown into the ocean and to certain death, and I was so wasted I didn't care.

Where was Lily?

Two large men, standing along the shoreline, shouted at the top of their voices so they could hear each other against the high winds and crashing waves.

Their accents German but they spoke English.

Rain whipped around in circles of wind trapped inside the night, but I couldn't feel water hitting my skin, or the true temperature beyond the false heat of the booze I was in.

The two men were closer to the sea than I was and walking into the ocean; they would be killed.

I looked back up the beach and a large shadow of a man, bigger than the two Germans, ran towards them screaming in broken English and Cambodian.

He was shouting at the men to get away from the ocean.

The two German men got the message but kept walking towards the sea and shouted back they wanted to die.

They yelled *To Death* but turned away from the crashing waves to face the fast approaching Cambodian man, who I'll name King Kong.

I sat and watched these two massive six foot three suicidal Germans stand in front of the six foot five Cambodian monster.

The Germans stopped screaming.

Faced with two crazy Germans and King Kong about to fight each other next to an ever expanding storming ocean any rational person would have called it a night.

Instead, I stood up, and ran towards the Germans.

Kong grabbed one of the Germans, not by the throat, but by the arm and pulled him away from the sea.

I ran and fell; a drunk running backwards in large shoes on a surface made from the oily backs of fish, as I got closer to the group I could see the two German men were crying.

This wasn't the kind of crying a man might do in a cinema at the end of an emotional kids film, hoping to hide his tears from the children around him, this was screaming out-loud blubbery crying, indicative of complete loss of mental control.

They were probably on their fifth consecutive day awake after drinking never ending buckets of red bull and whisky, and their minds had given up trying to power their massive bodies.

They could be me tomorrow; after all, I was already sitting on the beach.

I was just a few more whiskeys away from the waves.

And then I was in the middle of them; Kong grabbed the arm of one German and I grabbed the arm of the other. Mine wrestled away my grip and the other screamed to be let go.

Rather than being in the middle of a fight, I was in the middle of stopping a double suicide.

Kong's German threw a punch that cracked at the side of his head but Kong didn't flinch and he didn't release his grip. I turned to face my German and Kong shouted something in Cambodian and I grabbed my Germans wrist and felt a blow land on the side of my head, which put me on the floor, but I still had hold of him.

Four more men appeared from the darkness, through the howling rain, and three of them grabbed my German and wrestled him to the floor, and the other guy helped Kong take his one to the ground.

The Germans were dragged back up the beach for their own safety, and I watched on as they sat on a wall and smoked cigarettes given to them by the men who had fought them to save their lives.

The two German men shook with cold and sat, wet up to their knees; they had rang the doorbell of Death, fortunately for them, nobody was in.

We all sleep in our talk.

I looked at the two German men and wondered how long it would be until I broke down; perhaps this was me breaking down.

Kong walked up to me and through my whisky mist a oar-sized hand appeared that I shook.

He asked me if I wanted to go somewhere and smiled.

He looked like the kind of guy people go with and never went with people.

Kong said something in Cambodian to the group of men standing around the Germans.

I noticed two of the men from the bar earlier in the night, sitting at the table with the captain of the Cambodian mafia; Kong was big enough to be the guy who picked me up and carried me out of the bar, like he was lifting a baby out of a high chair.

If I hadn't been so drunk I may have been concerned none of this was coincidence.

I was put on the back of a moped by Kong and we zipped along the Cambodian coastline as the sun rose over the ocean. Along the way I had time to ponder, and the thoughts of my ponderings led me to seriously consider jumping off the moped to escape.

Was I about to be killed by the mafia for something I couldn't remember doing? Was I about to be arrested then beaten by dodgy police officers until I hand them all of my money? Maybe they'll make me their mule and use me to smuggle drugs across the border.

The sunrise was beautiful.

Whatever happened, the moment was not mine to control, I was relying on the kind hearted nature of flat-faced practitioners of organised thuggery.

The moped turned right, away from the coast-line and beautiful sunrise, and wound through fields of green then through back streets and cluttered doorways, into a town with bars and early rising elderly women shuffling along carrying dead animals on sticks tied together with pieces of string.

We stopped by a small market stall. The market stall looked like any other. The stall itself was a small vending machine with dead chickens hanging upside down inside the glass, and behind the market stall was a table.

Two men sat around the table in early morning silence.

Behind the men was a small tent.

I was invited to sit at the table and join the two men.

Kong pointed to me, said something in Cambodian, and the two guys around the table looked up and nodded.

One put a beer on the table in front of me; the other slapped my back.

No smiles.

I sat on a chair and took in my company.

Three men, including Kong.

Three men and a little baby, including me.

The chair at the head of the table was empty.

In front of me was another massive guy.

His muscles pushed the resistance levels of his white shirt, his skin tanned, cold-blue eyes and short blonde hair.

His nose pressed up against his top lip in a bewildering statement of misplacement; a man found on his kitchen floor looking into a washing machine for sausages.

The man said hello but did not say his name.

No smiles.

By his accent I could tell he was Dutch.

Saying hello is mostly hell.

He said he had heard about me; he'd been told tonight I was not afraid to help some people in need and I had put myself in danger by doing so.

I don't tell him I was so drunk just before running towards the Germans I was talking to the waves, and they were telling me to walk towards them too.

He told me he was from Holland but could never go back home.

I asked him why, and he said never ask why.

The third guy at the table with Kong and the Dutchman was yet to speak and he looked out of place.

Kong was relaxed; the Dutch guy was Dutch and had an air of confidence about him, suggesting he knew he could swipe the head off a bear if needed, so didn't need to impress anyone and wasn't going to try.

The third guy was small, white and skinny.

His hair was side parted but thin, the expression on his nervous face reminded me of a rat escaping a drowning ship who knew it stood no chance of swimming to land.

He couldn't stop smiling.

He had too much energy, as he spoke he bobbed up and down and jiggled his legs.

His fingers wrapped on the table nervously and his eyes darted as if he trusted nobody.

He sounded English, but given the scenario I found myself hoping he wasn't.

The guy smoked a cigarette and held no eye contact, but didn't stop smiling.

His nerves made me nervous and I hoped I wasn't about to watch him get shot, or he wasn't nervous because he knew they were about to shoot me, and he was the man told to do put the gun to my head and pull the trigger; to prove his worth to the others.

The chicken stall was busy for six in the morning.

A little old lady walked out from inside the tent holding a flapping chicken upside down in her hands.

She looked quite sweet, compared to the rest.

A kind face.

She walked slowly up to the upside down chickens and pulled out a large machete from a drawer underneath them.

She turned, machete in hand, looked at the scared English guy, and walked toward the table.

I wondered if I would see Lily again.

She put the chicken on the table, gripping the chicken hard by the legs.

The chicken flapped around, trying to fly, trying to move, trying anything the chicken could.

The old woman raised her machete above her head, and brought the machete down in one swing, into the chicken neck; separating chicken body, from chicken head.

Blood splattered across the table, and indiscriminately left marks on all of us.

I was out of my depth, but still drunk enough to act like I could breathe whilst standing on the bottom of the sea.

I wanted to look away, but stayed sitting, facing the same direction as everyone else, not wanting to rock the apple cart.

The chicken's wings still flapped, and with each flap the men around the table clapped their hands, and now everyone was smiling.

Kong touched my elbows and encouraged me to clap, so I did.

With each flap the headless chicken body made, we clapped.

These claps felt hollow; a standing ovation at a pop concert after the artist mimed everything.

The flapping chicken wings slowed, and so did our clapping.

The wings stopped completely.

The chicken's head was on the table in front of me, there wasn't much blood on the head, which surprised me.

The chicken's eyes were open, beak closed.

The old lady held the machete.

Kong nodded at me and said one word: *lucky*.

Not for the chicken, I thought.

The old lady looked at me, did not nod, or smile, and turned and walked slowly back into the tent.

Kong stood up and handed the nervous guy the body of the chicken.

Blood everywhere now, all over the table.

Kong handed the flapping chicken body to the guy who got up, shook my hand too many times with the hand without the chicken in, jumped on one of the many mopeds parked at the stall and drove away.

We sat in silence.

The Dutch guy spoke of Holland and how he missed his home, he spoke like he always spoke sitting in chicken blood.

What was I to know?

He told me he had a daughter he knew he would never see again.

Does nobody care about the chicken blood?

He was wanted in Holland for something, some crime meaning he could never return to his country or contact his family.

I asked them what the story was with the nervous English guy.

He was Cambodian, the head of the Cambodian Police.

The Dutch guy told me the more the chicken wings flap, the greater the gift; and the woman had handed a great gift to the head of the police.

Kong told me the old woman who cut the chicken head off was the head of the Cambodian mafia, and she wanted to give me the chicken head for luck, as a present.

I sensed it was an offer I couldn't refuse.

He was unable to explain anything else, because his English was no good.

He nodded to the chicken head on the table, and I picked it up, thanking him for his gift.

I put the dismembered chicken head in my pocket, and all I could think was I wanted to get back to my hotel room, have a hot shower, throw the chicken head in the bin and stay in my hotel room until time to return to Thailand to meet Lily.

I was sobering up; covered in chicken blood, and had a chicken head in my pocket for luck.

The eyes were open.

I told the guys I needed to leave; I'd been up for three days and needed to crash.

They shook my hands, strong grips.

No smiles.

As I walked back, alcohol wearing off, thumbing the beak of a dismembered chicken head in my pocket, I thought about how I would soon meet Lily at the airport and how we would head back to Thailand for Christmas and celebrate New Year's Eve together.

We would be us again.

I would wake up with her next to me, and it wouldn't be a dream.

"WHAT'S THAT BEHIND YOU?"

Friday 24th October 2010

My kitchen is so cold my hands need gloves.

The overcast day rests on my skin as the London rain pelts against large lime green windows.

I'm looking at a pile of broken wood stuffed in the gap between the side of the oven and the side of the kitchen cabinet. The oven itself Mohammad assures me is new and state of the art, but I've never seen a new state of the art oven with no timer or temperature control.

When I use the oven smoke pours through the hot plates and towards the ceiling, where Mohammad has intelligently placed the world's largest and most sensitive smoke alarm.

The smoke alarm is in the same place in every room, above the same cheap oven, and they're all connected. So when one smoke alarm goes off, every smoke alarm in the building goes off too.

The alarm is so powerful and high pitched the second it's activated dogs sitting on porches within a ten mile radius evaporate and people with fillings in their teeth hear ten seconds of boxing commentary from the 1974 fight between Muhammad Ali and George Foreman.

The only way all the alarms can be turned off is via the main control box outside Mohammad's front door.

Regularly an alarm will pierce the peace then footsteps are heard running from a flat above, to the ground floor, to outside Mohammad's apartment.

When the footsteps stop I hear the voice of Mohammad; impatient and rude.

The broken pieces of wood resting between the oven and the kitchen cabinet are the remains of the chair I sat through weeks ago.

When a person falls over a chair and no one is around to hear trees write silent philosophy.

The chair is in five smaller bits of wood and one larger piece, all piled together; the broken corpse of Pinocchio.

I've been meaning to throw away the pieces of wood but haven't found the right moment, the right moment being when Mohammad is not around.

I haven't heard Mohammad this morning so think he may be out or sleeping.

I place the broken pieces of wood into a black bin bag, leave my flat, and head down the stairs to the main front door.

As the heel of my left foot touches the last step Mohammad's front door opens, as the flat of my left foot displaces my weight across the step he walks out of the door; my right foot joins the position of my left, and by the time it does, Mohammad is standing in front of me.

He holds an empty glass in his hand.

I suspect he was holding the glass up to his ear, leaning against the inside of his front door so he could listen out for any signs of life coming down the stairs.

Mohammad leers at me over his glasses, and asks me what I'm doing.

His playful smile lets me know he's planning on coming with me.

I'm tempted to tell him to mind his own business, but instead I tell him I'm throwing out the chair because I fell through it.

I'm hoping he might offer to pay for a new one, or apologise for giving me a chair in the first place that could have caused me injury, but he suggests he takes the bits of wood and gets the Polish builder to glue the chair back together.

I suspect the chair has been glued together before, and that's why I fell through it, so I decline the offer, thank Mohammad, but tell him I'll get a new chair at some point.

I move towards the front door and Mohammad walks with me.

Mohammad is coming to help me put my bin bag in the bin.

Outside a million invisible piranhas nip at my face.

We walk down the concrete steps, then a few feet down the path and to the two bins standing side by side.

There's nothing special about these bins.

The green bin is for recycling, the grey bin is for normal rubbish; two standard bins and a standard bin bag.

Mohammad and I share a moment looking at bins.

A red bus drives by and I look up and catch the eye of a man on the top deck, looking down on us, likely thinking Mohammad and I are an ordinary couple who enjoy taking our rubbish to the bins together on cold days.

I open the bin lid and Mohammad touches me on the shoulder and asks a stupid question, but with such sincerity part of me wants to keep him in a small cage and smother him in cotton wool.

"Do you know Colossus? Do you know how to put the rubbish into the bin?"

I tell Mohammad I know how to put rubbish into a bin, I go further, and tell him I've done it before and I'm good at it.

I open up the lid to the bin, raise the bin bag, and as I'm lowering the bag into the bin I feel Mohammad pull on my elbow again, and again he speaks; intent on offering me advice on how to lower a bin bag into a bin:

"Yes. Yes. Lower the bag with all the wooden parts being inside."

I lower the bin bag and Mohammad gets annoyed.

"No! Not there! Put the bag at the back. More at the back so it is."

His words are aggressive, like he's slapping a child's wrist for hugging a boiling kettle with his face.

Still gripping the bag I look at Mohammad to check if he's serious, and from the intent in his eyes, he's never been more serious in his life.

Instructing me on how to lower a bin bag into an empty bin is his charge of the light brigade.

I move my hand out a bit and the bin bag moves a little further to the back of the bin.

I look at Mohammad to see if the new position is correct.

Mohammad nods his head, he doesn't smile, but his words are more positive:

"Yes. This is very good Colossus. This is very good in the bin of the rubbish putting."

I raise my eyebrows and ask if I should let go of the bin bag, if he's sure; Mohammad shakes his head in frustration like he's trying to pass down the knowledge of how mankind came into existence and I'm not capable of understanding.

"No! The bag more in the middle! More in the middle! Yes. Yes. Lower it now so it is."

I start to drop my arm, so the bin bag lowers into the bin.

Mohammad stares at the bin bag and takes me through the dropping process like he's telling someone how to reverse park their expensive car into a tight space.

"Yes. Slowly. Slowly. A little more. A little more."

I feel the bin bag hit the bottom of the bin but before I let go Mohammad speaks:

"Now you can be letting goings of the bag."

He must be joking, but he isn't.

I can tell from his face he truly believes he's just taught me how to put a bag of normal rubbish into a normal bin.

In a way, it's sweet, and throughout the process he's yet to say anything racist, sexist or abusive towards me.

I sense he is sensing we're bonding.

Mohammad shuffles back with me from the bins and into the hallway of the house, where I know he's going to want to talk to me all Saturday on my day off, and I just want to go back to my room and be left alone.

I truly don't mind talking to Mohammad because deep down I sense he's lonely, confused and fearful.

All the things I am, in a way.

Only I've accepted my life and don't need to be around others.

He's from a different time, a time where amusement is company; and reputation is golden.

Mohammad has lived a life afraid, and when you live a life afraid you end up afraid to live.

The reason he's afraid is likely not even his fault, because life is a series of events ours to experience not ours to control.

Mohammad tells me about the problems he's been having with the tenants.

I knew it would happen, I knew if I couldn't get away I would end up hearing stories of hate, stories where he wants to put ideas in my head about other people, stories convincing me to side with him in the war in his head.

Mohammad says the couple upstairs are terribly disruptive. He tells me many years ago he had a similar experience when one tenant tried to turn all his other tenants against him.

I tell him maybe the couple aren't doing what he thinks, and he ignores me and keeps speaking in monologues.

I don't know if he's recalling actual memory, or being paranoid.

Mohammad asks me if I read the sign on the communal toilet door yesterday:

 "Dear Landlord – we respect your privacy, please respect ours."

He'd been caught going through someone's room, like he admitted he does, and the tenant had quite rightly reacted.

Mohammad tells me *the people at the tops of the stairs* are turning people against him.

I point out to Mohammad apart from the couple at the top of the stairs there is only me and one other girl in the building, and I'm not swayed by events because I don't care either way.

And I don't, I want to go upstairs to my flat and leave behind the small minded squabbling.

Instead I'm standing here listening to Mohammad be negative.

Mohammad tells me the message was up for weeks.

I tell Mohammad the message was on the toilet door when I went to work yesterday morning and gone by the time I arrived home, so the note was up for less than a day.

Mohammad shakes his head and looks down at his shoes as he speaks; his words confirm he isn't listening to a word I'm saying:

"Weeks, maybe bloody months."

I tell Mohammad for arguments sake let's say the note was there for *years*.

He looks up and his eyes widen, his tongue rests oddly out of place on his bottom lip in a state of bewildered confusion, a trainee mechanic tasting the bonnet of a crashed alien spaceship.

I tell Mohammad the note could only be read by the people in his flats, and that number hasn't changed, so the amount of time the note was on the toilet door for does not increase the note on the toilet doors audience.

He stares at me, thinking about what I've just said.

He's listening, finally.

Mohammad's tongue shoots back into his mouth, he looks back down at his shoes and shakes his head.

"Years?"

His brain is a ball-less abacus; a rusty bar with nine chewed strings dangling in the wind tying up words he can't remember, laces on someone else's shoes.

He whispers again like he's whispering a fact;

"Bloody *years.*"

Because of the narcissistic nature of Mohammad it truly doesn't matter what I say or think. He uses me to validate what he thinks and ignores anything contradicting what he wants to believe.

This chat, like all of our chats, isn't going anywhere.

He stares at me as I try to find a moment I can tell him I must be going.

Instead, in a voice crackling with revenge for tenants he should be letting get on with their lives, he asks me into his flat for a cup of tea.

I should say no, but I say yes, and Mohammad leads me into his flat at the bottom of the stairs.

The first room in his flat is his front room and it's notable for the lack of television, the ridiculous amount of A4 white paper stacked floor to ceiling high, and cardboard boxes seemingly empty.

There must be a floor but if there is it cannot be seen, and if there's a window it's never been opened.

In the corner of the room I think I can see the edge of a black leather sofa, but it's impossible to say because it's drowning in old newspapers, and fliers taken from telephone boxes advertising local escorts and female models happy to fulfil old man desires.

There are so many pieces of paper and boxes to manoeuvre past them I have to turn sideways and walk slowly through the only available path behind Mohammad, all the while hoping he doesn't tell me about why he has a collection of fliers for prostitutes.

I make my breathing deliberately shallow, an attempt to put less stale smoke in my lungs.

Mohammad does not explain his home; but the front room is the room of a madman, of that I'm certain.

For all I know a dead prostitute could be buried under all this paper and nobody would ever find her.

I must leave as soon as possible.

The room with a million stacks of paper, pictures of comparatively young naked girls with bad history in their eyes and cardboard boxes, leads to the only other room in the flat. The kitchen.

Where does he sleep? Where's his bed?

Maybe he doesn't sleep.

I take a seat and Mohammad asks me what I want to drink and I ask for a cup of tea.

The kitchen is small and cramped.

The ceiling and walls are stained yellow with nicotine.

The sides are littered with ashtrays full of used cigarettes, and the only sign of food consumed is a creepy Prince Charles and Princess Dianna plate placed in the middle of the lime green and white polka dot table-cloth in front of me.

What is it with Mohammad and lime green?

Mohammad sits down and hands me a cup of coffee.

I choose not to remind him I asked for tea.

He stares briefly at Prince Charles waving to an invisible off-plate face and looks up at me and explains he never went into the room of the tenants, but why would they accuse him of doing something he didn't do, if the consequence could get them evicted?

Mohammad tells me one day he was in the garden and he saw the light was on in their flat, so he went in to turn it off, but he's never ever been in their room in the day when they weren't there.

I can see the tenant's problem because Mohammad has just admitted to me he's been in their flat whilst denying he's ever been in their flat.

Mohammad's attention turns from the couple at the top of the stairs to the only other person staying in the building; a Spanish girl who, like the couple, I have never met.

How I like it; the reason I moved here.

To be alone.

His mood darkens.

I watch as the grip around his cup tightens and his fat nostrils flare with momentary rage, he positions his tongue back on his thin lips and explains.

I can't imagine what this girl could have done, missed a few rent payments perhaps, that would cause the waves of rage crashing behind the land of his pupils.

I do know Mohammad has an odd fascination with women, and it appears to come from a dark place; from hearing him in conversation, and from seeing him at the bar that time, to him women are second class citizens, used for his sexual pleasure.

Not that I know what sexual pleasure a man of his age needs.

Mohammad shakes his head; his ear lobes wobble either side of his cheeks.

"She knocked on my door and asked me to lend to her a plate, do you know the word plate? For the eating of various foods."

I stare at Mohammad and nod my head.

"Later, she comes to me and asks if she can borrow a knife and a fork, you know, for the eating of the things we put in our mouths."

I stare at Mohammad waiting for him to get to the source of his anger.

Mohammad stares back.

One of his tenants asking for cutlery is the extent of his complaint.

Mohammad shakes his head and speaks again, a little calmer, but still in a tone like he's discovered his car tyres have been slashed overnight.

"Unbelievable isn't she not!" He states in the quite likeable way that he speaks.

I tell Mohammad I don't think the request is anything to worry about.

I look at the yellow clock on the stained wall of Mohammad's flat.

I took my bins outside two and a half hours ago.

I want to leave but recent history has taught me I'm too polite to tell him.

Oxygen is no easier to find in this room than the other.

The only other room here is his toilet, and a door leading to the garden.

Mohammad rakes my mind with negative words.

"She only puts in one bra into the washing machine so she does. One bloody bra. She never does full washes. This is wasting my water isn't it so? I told her if she wanted to she is quite welcome to go and use the launderette around the corner. And she complains it is too cold, every day she is complaining of this."

I know Mohammad is wrong but I'm defeated by his relentlessness and agree with him. It's been too cold in my room because Mohammad refuses to put the heating on during the day, even though winter has come early.

He's also invented a rule nobody can use electric heaters in their rooms without an increase to their rent.

And the idea he's thinking a tenant has to use a laundry service and pay for it in the shop over the road completely negates the fact the tenant is paying a lot more to use the washing machine he provides.

Nor do I appreciate the image of an old man smelling the bra of his young tenant.

This is my life now, my life with Mohammad.

If I make a stand, he will make one against me.

And I would be evicted.

Another fact I have learnt; he evicts people in the night, by slipping a little note under their door, telling them they have a week to leave.

I sometimes hear tears and shouting from my room.

My new best friend is a complete bastard.

And I am a coward.

"FROM HEROINE TO HEROIN"

December 31st 2007

I was standing, looking around; taking in the surroundings of Bangkok airport in Thailand.

Waiting for Lily; fingers in my pockets, then out of my pockets, then back into my pockets as I moved from one foot to the other; not knowing what to do with the excitement rippling through me with every heart beat and glance towards the clock.

The clock, informing me she had landed, and would be walking towards me any moment.

The airport was blue; a blue flashing neon sign wrapped around a large pair of sunglasses in the front of a window display, urging tourists to buy products to protect them from Bangkok sun rays.

Tired women in dark blue skirts and light blue tops, hats with matching skirts, shuffled along in rows jostling for positions in queues so they could purchase desired objects on their break from delivering dishes on planes to travellers with one eye on the mile high club record, which they secretly hoped to make.

There were so many people.

Some waited for love, some said goodbye to love, and some shouted into booths at blank faced staff trying to explain and apologise for love delayed on late arriving planes.

And there was me, standing alone in silence, my lips thirsty for a simple kiss.

I imagined Lily walking towards me and the sea of people parting before her, like she was Moses and the people were fish flung from their homes, flapping up trees, gawping for oxygen before dying through no fault of their own.

And there she was.

A flash of pink obliterated the blue, and the tedium of life was forgotten as I saw her as she saw me. We locked eyes, night-time sunrise, she yelled my name but couldn't get through because of the amount of people, I called her name and she ducked under one elbow then around the waist of a large women in blue; I dropped my bag, she ran the last few feet into my arms.

I felt her arm around my neck, my hand on her back.

We held each other close; I smelt her hair, her skin and I was reminded of olive branches in Greek fields, waterfalls, laughter, my home and the need to care and look after.

I felt her warmth and melted.

I was an ice swan in a sauna forgetting all sense of myself, relieved of all pressure to pertain to one state; knowing from the moment of our embrace Lily had transferred me to an alternate space.

Her eyes watered, tiny watering cans pouring over flowers growing in sand, we kissed, and I remembered seeing stars in a club years before whilst our lips touched on a London dance floor.

I kissed her nose and forehead, held her face in my hands, she gently held my wrists and we stood staring into each other's eyes as universes collided, recalibrated, and were forcibly reminded of the misfortune infinity is no substitute for being alive fleetingly.

Lily breathed me in and I breathed her out.

My hands said hello again to Lily's hands and her toes said *'long time no see'* to mine as they wiggled independently down at the end of our feet.

My chest said *'together at last'* to her chest as my lips screamed *'remind me'* to hers.

Our eyes said nothing but exchanged more information than it would take a lifetime for a mathematician to count, and in a moment no writer could capture in a thousand attempts no matter how hard he tried to write it down.

Lily looked beautiful, as always. Long blonde hair waved down her shoulders, her pale blue eyes glistened seductively behind eyelashes brushing gently against her tanned face and skin, that to hide behind makeup was a sin.

Her watering can eyes dried and flowers grew on the path ahead as I took her hand and she wrapped her arm around mine.

We headed out of the airport in search of a taxi to take us to our hotel.

I was pretty sure I must have looked overweight yet somehow drained, white faced and red eyed like a stoned lobster trying to read the Financial Times, but if I did, I never saw the recognition of my state in her eyes.

We spent two nights in the hotel and headed down the coast of Thailand, exploring golden sands and deep blue shores until we found a flyer for a New Years Eve party in a jungle nailed to a tree, and we decided to travel to the jungle and go to the party.

After a coach ride and a boat trip, then another coach ride, we found ourselves on New Year's Eve in the middle of a jungle in Thailand surrounded by two thousand people from all over the world; drinking, dancing and hugging.

The first guy I spoke to was a young Israeli hippy. His hair was long and dusty and his fine ginger beard was so beautiful he deserved to have an employee following him around slow clapping everything he did.

He wasn't like some of the hippies in England, where the qualification to rebel is planted by the guilt raised from being a spoilt child with a good education; he was a real hippy born from being forced to kill for his army until he was twenty one.

He had long hair because he was in the army until he was twenty one.

They made him shave his hair.

The army made him shave every day too.

So he had a beard.

His face for a long time was not his own.

When this guy said he was all about peace he wasn't talking about peace because his mum never got him the horse he wanted for his eighteenth birthday, he was talking about peace because he'd seen war.

He talked about love because he knew hate; hate for those above him, hate for those he had served with, hate for enemies not born his but who became so and, lastly, hate for himself for how his mind was controlled.

He talked about life and living because he had seen death and had been the cause of it.

I really liked my new giant ginger bearded friend; his life until then had not been his own making, but he was taking it back.

Life is what you fake it.

Night fell; Lily and I danced and drank.

I met a tall old hippy from America dressed like a cowboy and he offered me acid, warned me I should only take one, so I thanked him and took both.

I was sitting on a bench and talking to a Thai guy and he put his arm around my neck. I observed the Thai guy wasn't drinking alcohol and when I felt his hand on my neck I thought it strange, because we hadn't been talking for long, and I wasn't getting a friendly vibe from him.

Behind him on another table he had four other Thai friends, also not drinking; the friends were not dressed for a party in a jungle, they leered across the bar throwing judgemental daggers at inebriated partying revellers.

They looked like they were trying to act like they hoped they were perceived, so they stood out to me in a jungle full of hippies whose basic philosophy is be yourself.

The guy with his hand on my neck laughed and I smiled, but I kept my mind on the sensation of my neck, and felt his fingers moving.

I stared into his eyes and looked into darkness, his eyes were completely black; no pupils at all.

His face was flat, punched by a steamroller, his teeth stained yellow and his moustache thin and wispy.

Eight black chunks of hair rested on the top of his face creating a greasy dark thatch on his head, a spider feasting on his brain gripping his forehead for composure.

My necklace fell from around my neck; it wasn't worth stealing because it was just a piece of string with a dark blue stone that looked like a heart.

The value was minimal; there was no point in trying to steal it.

I caught my necklace in my hands between my lap, which, situation aside, made me feel pretty cool.

I gave the guy my *why are you trying to steal my chain* look and he immediately couldn't speak anymore English. I told him I knew he tried to steal my necklace. He said something in Thai, then stood up and walked away to join his friends.

I wasn't going to make a big deal out of it and he had four friends with him, so easy come easy go.

It was after the acid kicked in events became challenging.

An hour later I was pleasantly drunk, on acid, Lily and I danced.

My lips smiled into her eyes as we moved to the rhythm of the music. I stared up into trees at fluorescent man-made butterflies, giant mushrooms glowing against large leaves, and felt connected to the night sky above, hugging the edges of belief.

I stared into the stars with a large smile on my face and a sense Lily and I had made it, I could relax, we were dancing in a jungle on acid on New Year's Eve, we had been apart and reunited, been divided by ocean and land, and overcome the laws of man to be one again.

Nothing could stop us; nobody could take away our b iss in; one more year behind us and a lifetime of years ahead.

The stars were so beautiful above me, so bright and glimmering; I wanted to show them to Lily so I movec my grinning face away from the galaxy, away from the stars and directed my gaze back to her, so I could explain with words what my eyes were describing to me, but Lily was already standing close and staring back at me upset visibly.

I knew instinctively this look was out of the ordinary and something serious had happened because Lily looked vulnerable, and in all our years together I had never seen her look vulnerable.

"The man, the one who tried to take your necklace. He touched me."

It was raining on her face but the sky was dry.

Lily looked down and indicated the area violated was her lady kingdom and Lily looked up and I heard her words loud and clear:

"Do something."

My mind raced a hundred thoughts in half a second before I gave Lily my response. To Lily, there was no pause, but in my mind I took five years to answer her words, and in that time I had trained naked up a snow covered mountain to become a warrior.

What am I going to do?

I have to do something but, I can't fight the guy. I mean, shit. Maybe I will have to fight the guy but he's with at least four tough looking friends and I'm wasted on acid.

What if he knows Thai fighting?

What if he knows any kind of fighting?

Think...think.

You have to do something or your girlfriend is going to think you less of a man, but you also don't want to get killed.

Shit.

You are on acid, you idiot. What are you going to do? Hug them all to death?

Talk philosophical nonsense about the nature of violence?

You need to answer Lily before her look turns into her storming off and New Years Eve is ruined.

Speak Colossus, say words:

"Let's go."

I took Lily's hand and we walked from the dance floor up to the bar.

As we walked I had no idea what I was going to do; this was my John Wayne moment only I wasn't a cowboy, a fighter or anything like John Wayne.

I was about to take on five men in what could become a violent altercation on acid knowing if I got punched once in the face I would cry.

As we entered the clearing and the bar area my last thought was simply I had been beaten up before, and from what I remembered it wasn't *that* bad.

The bar was busy with chatter, but typically there was a clear and unobstructed view from where Lily and I stood all the way to the bench where this guy sat and laughed with four friends.

There was no escaping this moment.

I had to *do something*.

I walked towards the men and they stared at me; as I walked the man who touched Lily pointed at me, they all laughed in a clear declaration of war.

Think.

I stopped in the middle of the busy bar area and got the attention of every single person by screaming at the top of my voice:

"Ladies, Gentleman, hippies and festival goers! I have something I need to say to everyone here and it's *very* important."

A crowd of over three hundred people, at various levels of inebriation, stopped what they were doing and stared straight at me waiting for me to speak.

That was easy.

I walked up to the man sitting with his group of friends and I pointed straight at him:

"This man does not belong here. He is not part of the party. This man has just sexually assaulted my girlfriend on the dance-floor. This man is not one of us. This man does not belong here, this man is negative energy and if you see him please be on guard!"

The Thai guys sitting on the bench stopped laughing and their smiles turned to looks of horror.

They looked to the floor.

Tried to hide their faces.

They stood from the bench and stormed at speed towards me.

I was going to get hit in the face, probably lots of times.

They stormed toward me.

The crowd, remarkably, jeered them.

The Thai men stopped, surrounded by many; not so sure what to do.

The fight was no longer five on one; this was five against hundreds.

The few people who hadn't noticed the commotion stopped, turned and watched, not just the bar full of people, but the chill-out area, the people working behind the shops, and the people buying bracelets to remember the night with; they all watched.

Everyone booed the men; the men stared at the crowd, then back at me with wild cuckoo clock eyes.

I stood in a large circle made from friendly faces, with the guy who touched Lily and his angry faced friends.

At least four hundred people joined the circle and booed the men.

A woman screamed for the men to get lost and go away.

Another shouted they weren't wanted.

A guy screamed *you have no place*!

Another guy shouted *leave the jungle*!

I had created an angry mob, made from hippies missing pitchforks.

The men ran.

The circle parted, the men ran out of the circle, down the path, away from the bar, the shops, and the chill out area; into the jungle like cowards.

The man who touched Lily stumbled, as he did the crowd cheered.

Lily squeezed my hand.

"That's why I love you."

She said.

We kissed and the crowd cheered; I was a hero, I was brave, I used fists of peace to beat the Thai guys around the heads without using my hands.

We stopped kissing and the crowd applauded me, Lily squeezed my hand and, for a moment, I was king of a little jungle somewhere in Thailand.

Men and women asked Lily if she was okay and congratulated me on how I handled the situation, though the truth was the situation handled me.

Sometimes taking the only option we have, makes us appear to have chosen the right option.

I was glad to not be unconscious on the jungle floor with blood pouring from my ears, but five Thai guys still roamed the jungle, five men waiting for the right time to punch me in the face.

There was no way I could relax.

Not on acid, certainly.

Security guys asked if Lily was okay and she said she was fine and the people who ran the festival checked she was okay, they thought I handled the situation in the best way.

Little did anyone know my brain was a twitching paranoid mess, fearful of retribution for publically embarrassing the festivals equivalent to Biff from Back to The Future.

I was the heel of Achilles. A general; but of the Light Brigade. Samson's hair removed.

The burnt wings of Icarus.

A fat fish in a thin barrel leaking water, my time running out.

The music turned back on, making me realise the DJ had stopped playing music so my words could be heard.

People separated into their own fractions; the party began again.

A beer was handed to me and I tried to relax; tried to forget.

On the stroke of midnight as I kissed Lily and hugged random people my guard dropped and in that one moment, distracted by a year ending and a new one beginning, Thai Biff took his revenge.

A guy smiled at me to the backdrop of wild midnight cheers; we hugged and shouted Happy New Year.

He was smoking and asked if I wanted some, I asked him what it was and he said a spliff.

I gave him some beer and shared some of his spliff.

The second I breathed in I knew what I smoked wasn't a spliff; whatever I smoked tasted of death.

Cold, dead, nothingness. The edges of space.

A child waiting too long outside school gates, unable to see the car crash around the corner.

A dog washed up on shore, thrown in by children bored of Playstations.

A bitter taste, flat darkness.

The waves taken from the sea, sand on beaches replaced with crabs.

I handed it back and asked him if he was sure it was weed and he laughed and pointed out of the dance floor, to the start of the jungle, to a tree where Thai Biff waved and smiled at me.

I fought an urge to be sick; the jungle span like I was witnessing the party from inside a washing machine, the joy of the acid overpowered; my first steps into unknown footprints.

The guy grabbed my shoulder, his face suddenly right in mine, so close.

No escape.

"*Heroin*, frieeeend...*Herooooinnnn!*"

My head fell onto Lily's shoulder and I muttered weakly *take me back to the tent*, told her I smoked a spliff and was spinning out; Lily laughed, got me back to our tent, unaware of the incident.

There was little point in worrying her; I just needed to collapse and ride the journey out.

I sat down inside the tent, my brain rushed faster than I could understand what thought to follow, Lily wanted to go back and dance so she returned to the jungle; I was alone inside our tent staring up at the ceiling convincing myself I wasn't a rabbit.

I had a book and thought if I read the words they might distract my mind from breaking, by putting a dam composed of someone else's words between my brain and the torrent of rabbits desperately trying to turn me into one of them.

The book was Man and Wife by Tony Parsons and the read saved my life, I read from half past midnight right through till five in the morning, and as each hour past my mind filtered back into my brain, and the rabbits withdrew to some place they've stayed ever since.

I was so messed up on heroin, but able to focus on one thing exceptionally; once I read the book for the first time I had no memory of what I had read, but I knew I enjoyed the experience immensely and the words kept my mind on beautiful things.

Lily came back to the tent to sleep and as she rested on a pillow a rabbit popped its head over the dam, I stared at the cover of the book and thought I should read it again.

Lily slept for six hours, I read the book again, and by the time I finished I was almost feeling normal.

The rabbits subsided, my mental dam plugged with enough carrots to get me well into old age

"WE DON'T PLAY HEROES IN SPACE"

Sunday 14th November 2010

I'm in my flat drinking a glass of wine and waiting for brown rice, tuna and cheap curry sauce to come to the boil, when there's a knock at my door.

I don't know anyone.

Maybe it's not for me.

I look at the time, ten in the evening.

I'm wearing something not suited to sharing with landlords, but, I answer the door hoping my attire offends Mohammad because I want to tell him what I wear in the privacy of my own home is up to me.

I open the door, but it's not Mohammad.

Standing in front of me is a young girl.

Long dark hair falls to her waist and her skin is tanned naturally.

She's short, a little over five feet.

Her full lips cover her lower face and her forehead is all eyes.

The girl introduces herself as Alicia from Spain and I realise this small, fluffy, innocent looking creature is the fanged monster who dared to ask Mohammad for cutlery, and chooses to wash her clothes in the washing machine provided.

Her Spanish accent is quite thick; as she talks she gets some words backwards, and borrows passages from other sentences that have no place in the point she's trying to get across, which I'm trying to get at.

She speaks fast, with hardly a gap between the end of one word and the beginning of another; her voice is fun, and the backwards words come thick and fast, occasionally punctuated by high pitched tones.

Alicia tells me she thinks Mohammad is crazy.

Her forehead blinks brown pupils at mine and she chews her bottom lip, pondering if what she just said made sense.

She tells me she's concerned Mohammad is trying to steal her deposit and he's refusing to answer her questions, or give her information on what he's done with it.

Everything she says is a question, she's unsure how to be certain; Alicia winds down her voice, the engine from a plane after landing, and looks up, blinks a million eyes, my turn to respond.

I tell her Mohammad is weird, very weird, but has an odd moral system I think means he would never take anyone's deposit, and it's probably a miscommunication between the two of them that can be resolved.

I explain to Alicia the time to worry about where her deposit is, will be when she moves out, at that point she'll find out if he's going to keep her money because he won't give it to her, and if that happens she'll be able to deal with the problem then, once she knows she has one.

Alicia laughs because she thinks I'm weird, and I chuckle for no reason other than to fit in.

Believing I have calmed Alicia's nerves and done my bit for the community outside of my door I nod my head, plan to close the door and return to my evening of rice and wine. However, as I nod my head Alicia takes a seat on the floor and stares up at me cross-legged; a lost puppy catching wind of a something familiar.

I'm not sure if I should invite Alicia in, because I've only just met her and don't want her to think I'm being inappropriate; I'm thrown between two options and neither work well for me.

I could close my door, but imagine her happy face dropping into sadness as she continues staring up waiting for me to return or, I can leave my flat and sit with her on the floor.

The problem with option two is I'm wearing a moo moo.

So far I've hid behind my door so Alicia hasn't seen what I'm dressed in, if she sees what I'm wearing she may question my mental health too.

I'm wearing a blue moo moo with matching penguins on the front.

A moo moo is a long woolly dress falling to just above the knee; a man nightie, not intended for men.

I take a breath.

I open my door, and join Alicia on the floor outside my flat.

We sit on the floor at the top of the stairs.

Alicia is easy to talk to and because she's so chatty I don't have to do much talking, which I find peaceful.

There's no light on the landing outside my door; every now and then in the darkness we hear a creek from the bottom of the stairs and stop talking, hushing and huddling, in case Mohammad is coming up the stairs; two children staying up past bedtime, parents downstairs catching up with who they were.

I explain my moo moo to Alicia and let her know I'm not normally dressed like I chase plastic bags across busy roads.

We talk about travelling and life; I appreciate the company.

Alicia tells me she has no television and I tell Alicia I have no chair, I joke she can watch television in my room and I can have a sit in hers.

Alicia tells me Mohammad treats her bizarrely.

She tells me she came home late one night and he was there, standing in the doorway, waiting up for her.

As she walked up the stairs she turned back, sensing she was being watched, and he stood looking up at her in darkness, then placed a frail hand on the rail, the one place illuminated by a beam of light coming from the outside night.

She stared at his old hand.

She looked up, not sure if she should break his silence.

She froze, Mohammad said nothing.

She thought he was going to attack her.

He finally spoke, telling her she was getting back too late, asking her where she had been.

I tell Alicia Mohammad is like that with me too, and on occasions I've returned to find him standing in the darkness staring at the back of the main front door. I tell Alicia we have to accept he's old and will never change his ways, and therefore we must change our mindset in how we approach his behaviour, because we have the strength to do so, whereas he does not.

If those in power do not build paths toward peace, then all roads lead to war and nobody wins.

I recall the story of me going out with Mohammad, Alicia laughs, and tells me about the time she came home and found Mohammad in her flat.

Both of her stories are sinister; to come home as a young girl of twenty three to find an old man in your flat is wrong.

Alicia tells me she thinks Mohammad hates her because she asked him to turn the heating on, and she asked for a plate to eat from.

She explains a friend stayed over and used the washing machine and Mohammad complained she shouldn't be using the washing machine.

I'm becoming involved in the issues of the house.

Mohammad has been blaming Alicia for his own shortcomings as a human being.

By not correcting Mohammad when I was listening to him complain about his other tenants I reaffirmed in his head his crazy, ridiculous judgements about how people should use their free time and will are correct.

Alicia says she likes music; I lean over to my slightly open front door and push my door with my right hand, so the door swings open to reveal my keyboard, so Alicia can see.

The door swings back towards me, then closes, locking me outside my studio flat.

I'm locked out of my home at eleven in the evening wearing a moo moo, and the only person who can let me in is an old man who will hate me forever for what I'm wearing.

I tell Alicia I'm going down to get Mohammad to let me back into my room and we say goodnight.

I head to Mohammad, the world's most judge*mental* landlord, in the gayest clothing possible.

After tonight I can expect a note pushed under my door informing me, because I'm gay, I have to move out immediately.

I knock on Mohammad's front door, but get no answer.

I knock again.

If I can't get into my flat I'll be going to work tomorrow dressed in a penguin nightie.

I walk to the top flat to knock on Alicia's door to ask is she can ring Mohammad for me, because my phone is locked inside my flat.

Alicia tells me she has no sim card so doesn't know his phone number. She proclaims the only way of getting the number is to knock on the front door opposite hers, which to my surprise is answered by two Spanish twins, both attractive, in their early twenties.

They look me up and down and laugh and Alicia joins them, and I stand in a hallway at eleven at night in a man penguin nightie, laughed at by three attractive women.

The second twin points at me, the other buckles in half.

Alicia says something in Spanish I don't understand, and they share a private laugh at my expense.

The three women compose themselves and I ask if either of them have Mohammad's phone number but, as I get to Mohammad, the girls laugh again.

The two twins hold onto each other's shoulders for support, the laughter rendering their legs weak.

Tears form around Alicia's eyes.

If I'm ever having sex again, it's most likely not going to be with any of these women.

I stand and they laugh, and I look down and stare at my bare feet because it feels less awkward.

I have quite nice feet.

The girls get a grip on their laughter, move their hands in front of them like they're riding invisible bikes to compose themselves.

One dings a bell I can't see, and tells me Mohammad no longer has a mobile phone because his phone was stolen by Somalians.

I thank the Spanish twins and leave them to die laughing behind closed doors, Alicia comes with me to Mohammad's flat to help my cause.

We stand outside the front door to Mohammad's lair.

Alicia bangs on the door in a way perhaps only a woman can, she bangs with intent and purpose; I realise there was no chance Mohammad would have heard my polite knocks from earlier.

The fifth blow sounds like trees crashing into castle doors and Mohammad's croaked voice comes from the other side.

"Who is outside being?"

He sounds spooked so I move to reassure him.

"Colossus. I'm locked out."

"Are you alone so it is?"

That strikes me as an odd question. Given the strained relationship between Alicia and Mohammad I say yes, and nod up to Alicia's room, to indicate she should leave.

Alicia and I mouth goodnight.

Mohammad opens his door wide-eyed and in a panic.

I tell him it's okay, it's only me.

He speaks through the gap in the door, a paranoid crack dealer high on his own supply.

His voice is weak and brittle, fishing line caught in a tree, snapping the only way to break free.

"Are you being on your ownings?"

"Yes Mohammad."

"I am hearing the voices though, *voices.* The voices sounding bloody Somalian Colossus, so they did."

I tell Mohammad there are no Somalians, he heard me talking to the girl living upstairs.

"The little evil bitch one? Do not be giving your trustings to her; do not be listening to the things she be sayings about me. She is a little evil bitch! Evil. Little. Dirty. Bitchings!"

I tell Mohammad she seems like a good person to me, and to calm down; I tell him he is safe.

Mohammad's face lunges towards me from the darkness, his face barks at me from underneath his door-chain like a crazed monkey trying to claw its way out to escape the bananas in its brain.

"I be hearing the *voices so it is*! Who are you be talkings to? I heard bloody Somalians! Many bloody Somalians!"

I realise something sad, and shocking.

Mohammad, is showing, and probably has for some time, all the signs of someone facing the early stages of dementia and possibly Alzheimer's.

The paranoia, the need to have the front door double locked from the inside and out, the reclusiveness, the wild look in his eyes; his Somalian obsession now makes sense.

Even the unnecessary aggressiveness could be explained by this morphogenesis.

I attempt a different approach.

I use my softest cloud-waking-up-in-the-morning voice:

"Mohammad, it's okay. There's nobody in the house who shouldn't be here. You are completely safe."

The word "safe" appeases him and his wild monkey-in-a-cage-trying-to-avoid-thinking-about-bananas look gives way to an expression more of bewilderment and less of rage.

"What do you be wantings?"

I explain I'm locked out of my flat and Mohammad closes his door and disappears into his house of a thousand papers and ashtrays full of stale cigarettes and, eventually, returns with a spare key.

He insists on showing me to my room how the owner of a bed and breakfast in Blackpool might show new guests to theirs.

He moves ahead and I walk patiently behind him.

He points out the plant pot at the bottom of the stairs, tells me about the plant, and how he waters them on Thursdays.

As we slowly walk up the stairs, I get a running commentary on the history of each step.

"The stairs are not creaky in this building like in many old buildings isn't it so? And up here at the top of the stairs you will see on the right the communal toilet, which is always very tidy because my wife cleans it very well, she is very proud woman."

I let Mohammad continue with his tour guide and as we get to the top of the stairs I thank him.

He turns wild eyed, and with bananas in his eyes he moves his head nearer to mine, I suddenly wish there was a light nearby; he can be quite frightening when alone in the dark with him.

"Is there somebody being in your room?"

I take a step back and again, in my softest voice, reassure him.

"No, there is nobody in my room."

"Who were you be talkings to isn't it? I heard voices. Bloody *Somalian* voices."

"There are no Somalians in my flat."

Mohammad holds his stare then looks down at his feet then back up to me, his shoulders slump, the walk up the stairs has exhausted him.

He shakes his head and says goodnight, I say goodnight too and he walks slowly back down the stairs.

I'm about to close my front door when I hear his voice.

"Colossus?"

I turn around; he's half way down the stairs, looking up at me; one frail hand on solid railing.

"Yes Mohammad."

"What are you bloody wearing?"

"Something comfortable for the evenings."

"A bloody dress isn't it so?"

"I don't wear dresses."

"Bloody better not. Bloody Somalians wear dresses and I won't be having Somalians in my bloody house."

"No Mohammad, goodnight Mohammad, I promise I'm not Somalian."

"Good because a Somalian is one bloody thing; that would be eviction, but a bloody gay Somalian would be something entirely more bloody serious, entirely more punishable by the ending of your life isn't it so?"

He just threatened to kill me, in that quite likeable way which he speaks.

I say nothing. Aware no words I say will be the right ones to speak.

Mohammad turns and angrily walks down the stairs.

As he reaches the last step, he hits his wrist hard on the banister.

He turns, and I watch his dark silhouette shuffle into his house at the bottom of the stairs.

I am his only friend, and he wants to kill me.

"OUT OF OUR DEPTH"

January 6th 2008

I cannot recall any details or specifics of any of the smaller arguments Lily and I had, but I do recall with ease and detail all of the good times.

Maybe this means time holds true what's dear, and arguments are rows for rows sake, rather than some terrible act by an individual, or maybe I never listened to the arguments.

After the New Years Eve party in the jungle we moved down the coast of Thailand and to an island called Ko Lanta.

Lily and I stayed in a little hut on a beach. The little wooden hut was idyllic; inside the hut was a double bed with a large mosquito net and a small wooden table. The hut was made from real bamboo, held together by rope; a minimalist wooden dot in a vast painting of beauty we were too tiny to understand, painted by the hand of unexplainable mystery.

The little hut had a small wooden porch with two hammocks at either end and a table, so in the evenings we simply watched the beauty of life unfold before us.

The days were so warm, so bright, and the nights never cold, full of stars, free from light pollution, the nearest city far away.

The lungs of peace could not be punctured by the desire of people to let others know they exist, because the huts had no electricity powering them.

No music, no televisions.

A little bar around the corner had small concrete tables and chairs and opened to provide food in the day, and ear y evenings; we were one of only a few couples staying in the huts, so we had paradise all to ourselves.

And this was the scene, the perfect scene; stunning views of flat ocean, white sands in our toes, blue sky above, lanterns swinging in early evening breeze, sincere smiles from Thai people as minds buried heads under a thousand words from more reading material consumed, in peaceful abundance, peacefully cohabiting inside the heart of the wondrous.

This place, this stunning place, was the scene of our first argument since Lily arrived in Thailand.

The memory is strange; I cannot recall what the argument was about. Lily was upset, so emotionally upset she screamed at me in the sea.

I tried to ascertain some logical point of reference but there wasn't one, Lily poured her mind and heart out to me and, through her tears, it became clear underneath the surface of our perfect environment was a relationship Lily felt was failing to make her happy.

I remember Lily waist high in water, in her bikini, looking beautiful, but being so angry with me she smashed her fists into the sea in frustration, it was clear I wasn't understanding, or I was missing the point, or I wasn't feeling how I should be feeling, or I was somehow not becoming the man she hoped I would, forever fighting my true nature to be good.

I remember walking to her in the water, joining Lily, trying to calm her down and asking her what was wrong and to stop shouting, but telling her to calm down made her angrier, I could feel the wheels falling off and I didn't have the skills to put them back on.

Lily walked out of the sea and away from me in tears and I followed, and if I knew her at all I would have known what was wrong, but I did know her, knew her well, and still couldn't find land, or common ground; because the argument, to me, seemed born from fog.

Lily walked away and onto the beach and I followed her around the corner until we stood in a street outside a restaurant packed full of people enjoying paradise, and she screamed at me and I tried to understand what was going wrong as strangers looked on, judging me, for something they all thought I had done.

When the fires lessened, through the fog we held hands, she pulled me close and in her eyes I could see she thought less of me.

Lily told me she missed how we were, years ago, when we first got together; when we used to feel each other's energies and share auras and I would pick flowers for her hair, and she would wear them until she had to wash, and they had no choice but to fall off.

Lily thought we were not the same, and I agreed, but I thought the place we were now was better, more beautiful because of the growth; I said I didn't want to stay the same forever; I wanted to grow up together and enjoy all time delivered.

I thought someone or nobody, perhaps her own observations, had planted a seed that had shown Lily perfect love was possible; and I was perhaps preventing her from having it.

I felt inadequate. And as I felt inadequate I said less, and the less I said and the quieter and less expressive I became the more worried she was, until there were moments when we sat feet apart, but felt world's away.

The physical distance we had endured between us had placed an invisible wall I couldn't see, but could feel, and if I looked at Lily and held her gaze soon enough she would look away, or smile a little nervously, like she wasn't convinced anymore about what she saw when she drew me close and judged my brain.

We were still us though, and we talked life through and moved on and made up, and decided to move further down the coast.

The look in Lily's eye didn't change though, and sometimes when I stared closely around the edges of her blue pupils I could see our relationship burning in flames.

We travelled from the wooden huts and kaleidoscope sunsets of Ko Lanta and spent a day on a snorkelling tour; the snorkelling tour was a journey around some of the smaller, more isolated, less populated islands dotted around the coast of Thailand.

We landed on one island called Ko Rok and Lily wanted to stay for a couple of days. The scuba instructor had made it clear to everyone on the boat nobody was allowed to stay overnight, on any of the islands, but Lily to her credit wanted to stay and usually if Lily wanted something she was determined enough to ask, and nice enough to get.

I was unsure because I didn't want to rock the boat and upset the guy whose snorkel tour it was after he had specifically asked us not to ask to stay the night, so I expressed discomfort, which Lily read as negativity, so I accepted Lily was usually right about these things and stayed quiet; and watched on as Lily made plans for us to stay on the island.

Over the years I learnt if Lily and I disagreed on something, ninety percent of the time I would be proved wrong, and the other ten percent of the time I think she let me be right, so I didn't feel completely useless.

At times I was less use than a broken cog watching functioning machinery from a hill through stolen binoculars.

Lily asked one person if we could stay, then another, until someone agreed we could stay and we would be picked up in two days time.

They provided a tent.

Lily and I stood on the shore and waved goodbye to the tour.

The island of Ko Rok was like the bogie of God; small and green and the home of many strange and bewildering creatures that clung onto the island for life, or rest, from the surrounding seas.

The island was so thin we stood in the middle and watched the sun rise in the East and set in the West.

The sea around the island was clearer than raindrops falling onto the face of a snowman made from crystal, and warmer than baked bread delivered fresh from an oven by a neighbour with rosy cheeks, whose mild manner and take on life never got old.

Above us the sky was clear and beneath us the sand was white and fluffy to walk on, as if the clouds had fallen from the sky and landed on the shore.

Away from the beach the tiny island melted into a small area of woodland, and we followed a path to the summit of the island; a five minute walk, up a small hill.

From the summit we saw the island was no bigger than a football pitch, the beach stretched around half.

A warning sign at the top of the path stated instructions about what to do in the event of a Tsunami, but it was pointless, because if a Tsunami ever hit this small island everyone on it would die because there was no ground high enough to run to.

We walked back to the white cloudy beach and walked to its natural end, the sun beating down on us; a book being read to a sleepy child at night by a friend.

At the end of the island we noticed another.

We were in the middle of the ocean, and these two islands submerged for parts of the year.

We figured we could *probably* swim to the island opposite.

There were signs of life on the island we stood on; an area with benches, a few Thai people milling about who offered us food, so we were not completely alone.

On the island opposite, we would be.

Swimming to the island opposite would be something out of a film, or a really brilliant book you can't put down.

How far away was it?

The island didn't look *that* far away, a ten or twenty minute swim at most.

How far can I swim, how far can Lily?

We sat on the beach and discussed the probability of making it to the other island.

A philosopher would have told us we were already on a beautiful isolated island, and to still look for something better than what we had was to define the fallacy, and wonder, of man.

We would likely get to the other island and look back at the one we left and realise only then how beautiful it is.

Like how men leave relationships, then look back with regret.

Despite our quarrels and uncertain looks, we shared a sense of recklessness and adventure so as we sat on the sand staring out across the ocean at the other island, we already knew we were going.

The only question was who was going first.

"Ten minutes I think Lily, we could be on that island in ten minutes."

"I could make it in nine."

"I said ten because I was factoring in slowing down for you by two."

We laughed, stood, and it was decided; we smiled and looked into each other's eyes and when it got too much Lily came to me and made our look a hug.

We walked into the warm bread sea and swam.

At first we were fine; but after ten minutes of swimming towards the island, the island was no closer, yet the island we left behind was decreasing in size and becoming smaller.

After fifteen minutes the Earth beneath dropped away; the ocean temperature turned cold, as we swam across a stretch of ocean likely miles deep.

This wasn't swimming across a swimming pool.

This was the fucking ocean.

What the hell are we doing?

We kept swimming.

The silence told me we were both thinking the same type of thoughts, thoughts people don't always share.

A horrible feeling, knowing land is miles away from your feet.

Even on a plane feet touch floor.

We were the something that could go wrong.

Swimming across something so deep, the mind wanders; you starts to think about what life is beneath you, creatures you can't see, creatures at home in the deep.

In the shallow, beautiful sea of earlier, the sea had been a beautiful light blue.

I don't know why neither of us considered the depth would change between the islands.

The sea turned black.

The sea turned freezing cold.

I swam as close to Lily as I could because I thought, because of the depth, if we were caught by a current we could be dragged under, or away from the islands, where we would surely drown because nobody knew we had left.

As far as any paperwork was concerned, we were on a tour boat, on a tour boat with everyone else.

If anyone had seen us doing this we would have been stopped for our own safety.

"Colossus, it's further than I thought."

"Keep swimming."

"It's really deep."

"Keep swimming, don't think. Keep kicking."

But don't kick too hard, because every kick we make attracts sharks.

I swallowed seawater, the ocean reminding me who was boss, not that it needed to.

We swam in silence.

I chose not to share my thoughts.

I didn't want to panic Lily because the more she panicked the quicker she would exhaust herself.

We were only about half way across so, either way, if something went wrong now we were dead; but Lily was reading my mind, as I swallowed away a negative thought, Lily spoke my mind out loud.

"What about Jellyfish?"

"Jellyfish only float near the surface near shorelines, out this deep they'll be on the bottom."

Lily didn't answer.

Lily took a gulp of seawater, choked, and stopped swimming.

"Keep swimming! Even if you are coughing, keep swimming. Don't start treading water!"

I saw Lily treading water, kicking and punching underneath the ocean faster, more of her legs dangling beneath the surface, dangling in the cold. Sharks swimming around us we couldn't see.

Don't tread water, for fucks sake, don't tread water.

Start swimming Lily.

She did.

Lily kept swimming but I could tell, because I felt the same, she was aware the idea of swimming across the Indian Ocean to get to an island, when we were already on an island, was more stupid than climbing the Napali coastline without food or water.

I lied about jellyfish; I had no idea about the habits of Jellyfish and I didn't want to think about them because if either one of us was stung out here, in the middle of the stupid Indian Ocean, we would drown.

I knew what was coming, because I was thinking it too.

"Are sharks in the Indian Ocean?"

I was sure there were sharks in the Indian Ocean, and not just one or two, but that the Indian Ocean housed the biggest shark population of all the seas because of its climate.

"I read in the Lonely Planet it's too cold."

Lily didn't respond again.

We kept swimming, but I looked over and could tell from her face she was thinking something.

"Just keep swimming babe, please, we're almost there."

The island was getting closer, over the half way stage, but the ocean was still freezing cold, black; we were two irrelevant specks, and if nature decided, our bodies would never be found.

I was thinking if I was a shark, what better place to be than around two islands in the middle of the ocean, surrounded by an environment teething with wildlife.

"There was a shark in the film The Beach, that was in Thailand."

"Swim faster."

Lily and I raced the second part of the swim in panic and fear, in the desperate hope we wouldn't get eaten by a shark, stung by a jellyfish, caught up in a powerful current, seize up with cramp, or drowned by a wave.

The ocean slowly turned blue again, the temperature warmed and our fears subsided a little.

We manoeuvred around uncomfortable, welcome rocks that turned to sand.

We pulled ourselves out of the ocean and collapsed on the beach exhausted and out of breath, like two people who had fallen overboard and managed to swim for their lives to a deserted island.

And we laughed.

Safe on the shore, we laughed.

The swim in total took forty minutes, I teased Lily I would have completed it in thirty eight if I hadn't had to slow down for her.

We still had to make the swim back, but at least we could now mentally prepare ourselves for what the swim truly was.

There was no food on this little island, or tents, or people, so we had to swim back eventually.

We walked hand in hand around the little piece of sand poking its head out from the sea and basked in the glory of having our very own island, and for a while we needed nothing and no-one.

We found in the sand two snorkels, put them on and floated on top of the ocean for a while. I stared down at the coral below, at the millions of tiny towns full of life, daytime drunks, poets, manual labourers, office drones; stay at home mums and dads watching their children darting in and out of the underwater world that from the surface looked just like ours, but without the poison and insecurity of minds complicated with doubt.

I took a breath and dived deeper to the bottom of the ocean and looked back up at the sun breaking into the sea and pouring down around me; Lily swam through the sunlight above and I watched her body move in the ocean and, to my shame, I thought for the first time she looked old.

I had no right to think the thought, but it was like an instinct from within me I couldn't control. I didn't want to think it, and not only was it wrong to think the thought was factually incorrect, because Lily was a beautiful women and will be for her entire life and I was the partner punching above his weight, lucky to have her.

Yet still the shallow thought tumbled across my mind as I watched her from the depths, and I wondered if it would be me who couldn't hold the connection of our eyes next time they met.

Perhaps that is how we work, man and woman.

The man a shallow creature and the woman deep; the man falls out of love with what he sees, but the woman can see what she chooses to, if her heart and thoughts are believed.

"LIFE KNOCKS"

Friday 19ᵗʰ November 2010

The night is cold and the wind howls outside my flat. I've closed the two doors between the main room in my flat and the kitchen to try and keep at least some heat in the part where I sleep.

I'm wearing a jumper and under the covers of my bed, trying to retain heat.

The kitchen, beyond the two doors, will soon become a barren wasteland of ice and polar bears.

I prepare myself mentally to be woken, in the early hours, by an Eskimo tapping his frozen nose against the other side of the glass.

There's a knock at my door; it's late again, around ten in the evening.

I open my front door and look down at giant eyes staring up at me, full lips break into an awkward smile.

Alicia tells me she was at work and Mohammad placed a letter under her door telling her she is no longer welcome in the flat, and she must leave immediately.

I don't know if this is legal but I do know Mohammad cares for the law like a child cares for the life of a single ant.

Alicia's eyes bulge across her forehead and water swells along her eyelids.

I tell Alicia not to worry, and if she needs somewhere to stay she can stay with me.

Alicia says Mohammad wouldn't like that; she is afraid of the old man.

Those who live through bad experiences and don't become a person who gives bad experiences to others are the only important people in the world.

Mohammad is not one of those people.

Mohammad is afraid of the Somalians inside his head and the world outside his door and so he terrorises the people unfortunate enough to live inside his building, and by doing so he is no better than his own fears; a quality I don't admire.

I tell Alicia she shouldn't worry about Mohammad; he listens to me, and if she wants I could talk to him and try to get him to change his mind.

Alicia tells me she can't believe she's the only person complaining about the cold, as she speaks I glance behind me, an Eskimo stares at me from the other side of my kitchen doors.

I have taken the stance, because I live with others, there will always be someone who'll complain before I need to.

My flat has been freezing cold and by saying nothing I've pushed a girl less able to defend herself into the ring for me, where she has been metaphorically battered to death.

Alicia manages to get her tears under control and she explains, through wobbling lips, she's paranoid she complains too much and is different to everyone else.

I reassure her it's cold in my room too and I should have complained but I'm not as brave; I tell her she should be able to wash what she wants when she wants without the landlord's permission and asking for a plate is not a crime. If anything, she has a counter case for invasion of privacy because what is the landlord doing going through her underwear in the washing machine?

She smiles, a weight lifts from her face.

Then her face freezes, her large eyeballs narrow, revealing for the first time a hint of forehead as she understands what I've just said, and the image of Mohammad smelling her bra by the communal washing machine fills her with dread.

Alicia tells me she isn't doing anything tonight.

I know because it's ten o'clock and she's talking to me about a pensioner.

I ask her if she fancies going out anywhere and she tells me she wants to watch the film Sliding Doors.

Alicia hands me a piece of paper with the words "Sliding Doors" scrawled along the top and underneath in Spanish "Dos vidas en un instante."

I tell Alicia because the film is so old I can probably find it to watch on-line; her eyes waggle and the lower half of her face brightens and smiles.

I don't want to ask Alicia into my flat because I don't want her to think I'm making a move, but the chances of us finding a cinema playing a film from twelve years ago are slim, but then Alicia invites herself in.

Through no instigation of my own, and without looking, I have a girl in my flat.

Perhaps there's some truth in the saying if you stop looking for what you want it finds you.

I've always thought the saying was nonsense, but here I am.

Irrelevance is full of relevance.

Perhaps if we choose to not actively participate in life, eventually life knocks.

Alicia says she fancies drinking and offers to go and buy some alcohol to say thanks for finding the film, and for being a friend when she felt alone.

I have a girl in my flat, who invited herself in, and the girl wants to get drunk.

Alicia returns with beers.

She drinks her beers, I drink my wine and I find the film she wants to watch.

315

I look at Alicia sitting on my bed and remind her I don't have a chair so we're going to have to sit on the bed together.

Alicia is totally fine with that.

Alicia and I sit with our backs to the wall, in the same bed, drinking alcohol and watching a romantic comedy.

Alicia seems depressed and I tell her she's probably over thinking and she asks me to explain.

I ask her if she's happy now eating the little carrot with the bit of hummus I have given her and watching the film, she says she is, but asks me how she can be happy now if she might not be tomorrow.

I tell her if she's happy now then she's happy, and she won't know how she will be tomorrow until she asks herself then.

We can see life as a mountain; or we can see life as land moving upwards with an awesome view.

The choice is ours.

The film is all about how different the main characters life could have been if she hadn't got on a train she wasn't meant to get on, and I wonder how different my life would be now if it wasn't for a decision I made at an airport.

The film ends and Alicia and I are in my bed, drunk, it's almost midnight and I'm curious to know if any of this has anything to do with Alicia wanting to have sex with me or not; or maybe not sex, but just maybe she fancies me a little bit.

Should I make a move?

It's not often I get a girl in my bed and in a way if I make a move and she turns me down I haven't lost anything.

My mind should be able to get more sex for my penis.

I know that much.

I'm turn to face Alicia, I lean toward her and she yawns and she says she'd better go.

Ask her to stay.

"THE INSTINCTIVE BUTTOCK CLENCHING MECHANISM"

April 31st 2008

Lily and I were back from travelling and finally home on our little Hawaiian island of Kauai, but our relationship ice cream car with chocolate sauce wheels was careering off the road as we both fell asleep at the wagon wheel.

Our friends had flown over from England to spend a few weeks with us and for the first part of their holiday Lily flew to Greece for her best friend's wedding, which meant we were apart again.

Our friends and I went drinking and I regressed to my former drunk self; me before Lily, and at the same time on the other side of the world Lily watched her best friend marry a man who had a decent job, harboured realistic goals for life, they had a child on the way.

Lily returned home from her week in Greece to a messy house, me unconscious semi-naked on the front room floor gripping a Playstation controller, and one of my Hawaiian friends masturbating in the kitchen sink high on cocaine; in hindsight, her growing frustrations were understandable.

Lily had been away from me when I travelled and spent time with an older man called Phil who always held a candle to her, and tolerated me; during my time travelling Lily was innocently meeting, in her mind, a friend; but in complete ignorance to the reality she was likely being groomed, every so subtly.

He thought he knew about energy, walked around like a wizard; spoke at length about these things whenever Lily was in ear shot, because he knew these things attracted Lily.

No different to a sleazy guy asking a girl *do you come here often?*

Different words, same intention.

A special man to Lily, to me just another jumped up idiot taking advantage of a woman during her greatest moment of vulnerability.

The man still had a penis and sexual urges, and the idea any man can transcend instinct is laughable.

Watching her friend marry in Greece, watching me behave like a baby, and listening to the plastic wisdom of Phil; piece by piece, in her mind, life was showing Lily she was setting her life up around the wrong man.

And she wasn't wrong, and it was all my fault and I blame nobody else; I was so drunk I couldn't see me at the time, or stop me to fix the problems.

The problems had nothing to do with our friends being with us, or the idiot Phil, the problem was between Lily and I.

I thought I would fix it later and after our friends had gone back to England I would make it up to her. Nothing was irreversible, we'd been best friends for years Lily and I, we travelled the world and filled each other's hearts with a great love, I would make it up to her and I remind her of the man she met.

Maybe I would ask her to marry me.

I knew I couldn't afford a ring, but I would think of something.

Rob, my best friend and Lego man chasing bendy sticks, Adrian, super spy, friend and famous bad joke teller and Becky; a kind soul and friend with an abundance of dark curly hair and a face full of smiles.

They all helped clean our flat; and before long Lily and I smiled again.

I reached for a beer, and somewhere between picking up the first glass and putting down the three hundred and twentieth everything went wrong.

*

I woke up being hit in the face by a stick, Rob happily poking me in the cheek.

On the forehead.

In the mouth.

I had no idea where Lily was.

I sat up.

This wasn't my front room.

I was on a beach.

Rob was using my face to test if his stick was bendy.

His quest continues.

The night before we all drank, grabbed three others in the shape of Zac, Jesus and Sean and the group travelled to the longest stretch of beach on Kauai.

We camped the night and took mushrooms.

Zac is a wild guy with short curly hair and a great sense of humour, the energy of a whippet on steroids chased by a horse and when he laughs he closes his eyes as if each laugh is a moment to relish he can't trust his sight not to blemish.

He was the first American I met in a bar on the island, we clicked with straight away; sometimes he would listen to me talk and laugh and then once he finished listening he would tell me he had no idea what I just said, but he thought it was the best thing he ever head; which speaks for the spirit of the man because what he couldn't understand he laughed at; whereas our television led instincts are built on hating and fearing what we can't comprehend.

Jesus is really called Josh, but Josh looks like Jesus and is nicer than Jesus, so we call him Jesus; I don't think I will ever meet a genuinely nicer guy on the planet.

He's a vegan, with long curly black hair, a warm smile and a child's laugh; he's always discovering things for the first time and each new discovery is a world of wonder.

He sees the world intended and never has a bad word to say about anything or anyone.

He's highly intelligent too, and I often thought if I died I hoped Lily would end up marry Jesus because that's how lovely he is; I knew he would treat her with kindness where I failed.

He's travelling the world now and the last I heard he was in Jerusalem with a big beard...wandering around being nice to people he's meant to fear.

Sean is as tall as a giraffe and as thin as a ballerina's leg, he has short black hair and was officially voted the last one in the group to still be living with his mum at the age of forty five. Sean always says what he thinks which makes him a refreshing character to be around; sometimes his views split rooms, but I always knew where I stood with him, he has a heart of gold and would never intentionally upset anyone.

The night before we laughed, hugged and danced under the brilliant lights of the Milky Way and theologised if life were moments, in this one we would ask to stay.

The waves moved in as we breathed out, the sand hugged our toes, the sky filled our eyes and all combined to make our hearts beat in our brains, and fill us with thoughts of being alive and the infinite wonder of experiencing friends.

Then we wondered where Josh was.

We'd lost Jesus.

The search for Jesus began; he'd never taken mushrooms before.

I found Jesus about half a mile up the beach; sitting away from the shore and by a tree naked.

I sat down with Jesus and, trying not to look at his penis, asked him how he found the mushrooms and whether he was having a good time or not.

He told me he thought they were excellent but he had taken too much.

I asked him if he thought he'd taken too much because he was naked.

"Oh no, not that."

"What then?"

"This tree just asked me to have sex with it."

"Jesus, have you just had sex with a tree?"

"No, I said sorry Mr Tree but I'm not making love with you."

Jesus told me he denied the sexual advances of the tree, but never explained why he was naked, on his own, with a tree.

The next morning, after being woken by Rob pocking me in the face with his stick, we all went our separate ways.

Adrian went home to freshen up, Lily and Becky went with him back to our home.

Jesus, Zac and Sean all left to go back and get some sleep, leaving Rob and I to wander the bars of the local town Kapaa.

We went on a pub crawl; took some acid, and found ourselves in a bar called The Olympic Cafe.

The Olympic cafe is a large bar and restaurant stretching across the rooftops of several smaller shops; it attracts a mixture of workers, locals and tourists.

The bar itself is long and wooden; the views out one side are ocean and out the other the town; the staff wear hideous green leaf t-shirts and white hats but you can, like every bar in Kauai, usually get a good random conversation.

Rob and I sat at the bar and ordered two pints and laughed at life and the universe and noticed the guy at the end of the bar, completely alone and staring into a large glass of white wine, with a face like he'd just heard his dog had accidentally fallen into a blender.

We offered to buy him a drink to cheer him up and he smiled, walked over and joined us.

The man had blonde thinning hair, white teeth and perfect tan, his facial features were all in proportion, but there was something about the look in his eyes that spoke of trials, sufferings, denials and secrets.

He told us his name is Roberto, which we immediately found amusing and coincidental because Rob's full name is Robert.

Roberto told us he was a pilot and had retired from the air force.

We drank more and the more we drank the more Roberto relaxed and the more his demeanour changed; starting with a flick of hair nowhere near his eye, then moving onto a hand on the shoulder in laughter, that ran down my arm and squeezed my finger.

When taking his change his wrist flicked with the type of elegance most men can never master; he occasionally glanced at me and smiled, but not like he was smiling at a friend, like he was smiling to someone much more.

As we drank more Roberto became the second most flamboyant gay man I've ever met, and it became clear he'd been suppressing a lot of who he really was, and that suppression was the reason for his isolated misery at the end of the bar when we first walked in.

Roberto had been suppressing his love for men to such an extent he was almost feverish with joy neither Rob nor I cared where he chose to put his penis for pleasure.

Kauai is a small town and Rob and I didn't need to be told Roberto would have been ostracised for his sexual orientation, and as we drank further we asked him outright if he was gay and reassured him we didn't care if he stuck his penis in men, animals, women, dead people or vases, we just wanted to know.

Roberto said he was and years of suppression boiled to the surface; as the wine took hold Roberto lost control like a big gay volcano erupting rainbow.

I went to the toilet leaving Robert with Roberto.

When I returned we ordered another round and as Roberto swayed to music playing in his mind, he came up behind me and put his arms around my waist.

I laughed but was too polite to ask him to try and keep his advance friendly; I wasn't that fussed because the poor guy had a lot to deal with, but by not telling him to not hug me he was encouraged, and the next thing I knew I felt Roberto's wet drunken lips on the side of my neck.

I was laughing and so was Rob whilst Roberto was entering a happy drunk world of his own; not wanting to offend the guy I tried to gently pry myself away from his hug, to let him down as lightly as possible, whilst mouthing at Rob for help.

Rob helped in the only way he knew how, and the only way a life-long friend ever would.

He grabbed his phone from his bag and took a photograph of me being molested by our new gay friend Roberto.

Through tears of laughter I moved away from Roberto's kissing lips and felt his hands leave my waist.

I turned and waved a hand at Roberto assuring him I was flattered but I not gay.

Roberto stood back a second and absorbed this information, he nodded his head and went to the toilet.

I thought it was probably a good idea, why he was gone he would splash some cold water on his face and gather his composure.

Instead as Roberto passed me he put his hand down my swim shorts and grabbed my penis and gave it a tug, all in one movement, so fast before I'd digested what he'd done he was already in the toilet.

Rob and I laughed, I mean, what else could we do; this was the most random story happening to us whilst on acid, drunk in Hawaii.

We could leave, but then we wouldn't know how the story ends. We could go somewhere else, but this was a lifetime memory. Maybe for all the wrong reasons, but at the time, reason was in the back seat and adventure was driving.

Rob smiled, so I asked him why he was so happy.

He apologised, and told me he didn't think things would go so far. I asked him to explain:

"When you went to the toilet I told him you're gay and no matter what you said you're in the closet and you've been waiting your entire life for the right man to pull you out of it."

I laughed and Rob laughed, because it was really funny.

Roberto returned from the toilet and ordered another wine and Rob, foolishly, decided he needed to go to the toilet;

leaving me with the sexually starved drunk Roberto and his thirst for man flesh.

I explained to Roberto, as he touched my bare thigh, I wasn't gay and had a girlfriend but he didn't believe me. I even showed him a photograph of Lily on my phone, but he was at that stage of drunk where anything I said compounded Rob's story as fact; the more I denied I was gay the more Roberto thought I was playing hard to get; just like Rob said I would.

I told Roberto Lily would be at the bar soon, and he would meet her.

That piece of information seemed to go in, as he took his hand off my leg and thought for a moment.

I told him Rob was gay, and the reason he'd told Roberto I was gay was because he'd always wanted to turn me, but couldn't and hoped Roberto would.

Roberto stopped stroking the back of my hand, we shared a drink, and waited for Rob.

Rob returned from the toilet and Roberto pondered new information.

Lily arrived with Adrian, now all freshened up, and Becky.

I gave Lily a hug and a kiss and introduced Lily to Roberto.

I witnessed the moment click in Roberto's head he decided Rob lied to him to cover his own insecurities about his sexuality.

I think he decided in the middle of a white wine coma he and Rob had a lot in common, both in sexual preference, and how they had to keep their true selves hidden.

I needed to go the toilet again, happy in the knowledge with the arrival of my other friends and Lily Roberto would calm, stop trying to touch my willy, and we'd all sit together and have a laugh.

I returned from the toilet and waited at the bar, Roberto appeared in front of me and put two of his fingers under my nose smiling.

Not thinking, I breathed in then took a step backward, not entirely sure I was getting his joke.

Roberto laughed and said his fingers should smell nutty and I realised he must have discreetly fingered himself and was making me smell his fingers, or his arse on his fingers.

Either way, it wasn't the best practical joke ever.

Rob stood in front of me with a look of shock on his face and it was clear he wasn't *quite* sure if the joke was still as funny as we first thought it was.

Roberto put his glass of wine on the bar, shook his head, realised how drunk he was, and staggered out of the bar; with most of his body weight supported by the wall.

Rob stood beside me, both our faces puzzled.

We stared at the exit, two children waiting to see if their drunk father returns with a belt.

He did not return.

Roberto was gone.

We smiled.

I spoke.

"He fingered his arse and made me smell his fingers."

"Colossus."

"Yes."

"It wasn't his arse he fingered."

I said nothing, Rob continued. We both stared at the exit.

"I was at the bar getting a drink and he came up behind me, stuck his fingers down my shorts, and into my arsehole."

We both held the look of the exit.

Rob continued.

"I clenched, instinctively, just in time. It was only my instinctive buttock clenching mechanism which prevented full penetration, had I been a second later I'd have probably trapped his fingers, possibly for good. He got as far as my ring Colossus."

I laughed because it dawned on me Robert got fingered by an oppressed gay guy called Roberto at a bar on acid; the kind of thing that just doesn't happen every day.

Rob looked at me and cut my laughter short by pointing out I smelt his arse.

I asked him if this made us closer, or further apart.

And without looking at me, he said he didn't know.

"MOHAMMAD AND THE PROSTITUTE"

Part 1

Friday 26th November 2010

The darkness of South East London and the alcohol content of my blood make it hard for me to put my key in the lock; I bump my head against the front door, but because it's midnight the blue tweeting birds normally flying around my head are sleeping on the stars inside my brain.

I haven't seen or heard from Mohammad all week which is highly unusual; although we don't see eye to eye on any subject I'll give him a knock in the morning to make sure he's not sitting in the corner of his flat, in his own poo, pointing a broken fork at the door wearing a paper boat hat.

I enter my flat and get a text message from Alicia saying we should do something this weekend.

My phone rings, as if hearing my thoughts, Mohammad's voice asks me in a bizarre whisper if I can come and see him in his flat immediately.

Usually I wouldn't appreciate the call, but I'm drunk.

I enter Mohammad's flat and manoeuvre through the smoke and stacks of paper, a soldier in a trench during world war one finding his way back to sense after a mustard gas attack.

The light is on in Mohammad's kitchen, which acts as a guide.

I make it to the table, sit down, and hope he offers cool water for my coughing eyes.

Mohammad sits opposite me.

I look around the tiny lime green room, to Prince Charles waving at me with his large smile and at Mohammad; he's wearing blue and white striped pyjamas and his hair's a mess.

Mohammad takes pride in how he looks, he's always clean shaven and his hair is usually flat like a grey pancake, but now grey stubble pokes through his dark skin and his pancake hair has flopped over the side of his saucepan forehead.

Mohammad drums his fingers once on the table and begins, his voice uncertain as he speaks; a boy stealing his favourite soldier from his friend as his back is turned during a fun war re-enactment.

"Tonight this bloody woman has come to my front door and is be ringing the bell. I was asleep. I woke up with thinkings of my phone alarm going off and thought it was seven in the morning. I set my alarm for seven because I like very much listening to the news on the radio. Do you know radio?"

Mohammad pulls a cigarette from his pocket and lights up.

I tell him I know radio.

He inhales smoke and exhales a slight decrease in his capacity to breathe; he splutters and coughs then continues.

He looks very much like an old bastard who hates the world; surrounded by smoke, lost in the hell he's spent a life creating.

"I thought it was a very short night's sleep and I was surprised morning had come so early, but then the ringing happened again and then again Colossus; I realised this was my phone ringing and not the front door bell. You know? With the noise that it makes? I thought what is bloody wrong with my phone, you know? Because it kept ringing."

I don't tell Mohammad ringing is a common feature on most phones.

He takes another long drag on his cigarette and I watch the moment, no longer than half a second, when his smile lifts off, before it's ripped from his face by a Tsunami of coughs.

He gathers himself and continues.

"I read the name on my phone and it says the name of a girl called Tracy. Bloody bitch she is. My phone kept beeping and I realised I had an answer phone message, so I listened to her message and it's this woman outside my house trying to get in."

So there was a woman outside Mohammad's house, tonight, knocking on the door and calling his mobile demanding to be let in; quite remarkable.

I ask Mohammad who Tracy is:

"Tracy is a bloody bitch. She is a common prostitute. A year ago I had sex with her for twenty pounds in my flat and we sent each other text messagings."

Twenty pounds for sex sounds reasonable.

I ask Mohammad why Tracy was trying to see him.

"I sent her one texting message and she sent me one back telling me it was disgusting and her bloody son could have read the text messagings. And she and her sister have kept the messaging and are going to tell my wife about the text messaging."

This is a *"who knew?"* moment.

Mohammad does have a wife, but they are just friends.

His wife lives down the road in a different house and pops in from time to time.

"She's coming to my house. The other day she rang the bell and my wife answered and she said it was Tracy and I was her patient. You know, because I do the holistic medicine. My wife gave me the message Tracy knocked for me when I got in. My own bloody wife Colossus, can you imagine?"

So Mohammad, the master of morals, the homophobic, racist, judgemental, sexist beacon of all things holy has slept with a prostitute and is being blackmailed.

He wants me to help him resolve the problem so his wife never finds out, and he can get away with using a lady of the night whilst accepting no responsibility for his actions.

The easy thing to do would be to walk away, but he's an old man and I can't help think the stress of something like this could kill him; he's such a stubborn old fool there's no way he's going to be able to handle this without his pride escalating events.

I ask Mohammad to show me the text Tracy has been offended by, and to let me listen to the answer-phone message she left.

The answer phone message is from an hour ago. I listen to the shrieking voice of a drunk woman slurring her words like she's drinking a slush puppy on a trampoline; her words are threatening and she's demanding to be let in.

The big bad wolf of Willesden Green.

I feel a bit sorry for Mohammad because this younger woman is trying to scare an old man in his own home, and from the strain on Mohammad's grey face she's succeeded.

I ask Mohammad to show me the text message she sent him.

I bring his phone to my face and read her words.

"Give me what I want or I will tell your wife and show her your disgusting text."

I ask Mohammad to show me the *disgusting* text message he sent started all this, the text that's got Tracy so riled and angry she's beating an old man's door in at eleven o'clock on a Friday night.

Before he shows me the text, he explains why he sent it, justifying, too afraid to just show me his words.

 "You see, I sent this text because she wanted to come round and give me the sexual intercoursing. You know? With the man and the women being inside of each other. I bloody sent the message to the number she had given me and when I sent it I didn't even know she had a bloody son."

Mohammad takes another drag of his cigarette and, as he coughs part of his breathing system back out into the air, his lips curl at the end, a ghostly smile he doesn't know he's making.

He finds the text message he sent and passes me his phone.

Part of me doesn't want to read the message, because it's easy to imagine he could be pretty sick in the head, and to piss off a prostitute with a sexual advance, via text message; I know the message is going to be pretty extreme.

I prepare myself for reading a text message about pissing in her mouth, her dressed as a baby. Mohammad in tight leather y-fronts fisting an elephant.

I read the offensive text message:

"Hello, I know you like bg c. How are you? I hope you are well Tracy."

Mohammad is worried sick about the text message he sent but, although his text message may have been considered rude in the Victorian era, in this day and age his text is the equivalent to accidentally touching a girl's shoulder at a picnic.

I tell Mohammad no child would think "bg c" stood for big cock. No one could prove he didn't mean "big cuddle" and, even if Tracy has a son, if she's having sex for twenty pounds she's putting a drug habit before him.

I tell Mohammad this is the act of a desperate woman with no case to obtain money from him.

Mohammad lights another cigarette, coughs for longer than he breathes in, leans forward and tells me he should probably continue then.

There's more?

Please don't end this by telling me Tracy is dead, her naked body is in your bathtub, and you want me to help you bury the body.

Please don't be that.

He tells me Tracy came to the house last week with her sister.

They walked by the house as he smoked outside, insisted on coming in, and he let them because he didn't feel he had a choice.

Mohammad tells me they smoked "hashish" and drank one beer each.

They drank the beer and asked him if he wanted sex for twenty pounds, which he declined.

He's having more sex than I am.

I tell Mohammad he's about to be blackmailed, but the girl in question has no case because her case is based on a man sending a non-sexual text message to a prostitute.

Mohammad tells me after he sent his text to Tracy he got one back from her telling him she had a wank with a b g orgasm, so she was not upset at the time.

"Do you know a lady orgasm Colossus? With the rolling eyes and the clawing onto your back until they are like the wobbly jelly."

Nice image.

We agree to do nothing tonight.

I tell Mohammad I will come and see him tomorrow.

He says his wife and son are coming to the house at eleven.

Whatever we do, we need to do it before then.

"UNPLUGGED"

June 21st 2008

Our friends left the island a few weeks ago and we enjoyed some of the funniest and memorable experiences of our lives.

Lily and I had not discussed the distance caused from my travelling, the despair she felt witnessing her friends marriage in Greece, the whispers of Phil, or my failure to provide anything a normal guy would; financial or emotional.

I woke up and Lily wasn't next to me.

I got out of bed, grabbed my dressing gown and walked down the narrow dark corridor into the front room where morning light, too bright, poured through large windows surrounding Lily; who sat on the sofa.

An angel with a letter in her hands.

Tears fell from her beautiful face, hitting the page; reading a book in a park beneath black clouds, out of the protection of trees.

The letter Lily clutched in her hands was from me.

Two days ago we'd argued again, and again the argument ended with Lily screaming she wished she wasn't with me, and I wasn't the man she thought I was.

This was often how our arguments ended; we'd taught each other how to love deeper than we'd ever experienced, but never learnt the most valuable lesson love teaches; how to concede.

The strength in weakness.

Lily stormed out, she often did during arguments; I used to when we first started arguing years ago.

Sometimes she disappeared for a few days and on this occasion she had too.

With Lily gone I had time to think about the words she used during our fights, and how upset they made us both, and so I wrote Lily a letter.

A letter saying I love you, but I'm worried I'm not mak ng you happy anymore; I'm worried I'm failing to be the man you should be with, and, if you really think you co.ld be happier with another I would be wrong to stand in your way. If you want to, if I'm making you sad, I'll leave because I don't want to be the kind of man who stops another from living; I don't want to be the kind of man who makes his girlfriend sad, and if that's the kind of man you think I'm being, I don't deserve you.

Honesty is the test policy.

Those words Lily read, crying thoughts running around her head, leaking out through her eyeballs.

I stood in the doorway to our front room, listening to her snort snot back up her nose to clear her airway, to make way for more pain.

My heart sank in my chest at the sight of the hands of the woman I loved, shaking uncontrollably at my words on the page in front of her.

I asked her if she was okay, a stupid question I know, but I was unsure how else to start what we both had to say.

Lily looked up, dishevelled beauty; I wasn't sure if the look in her eyes was love, loss, rage or pain.

I shouldn't have wrote the letter, if I'd said nothing things would be better.

She spoke; her voice tired, strained, the pain too much to carry.

"We see things in different ways, which is what we always do! You see me as a jealous, selfish, controlling woman, and that has a lot to do with the way our arguments go and why I feel so defeated."

I defeat her.

Where has she been for two days?

I hear myself respond but it's surreal, I'm disconnected from myself.

"Every couple has stress. It's not possible to not have stress! If you want to live like a recluse in a bubble and cut off all contact from people you care about because you might get hurt, then good luck to you. But it's not the way to live; it's five years away from being a woman with cats for hair."

What am I talking about, why can't I stay on topic?

Lily said she thought I thought she was controlling, but I didn't think she was, so why didn't I tell her I thought she was wonderful?

Instead I accused her of showing signs of becoming crazy cat woman.

We were talking, arguing even, but I couldn't listen to Lily's words for the statements my mind had pre-written.

Two more tears fell onto the page Lily gripped in silent rage, and as she spoke I heard impatience in her voice, as if she couldn't believe we were going to go through this *again*.

"I don't want this feeling of doubt anymore."

I tried to focus, to stay on topic and respond with the right words:

"Feelings of doubt because we're together or feelings of doubt because we're fighting? Maybe the cause of your stress is because you think you're with the wrong man."

My voice broke a little, just a little, I don't think Lily noticed, or if she did her eyes never flickered with recognition. She held my gaze and spoke through vocal chords increasing in tension:

"You said if I spoke calmly and stopped shouting we could talk things through, so I come home thinking about trying, and you give me this letter telling me you don't want me anymore."

I don't like the way Lily said she *decided* to come home; like she had an option of staying somewhere else. Like I was lucky she *decided* to come home at all.

Where has she been for two days?

"My letter doesn't say I don't want you anymore. My letter says I don't know if you want me anymore, and if your heart wants out I'll take mine away for you."

I needed to tell Lily I wanted her, to calm her fears. To love her without needing to be loved back, but I was being an idiot and couldn't concede, I couldn't thank her for coming home and nor did I want to reassure her because I didn't want to convince her of anything.

We were both insecure, both young; two people needing the other one to make them stay, neither knowing how to begin the uncomplicated process of simply loving.

I wanted Lily to want me without me wanting her because then I would know she wanted me, Lily wanted the same, and now we were in a position we couldn't stop and so we blamed.

"You think I'm selfish because I don't do the dishes or something, but when it comes down to it, it's me who leaves the place he loves. Me leaving the friends he's made, me leaving for *you*. When I told you forever and ever, I meant it. I never thought you would give up."

I had no idea what I was thinking blaming Lily for leaving England. Leaving England had nothing to do with the girl in

344

tears holding the letter. Young man, foolish ways. Nor was I responding to what she was saying. Even at breaking point I couldn't listen; couldn't hear.

"Colossus after four years we haven't sorted any of our problems, have we?"

I was annoyed with her new strife for idealism, because I knew these words were not from Lily; even Lily knew, or knew once, there are no perfect relationships and they all have ups and downs. I didn't know where she was coming from so my voice raised with frustration.

"We've sorted old problems! But life presents new problems! That's what life does! I'm sorry I went out and got drunk with our friends, I'm sorry. I let you down. I was stupid and inconsiderate but it's you who has to punish; maybe because you witnessed me having a laugh with others in a different way than maybe I do with you...oh look, what does it matter now? I'm sorry for how I behaved!"

Lily's frustration was in her voice now too:

"You were horrible to me when you were with them. You acted like you didn't want to be with me and wanted to be single. You resented me. Then before I left for Greece you were so nasty...

Lily's voice rose to a shout, fresh tears spilt from her eyes.

...it would have been nice if you wanted to spend a couple of hours with me before I left and you know what, I wasn't even expecting you to come home with me when I left the restaurant that night, but then you said you wanted to come with me so I waited but then, *oh no*, you didn't want to leave so I got upset, and then what followed was a whole night of what a jealous, controlling person I am!"

She was right too, looking back. I grabbed those days with my friends like they were our last because they could have been. And for a while there, for Lily, having me around was like babysitting a sixteen year old child. And for a short time I put our relationship in the backseat. I knew her well enough to know she wouldn't have stood for it; but foolishly thought I could make it up to her.

My priorities changed for a brief moment in our relationship and Lily hated me for it, and I resented Lily for hating me for it.

Lily was right, I was wrong.

"The reason I had such a good time with my friends was because I knew I was coming back to you, why can't you see that?!"

I wasn't listening.

Apologise for being a drunken arsehole before she left to go to Greece.

My words angered Lily, she snapped back, I wondered how we could be speaking the same language, and talking about the same subject, but failing to understand each other so spectacularly.

"I got upset with you one night because I was waiting all week to have fun with you guys and when it came to the night I could go out, you wanted to stay home!! What about when my friends and family were here? Again you took time off work and spent every day with them, and you never considered things like maybe helping me in other ways so I could spend more time with them...

I was being blamed for thoughts I didn't know how to think...

...You said yourself you took the chance not to do anything; well I was still doing everything! How much did we argue about doing taxes and filling out the immigration paperwork? Couldn't you have just done it? Couldn't you have made it easier for me? You don't make anything easier for me! You don't help me!"

Lily looked down and watched my words on the page smear with her tears; blue pen on white paper blending with the despair of hopelessness, tears jumped from the roof of her eyes because they couldn't stay inside her anymore, hoping the floor beneath was a door to some better place.

I knew I should speak, but I thought the right thing to do was for Lily to think over what was going through her mind without me interrupting. I thought this was the right thing to do, I thought this was brave but it was cowardly. My silence was viewed by Lily as me not caring.

I withdrew when I needed to be open.

I left Lily to make a massive decision on her own and blamed her for making it.

At the time, I didn't see it as that. At the time I thought I was being the good guy.

I thought if Lily came to her own conclusion she wanted me then we would be fine again, because I wouldn't need to reassure her, and she would just know we were right together.

What's wrong with love?

I wanted Lily to put down my letter, walk into my arms, bury her head in my chest and we would tell each other how much we loved each other and we would never argue like this again.

Lily wanted me to do the same.

And for whatever reason, the middle, the place we could meet, was invisible to us.

I tried to speak the truth from my heart, but it's hard when it's breaking and missing parts.

"You have a right to live the life that makes you happy, with or without me. Why did I write that letter? In every argument you run away! You tell me to 'fuck off' in every argument! You turn every argument into a statement about not wanting to be with me, and now I think maybe there's truth hanging from your barbed wire."

I sounded reasonable, desperate, and angry.

To Lily I sounded hateful at the one time she needed to be loved the most.

I took a few steps forward so I no longer stood in the doorway, but in the same room.

Lily was angry; and threw fire back onto my flames.

She shouted, I pictured two pink fluffy dice, untouched, gently swaying under the mirror of our red car.

"In every argument we have you say I should leave you if I'm not happy!! You tell me I should leave! Last week you said you wished you didn't have a girlfriend, and you said you were joking, but the you said it when we were arguing about directions to somewhere and the way you said it was serious!"

Lily was right, when drunk at times I'd been a dick and to the one person I should've been treating well. One night, driving to the beach, I said to Lily I wanted to go back to England. And she punched me. It didn't hurt, and she didn't mean it to hurt, she was literally trying to knock some sense into me.

For a second she knocked me out of my drunken slipstream of being an obnoxious cock.

I hadn't meant what I said, the booze was talking, but the words left my mouth, and the thoughts boiled in my brain before.

My words couldn't be taken back.

Now we were both off topic.

What is the topic?

What are we talking about?

What's going on?

Why are we fighting?

Where have you been for two days?

"And *this* letter! I'm trying to deal with my own emotions in a different way. I've come back home from clearing my head because before I left you told me you would listen, and you told me it wasn't going to end in a big argument, so I come home to find out when I was gone you got mad and wrote me a letter saying we should split up!"

The letter is not saying I want to be without you, the letter says I want you to want to be with me!

How can she interpret my words so wildly from their meaning?

The letter wasn't written in anger, but in open sorrow.

My voice softened as I reassured Lily my intentions were not for us to split up but to continue together forever, and to be stronger because of moments like these.

There was a cup of coffee on the table in front of Lily, and I wondered in what order Lily found herself reading my letter. Had she returned home and flicked the switch to the kettle and then sat down and read my letter, or, had she started to read then put the letter down because her need for a coffee was more important than the outpouring of the contents of my heart?

I blinked away a tear I didn't know I could grow and spoke softly; ignoring the smell of freshly ground coffee:

"The only reason I'm here is for you. I can't imagine having a kid with anyone else, in fact you're the reason I'm sure I want one. I'm sacrificing my life, my family and friends. I'm trying to give you everything. I'm giving you me!"

The television was on; ejaculating the news over the face of our front room.

I looked around, briefly; everything was how it normally was.

The morning coffee sat on the same coaster; the news spoke of people dying somewhere, and the blinds were open because Lily liked the morning light pouring through them.

Everything was normal but us; we were in trouble and this was more serious than any argument we'd had before, but although we were fighting what were we saying? Where was this going?

Lily's voice had a pleading quality but there was an audible coldness creeping in, an almost professional pattern and rhythm to her new words.

"I didn't realize you'd *sacrificed your life* to be with me because in England you were miserable! I'm sorry it's such a burden to live here! Okay, you're right, it's hard to be away from family & friends but if you really didn't want to be that far away from them you should have said something. Instead, you feel like you sacrificed everything for me, maybe that's why you're punishing me?"

351

This was impossible, I told Lily she was the reason I wanted children and I told her I sacrificed my family, not to complain, but to reassure her of my love; instead she heard my words upside down like we were reading each others words on broken mirrors.

This was a complete breakdown in communication and it wasn't Lily's fault. The reason she was taking my words the wrong way was because of the stupid letter I wrote which was meant to reassure her; but it was clear I had chosen the wrong time to write it.

I thought the *if you love someone set them free* approach was the right way to come at our problems, and Lily would reach the conclusion she couldn't believe I loved her so much.

But she thought I was kicking her out the door and now everything I said to try and keep us together was heard as a reason why I didn't want to be with her.

The television set, why was it on? Had she read my letter looking up at the television every few minutes between taking sips of coffee and checking her phone for any facebook updates from Phil, the guy I suspected I was being compared to; which was highly unfair considering she only knew Phil's best side because he was trying to get inside her with his penis.

Despite Lily putting Phil on mystic status, it was clear to me he was a divorced man in his mid forties who sensed vulnerability in an attractive girl, a girl he masturbated to in the evenings as he recalled the last time they hugged at a party.

I knew I couldn't share my thoughts about Phil with Lily because she would get defensive, so I didn't, however my patience was thinner than my frustrations and I snapped back:

"I'm not deliberately trying to punish you! I will give up alcohol for you, but even that isn't good enough!"

"I haven't asked you to give up alcohol for me! If you mean you've recognised you're often not very nice to me when drinking and that's why you want to give up, then that would be different."

"What difference does the reason why I'm giving it up make? Surely, the attempt to give alcohol up is, without saying it, bloody obvious, because I'm giving it up to be with you! If it was all rainbows and unicorns when I was drunk I wouldn't be giving it up!"

Lily cried again and I slipped a noose over my frustration, pulled it tight, and rode out of me on a horse called kirdness.

"I'm sorry Lily. I think stopping drinking should be seen as a positive step, not one needing immediate self reflection."

Why couldn't I just tell her I was going to stop drinking because I was a dick to the person I loved most in the world when drunk?

"You say you would quit drinking with beers in the fridge."

"That unfair."

"Then try taking responsibility for your words."

I bit back at Lily, spitting out my kindness as I did.

I tell her I do everything in the house, and don't expect applauding when I do.

She hated this, my implication being when she does something she expects the world to stop.

I pushed a button inside her, so she responded by pushing a button inside me.

She told me before we arrived I promised her I would cook and clean, and do the shopping, but when it comes down to it I do nothing. I don't even write books, she screamed.

Her voice rose with mine, and as she spoke she didn't like me anymore.

I shouted back I was writing books and she knew I was, I couldn't mow the garden because the garden was a fucking jungle, and I couldn't do the shopping because I couldn't drive.

I told her she knew I did everything I could, everything I fucking could.

She asked me if I thought *everything I could* was good enough.

A silence fell between us.

Neither wanted to go down the road our out of control love was crashing us into.

Two pink fluffy dice dangled under the rear-view mirror in my vision and I couldn't understand how they moved or why I was seeing them.

The silence squeezed my throat.

Lily continued speaking, her question unanswered.

Dangling in my mind, forever between us.

Her voice was calmer, more controlled.

Lily told me it's not about the things I do, but about the things I don't. She told me if I say I'm hungry, she makes me a sandwich. If I need a doctor's appointment she books one for me.

The things I don't think about doing but still need to be done, those things I don't do.

That's what this is about, she said.

I was confused, felt like I couldn't win, wrongly or rightly, maybe I wasn't good enough, in frustration I shouted back; she's winning, she's taken the moral high ground.

"But I don't ask for anything! If I get hungry I make a sandwich! And when have I ever asked for a doctor's appointment?"

My voice rose again.

Her voice rose higher, defying mine defying hers.

"You don't care about doing the gardening so why do it? You don't care about cleaning the car so why do it? You don't care about doing the taxes so why do them? You don't care about doing the shopping so why go? You don't care if the floors need to be swept or washed so why do them? You don't care if the bathroom needs to be cleaned so clean it?!"

People who don't carry bags because they don't care for the weight, end up carrying the third bag of strangers who can't go anywhere without everything they own. These people are the first to tut if you walk by them, and the last to help you carry your own.

Lily hadn't touched her coffee.

The people in the field who worked hard to pick those beans had picked them for no reason.

I shout at Lily sometimes nothing needs to be done even when she thinks something does.

I tell her there's nothing wrong with relaxing. There doesn't always have to be something needing to be done before we can sit down.

Sometimes we can just sit down.

Lily looks at her coffee.

She bites her bottom lip.

She doesn't want to cry. Her emotions fight what she thinks, her tears are the fallout from her internal conflict.

I can tell from her eyes she thinks she's talking to a madman; a box of frogs with a face drawn on.

But her heart reminds her she loves me.

She glances over at the television, and I want to scream I'm over here.

She wipes her face, sniffs snot up her nose.

We both know she's going to speak first, break this second silence.

This silence is hers, not mine.

She's built it up nicely, with glances all over the room.

Then she lets me have it, both barrels, her words hate me now.

Hate me more than they've ever hated anyone.

"You never clean the car! You don't care if the taps are polished so I polish them! You let me do everything if you don't think it needs to be done, and you don't care that you do! You *always* tell me I'm a psycho! You're constantly questioning my mental health, even in this fucking argument!"

I was just thinking how crazy she must think I am.

But, it's true, when Lily is picking on invisible dirt I can't see, eventually I snap, and sometimes call her a psycho. I never said it to make her question her mental health.

Until that point, I never considered people worry about their mental health.

I thought it was a given, everyone knows everyone else is fucking mental.

Why waste time wondering if you're more or less mental than the person next door, they're a person. Trust me, they're fucked in the head. And if they're always completely perfect, it's because they're medicated.

Some hide crazy better than others, some avoid people to hide crazy, some married men cut themselves in a place no-one sees, some American housewives get drunk and fuck each other when their husbands are away on business.

Our fear and loathing is the rent we pay to live inside us.

But I'd never explained any of this thinking to Lily.

I'm lost, completely lost, I shout back but not in anger, I shout back now angry with us, with the argument, exasperated we're here again, from a letter intended to create something entirely different.

"I don't care if the car is dirty, I don't even have a car, and I don't care if the kitchen taps aren't seriously polished rather than just rubbed a little bit...I mean, they're just taps? And this *is* crazy!"

"That's exactly what I mean! And I believe you. Sometimes I believe you when you say I'm crazy."

How can she not fucking be hearing me! I step forward, and shout.

The type of shouting you only ever show the person you love most in the world.

"I'm not saying you are crazy, this THIS is crazy, I'm not saying YOU are crazy I'm saying arguing over whether or not a tap is really shiny or just a bit shiny is fucking crazy! It's a tap, the tap isn't going to complain to the fucking tap authority and get us arrested for failing to polish his fucking face is he?"

Lily screams back, would throw something if she could.

The only object near her is a cooling coffee.

She leaves it, restrains her self, screams back into my face.

"I'm not talking about THE FUCKING TAP; I'm talking about why you don't think to care about the fucking tap!"

A silence falls again; a false calm, the eerie silence heard during war.

Usually during an argument this would be the moment we burst out laughing at the ridiculous situation we'd created; but this time when Lily finished shouting she didn't look at me, she looked at my letter.

That stupid letter, she was reading my words and thinking I wanted to leave and there was nothing I could do to make her see how I wrote the letter; the intention behind my words.

My letter was meant to bring us together, but instead it was validating all of her fears.

Lily looked up at me and spoke like there was something she was reading on my face I hadn't intended to put there.

"Now you're getting stressed and I'm feeling *really* stressed and I can't handle this feeling because it's the worst feeling in the world! And when I say I get stressed I'm talking more about the way you make me feel when I'm stressed. You constantly turn everything against me!"

I lost it, all along I thought Lily was turning my words against me, but Lily was thinking I was turning her words against her.

"I'm not turning anything against you!"

"You're turning me against myself and you don't even fucking realise it!"

 Silence.

The eye of the storm of our making.

A ghost drank Lily's coffee, I blinked and realised it was steam leaving nonchalantly.

Somewhere another Colossus and Lily banged at us through clear glass we couldn't see or hear, shouting at the top of their lungs to take a step back and remember our love.

The piece of string dangling from the mirror snapped and two pink furry dice tumbled from the mirror, one landed in the driving seat; the other disappeared.

When I spoke my voice was weak; unintended hope broke over my words, desperately hoping Lily heard my tone and would decide to forgive me for all the wrong things I'd done.

"You don't appreciate me Lily. Maybe for a long time now you've looked down your nose at me. Wondered in the back of your mind if you could do better? All you talk about is your stress this and your stress that, what about *our* love?"

She shook her head, tapped her feet, her fingers gripped above her knees, like she was on a rollercoaster with no flat bits to look back and appreciated the drops from.

"You never believed I fell in love with you; you always said I was ready to meet someone else, but I do love you and I've loved you since the day I met you and I will always love you."

I'd been insecure of her past loves, true, but never felt threatened by another man in the present. Lily was talking about meeting someone else; I wondered if a small wheel was turning Lily didn't want to face herself, but somehow couldn't entirely deny.

Lily wasn't finished. She had me on the ropes, a boxer about to go down, a vampire with a stake close to his heart, an enemy of the state sitting down for the last time in a chair.

"You make me question myself and wonder whether what I think is right! This is a form of abuse and I can't deal w th this, us, on a regular basis! Everything I do to avoid these arguments has failed. I came here wanting to talk after spending two days at a party at Phil's and now look at me!"

So she spent two days at Phil's house. I didn't point out she thought what she was thinking because she was thinking what Phil had thought to tell her, so she thought what she thought about me and therefore thought higher of he.

And two days at a party; part of me hated her back.

After two days at a party she would come home anyway, so did she come home to talk to me, or did she come home because she wanted to come home, and I was there, so she might as well talk to me.

Put the kettle on first, watch a bit of television; try not to wake him.

I could take the bait, could finally slam Phil and tell her what I really thought of him, but Phil was nothing, Phil didn't deserve to be in this conversation, even if she'd tried to put him in.

If I attacked Phil, and his plastic Hawaiian skirt, she wouldn't believe me, and would run back to him.

Or his party.

Whatever.

I never knew about the party, it must have slipped his mind to invite me.

This wasn't about Phil it was about me and Lily, though I wished she could have gone to a female frienc's house for a few days advice.

I remembered Lily's phone ringing one night at ten o'clock and she wondered who it was, it was Phil, and she never answered.

I wondered, briefly, if she would have answered the phone if I was still travelling alone.

If he called knowing she wouldn't answer, but to let me know he was around.

I let my thoughts pass and focused them on the positive; for starters I knew Lily would never cheat on us, this was just stupid male pride agitating me in a moment when male pride was the last attribute needed.

The positive; Lily just told me she loved me.

I ignored Lily saying I always had a warped view of her because the idea was preposterous, we'd been together for four years and in one argument Lily was saying I never knew who she really was, an offence to our history and also a subconscious justification for leaving.

She just said she loved me and would love me forever.

That was positive.

There was hope.

And then Lily sobbed into her hands and there was no hope; suddenly there was no hope for us.

I watched Lily cry and wanted to go to her but couldn't. I wanted to make it better but I wasn't sure I knew how. I wanted to be the guy who made her laugh like I could. I wanted to be on the sofa talking about crap movies, cleaning each other's teeth and brushing our noses, I wanted to cook her the dinner I never did and wanted to clean the taps.

I wanted to clean the fucking taps so much when she walked in she was blinded by the shine, I wanted to watch her smoke a cigarette and bounce up and down with joy on the front room carpet, I wanted to rest my head on her lap and look up her nose and think how remarkable it was that even from the view underneath her chin she managed to look like the best thing I'd ever seen, I wanted to show her I cared about her car, the letter she was reading was a mistake, if we could just start this again, without the letter, I would get her to see my intentions had been more honourable than she believed.

I wanted to fill out the immigration forms and do all of the tax returns.

I wanted to mow the jungle.

I spoke and felt disconnected as if I knew I couldn't take the weight of what needed to be asked, or what the response might be.

I was at one end of a long dark corridor unable to speak and my voice was at the other end blowing in the wind.

"What do you want to do Lily?"

Give me a lawnmower and I'll go out there and be back in ten years.

I will mow down every fucking tree, I will hack down every bush and I will make the island flat.

I promise.

I promise.

I will.

It must have been three seconds, maybe less, but it felt like a lifetime built up of an infinite number of three second moments pummelling down on me.

Lily looked up from my letter and finally held my eyes.

Tension sucked our air from the room, pulled the steam from the cooling coffee, making it hard to breathe. I felt my neck closing, the first time I remember the feeling.

My eyes moved from to her mouth, tracing the sound of her voice.

I studied her lips, lips I'd kissed a thousand times, lips I'd turned upside down and made frown, then turned back around by being a clown.

Her words dragged from her mouth slowly; old turtles with a hundred years to avoid a head on collision taking just over a hundred years to make a decision.

"Colossus...

Don't baby.

...I want you to leave."

We weep what we sow.

Lily stood in tears and my letter dropped from her lap and fell to the floor; my letter had shown the pen was mightier than the sword, but words are so powerful they cannot be controlled.

The sword has one point, one intention; the sword may be limited but is never misunderstood, words for all their power are misconstrued, and there's no point holding a sword if everyone else thinks you hold a twig.

Lily walked to the front door, opened it, and left.

Come back, we haven't sorted this out yet.

Have we?

I watched her back leave; I listened to her walk along the jungle and watched the top of her blonde head bob past the window until she was out of sight.

My eyes scanned the room and fell onto the coffee sitting on the table.

They say love can be once in a lifetime but they don't mention whose life.

Heat sailed into the air from the coffee on the table like it was just another coffee that could be sitting on any table anywhere in the world, but it wasn't, it was the coffee Lily had left to turn cold because I'd pushed her too far away by growing up too slow.

The television flashed images of old people advertising how to leave behind material possessions for the people dying behind them.

I could hear friends saying clichéd positives to try and pick me up and fix my wings, things like *there are plenty more fish in the sea,* but with over-fishing there aren't anymore.

Even if there are plenty of fish and plenty of oceans, what good does that do me if the one fish I want doesn't want me?

I was standing up, a little further into the room than before, staring at the coffee and seeing images of empty seas devoid of all life, and wondering what it would mean to drink the coffee symbolically.

When Lily entered the front room an hour ago she entered our house, but when she left in tears, she left me alone in hers.

As the engine of her little red car started on the driveway, I was a stranger in her home.

I closed my eyes and I was back in a summer field, on Blackheath common, four years ago.

The sound of marbles spilling over angel wings played delicately as I watched this beautiful girl walk out of the shadows and into the sunlight, walking over the horizon and towards me between two of my friends.

I watched her walk towards me from the moment I saw her on the horizon; not caring the sun was in my eyes, ignoring for a few moments the kid wanting me to throw the ball.

This time she didn't sit down, and I didn't say hello.

She walked right through me like I never existed.

A stranger I never knew then, who became a friend and a lover, then a stranger again.

I found it odd I wasn't crying; I wasn't sure what I was feeling, if I was feeling anything at all.

I was numb, like I'd disconnected or unplugged myself from pain somehow.

I grabbed a beer out of the fridge, which was a bad idea because if I stayed sober I could show Lily I was growing and learning to deal with stress like an adult, and not like a sixteen year old, but then again, I thought, we're over so what did I owe her?

The end of the first bottle became the top of another.

Sometimes; some days, some moments, some actions seem as futile as wearing sunglasses falling into the sun.

Lily didn't come home that night; or the next.

She didn't answer her phone or tell me where she'd gone.

I stayed in for the first night and the second in case she came back, alone with my tear-stained letter and the cold coffee I couldn't throw away, a shrine to all that was wrong with me.

I sat on the couch, drank and tried to call Lily.

Then drank some more and remembered how we bought the couch together but it was no longer mine.

On the third day of being alone and drinking I booked my flight home.

I was flying back to England via San Francisco and into joblessness, homelessness and oblivion, but I was an adult in body, I had no one to blame but myself.

On the fourth day Lily came back and told me she'd gone to a party and I couldn't help but think running off to a party in the middle of us breaking up spoke volumes, to me, about how bizarre our relationship was.

I told Lily my flight was booked back to England and I was to leave for San Francisco in two days, where I'd stay for a couple of nights before heading back to another life.

If Lily wanted me to stay, if her mind thought in that moment she didn't want me to get on the plane, her eyes didn't show it.

As Lily entered her house, I left.

I had no idea where I was going but knew I was going to continue getting drunk; the special sort of drunk only a man can get when feeling sorry for himself.

*

I opened my eyes and I was sitting on top of a waterfall.

Surrounded by jungle.

A tall waterfall, not really my scene.

I held a large bottle of Bacardi in my left hand, a bottle of beer in my right.

Nostradamus backwards (Sumadartson) sounds like "some of the dates are wrong."

One guy, younger than me, grabbed the Bacardi bottle from my hand, drank a large swig, looked down, smiled and winked.

He stood on the edge, closer to the edge than me.

He dropped the Bacardi bottle, and stepped off.

He was gone, over the edge.

I heard a scream, a splash, stood and walked away from the edge.

I walked down the rocks, away from the fall, and circled round so I could get a look at where I was.

The waterfall was massive and the drop was fifty feet easily, another guy appeared at the top of the fall and shouted my name and I waved, in disbelief, because I felt caught in a surreal dream.

Lily and I had visited most of the known and unknown waterfalls on the island but I had no idea where this one was.

I remembered the back of a black pickup truck, drinking in the back, the driver making large circles in the sand to loud music.

I remembered an altercation with some locals on the beach, nothing serious, but we were told to leave.

My clothes were wet, soaked through, I was shivering.

There was no way I would have jumped off the waterfall, no way, and if I did there was no way I wouldn't remember jumping.

How long had I been drinking?

Where was I?

I was pawing desperately around in the dark, an old man having a young man's dream.

I remembered the fight with Lily; I remembered drinking in the bars in town.

I had to leave and find my way out.

I still held the large Bacardi bottle and shouted to the two guys calling my name I had to go to the toilet, I would be back in five minutes.

I followed the jungle up a winding path and the jungle broke into another path leading to a road.

I emerged from the jungle at the same time as an unfortunate American couple and their daughter crossed the road from the other side; the father asked me if I knew where the waterfall was.

I tried to tell them but I was so drunk I couldn't speak and fell sideways. I tried holding myself up on the side of an aptly named pickup truck parked on the side of the road, but, I fell over like a new born giraffe on a frozen lake; the Bacardi bottle smashed and glass spilled across the road.

The ice cracked, cold water poured over my feet, and I was reminded of the thin line between beautiful scenery and slipping silently away from me.

The wife screamed and the husband ferried his family away.

I was not in control of myself and if a passing police car found me I would have been arrested.

I picked myself up from the glass and searched my pockets for my phone but it was gone.

I stumbled a mile down the road until I found a payphone, and I spoke to an operator who called Lily for me; the only person who could save me.

I blurted out the name of the nearest road sign and Lily Googled it and asked me how the hell I got there because it was on the other side of the island.

I said I didn't know and she shouted I had disappeared for two days, I told her I didn't mean to, she told me my flight was in a few hours and she was going to have to pick me up on the way.

Lily thought I spent two days away because I didn't care, but I hadn't, I blacked out completely because I cared so much I couldn't process it.

I told her I'd lost my phone, she told me I left it at home. She thought I left my phone at home deliberately so she couldn't call me but I hadn't.

When I left I simply hadn't been thinking.

I was trying to teach a child genius something he knew more about than me.

I was digesting the first sentence as he was finishing the book.

Everything was moving too fast, events seemed unstoppable.

There was no time to take a breath; no time left.

An hour later Lily pulled up in our red car, she handed me my phone, and we drove in thick silence the entire way to the airport.

I rested my head against the glass of the passenger side window and watched as the island of Kauai drove by me; I was seeing everything for the last time.

Lily was probably thinking I would think of something to say and, if I did, she would turn the car around, we would go home and talk through how stupid we'd been to let our argument get so close to separating us for good.

I just wasn't thinking.

As we pulled into the airport I was still drunk and the alcohol gave me a buzz, stopping me from feeling any of the misery or the reality of what was happening.

My heart held a megaphone and shouted at my brain to wake up, but my brain was wrapped in Bacardi sponsored soundproof glass playing music loud enough to block out pain.

I was aware behind the drunken false high was the devastating misery of being put on a plane, away from the island and the girl I still loved; but the booze made it easier to wallow in the pain, and the pain justified leaving.

We waited side by side for my flight to come up on the screen above us, in silence.

I listened to the crashing thundering of a tiny tear tumbling like a wave down her beautiful face.

This flight was only a small flight to another Hawaiian island; I would catch a plane to San Francisco the next day.

Perhaps it wasn't too late.

My flight number flashed on the screen and I walked with my two bags to the terminal and Lily walked in front of me, she was crying, this was it. This was our goodbye scene.

The last time I would ever see her face was the same as the first time ever I saw her face; the sun truly did rise in those eyes, and the moon and the stars were the gifts she gave.

I said goodbye and Lily said the last words I would ever hear her say; they were as honest as her first:

"I loved you."

Those words took a few days to sink in.

I walked away with my bags and it dawned on me this really was it, there was no going back.

Loved me? Was her heart moving on without me; I wasn't even on the plane yet.

I moved through security and, on the other side, I walked a little and turned.

Lily was still standing, facing me.

She hadn't moved, she was going to watch me walk away for as long as she could.

The woman who taught me *I love you forever* in sign language.

Two fingers to the chest, arms folded across the chest, finger pointed at the other person and a big circle.

If we were on different sides of the same room Lily would look over at me and sign *I love you* and I would sign back *I love you forever*.

We looked at each other from across the airport terminal, barriers between us.

Neither wanted to turn away.

She pointed two fingers to her chest.

Folded her arms across her body.

Pointed a finger at me.

Her bottom lip hugged her top, her face shook with tears.

A sunny field near Greenwich, her name is Lily.

I pointed two fingers to my chest.

Dancing in a club, our first kiss, fireworks exploding above us.

I folded my arms across my body.

Swimming across the Indian Ocean, the world beneath.

Pointed a finger back.

Made a tiny circle with my fingers no one in the world could see but me.

Forever.

We stood on different sides of the barriers taking us to different worlds and lives; all our moments between and simultaneously behind.

All our hate and love, all the pain we had put each other through and all the laughter we'd made.

In the end the bad times didn't matter; in the end, we shared all our best moments.

Standing on different sides of the same room, only truly getting our love across when we weren't destroying it with words.

Lily turned and walked away.

I picked up my bags, turned and walked away too.

My brain snapped, my heart slapped my soul.

Water flooded my eyes. Tears overwhelmed me.

I'd lost love; the emotion we never see landed on my skin like glass, cutting through barriers and making me feel for the first and last time in a while.

I was empty.

Life once poured in, flooded back out again; my heart leaked love through the holes I'd put in.

Love was no longer part of me.

Lily was gone.

"MOHAMMAD AND THE PROSTITUTE"

Part Duh

Saturday 27th November 2010

With a slight hangover I wake up and walk down the stairs to Mohammad's flat, apprehensive but certain helping him is the right thing to do.

My teeth are percussionists from the Royal Philharmonic Orchestra whispering into empty bean tins *one day you will be famous*.

Inside his flat, even in the light of day, there is no daylight.

I shuffle again between large pillars of paper and flyers for young women (I now suspect these flyers are not for show, and the reason he's often complaining about having no savings).

Mohammad offers me a cup of tea which I accept.

He boils the kettle.

I blink smoke from my eyes and stare at Prince Charles, again, waving to nobody.

Mohammad puts a coffee on the table in front of me, and I wonder if on some nights he waves back silently at Prince Charles with the lights off to feel less alone.

I note Mohammad, again, serves the opposite drink to what he offered and I requested.

Mohammad sits down opposite me and we both rest our hands on the small round table, very much like knights only less brave and able.

His grey hair still sprouts in directions it would normally not be allowed to.

He's still wearing his blue and white striped pyjamas; all is not well inside his mind.

He reaches into his pocket and pulls out his phone and shows me a text message he's planning on sending Tracy, the prostitute he knows too well, the burning sun to his Icarus wings:

You banged on my door all bloody night. I have already told my wife about the text. You are being an evil common prostitute and a horrible bloody woman so you are. I will be calling the bloody police so it is.

I smile deep inside because he texts how he speaks, which is cute, but on the outside I wonder how I got here, how I'm about to help an idiot get out of a stupid situation of his own stupid making.

I tell Mohammad to delete calling Tracy an evil common prostitute, as these words will only inflame the situation.

I tell him if he tells Tracy he's telling his wife then he has to tell his wife.

Mohammad lights a cigarette because he's short of breath and shakes his head; his ears wobble, as does the extra floppy piece of skin hanging from his neck.

He says no.

I tell him not to lie to Tracy in these messages because lies return to haunt.

He says he'll say what he likes to her, because she's a common prostitute.

Helping Mohammad is going to be a thankless task, and likely an exercise of saving him from himself.

I tell him to add a line saying if she contacts h m again, or comes to the house again, he'll go the police.

He drags on his cigarette and nods his head ir agreement; our first sign of progress.

He breathes out and coughs, but his eyes brighten, like he's just thought of an invention that will bring the moon to us so in the future the human race won't have to waste lifetimes travelling across space in a bus.

The road to hell is paved with good inventions.

Engulfed in smoke Mohammad tells me he wants to text a message to Tracy asking her how much she wants to leave him alone; with his brilliant idea being if she texts back with a figure he can go to the police and get her arrested for blackmail.

I tell Mohammad we don't live in a nineties television show and the police aren't going to come and arrest someone based on a text message.

I tell him as far as I know rarely are text messages admissible in a court of law. I also point out prostitutes are probably familiar with breaching the law, and so threats of the law are not as strong as he thinks.

Thankfully, for the first time ever, he seems to listen and the blackmail idea is forgotten.

Mohammad says he'll send the text later.

He tells me his wife will be visiting soon with his son and so I have to leave, which I'm only too glad to do because the other option would be listening to him talk for hours about holistic medicine, his favourite subject.

Or worse, the sign on the toilet door asking Mohammad to respect the privacy of tenants, the sign he's now convinced has been up for over a year.

I stand up to leave and he asks me if he should tell his wife.

I note since the start of this bizarre situation he's used the word "wife" on a regular basis, when previously he's told me he has no wife, specifically he has an ex wife who lives down the road and they're friends.

I tell Mohammad the most logical play is to tell his "wife" because then Tracy has no power, no bargaining chip, holds no fear over him.

Also, he doesn't have a wife, so he doesn't have a wife to lose.

I leave Mohammad's flat and walk up the stairs grateful for the smell of fresh air.

I receive a text message from Alicia asking me out to a party; I'm pretty tired and have a horrible landlord to save, so I tell her I want to, but some other time would be better.

Alicia responds by saying no problem, and ends her message with a single kiss; a new addition to our communications.

My text message, in response, ends with a smiley face.

A few hours pass in my room full of peace and tranquillity as I watch a television series and drink a glass of red wine, but as early evening approaches life knocks on my door, and life is Mohammad.

Mohammad invites himself in, because in his head it's his flat not mine; he's holding three boxes, and offers them to me smiling.

An unusually kind and thoughtful act from Mohammad; gifts from the horse's mouth.

I open the boxes and smile back, as is custom, but deep inside I wonder who he's really buying for.

The first box contains a new plug for the sink in my kitchen, when the plug I have is fine. He tells me I should use the new plug, because it will stop food going down the drain.

The second gift is a plastic box for covering plates in the microwave. He tells me no food will *now* go over his microwave.

Lastly he gives me a clothes hanger so I can hang my shirts over the radiator, and not where I hang them.

I like where I hang my clothes, my microwave is clean and I don't put food down the sink.

In return for helping Mohammad I've been supplied with three messages about what I need to change to stay living in his flat.

The only way he can think my microwave is dirty, is if he's been entering my flat when I'm at work and looking inside.

Mohammad pulls out his phone and sends the text message he showed me earlier to Tracy.

He looks up and smiles.

"Mohammad, you left out evil prostitute, right?"

"No, because she needs to know what she is, and so I am telling her so."

He sits on the end of my bed like he's planning on spending the night.

He's sure calling Tracy an evil prostitute and threatening to call the police will get rid of her; he genuinely thinks her response will be full of fear and apology, but I know it won't because his text message is antagonising, and he has no idea how to empathise with others.

Mohammad's phone beeps.

Tracy has sent a text message straight back.

Mohammad reads out the new text message, coughing between words as he does:

"I was not at your house last nite. Now I av two texts you have sent me and I will show dem both to youre[sic] wife. Tell who you like I dont care. Youre[sic] give drugs to children."

There's no way he could give drugs to anyone because he's anti everything, or at least seems to be.

I heard the answer-phone message from Tracy last night; she shouted she was outside his house, so Tracy isn't being honest either.

I find myself in the middle of two lying idiots.

One old idiot lying so his ex wife doesn't know he sleeps with prostitutes, and one young idiot lying to extort money from a marriage that doesn't exist.

In another life they would be quite suited.

However, one of the idiots is a pensioner with a brain like a broken sieve, so I have to persevere in helping Mohammad dig his way out of his own hole.

I ask Mohammad if he's told his wife what's happening, like I advised.

He moves a little on the bed and nods his head at me, then clears his throat before speaking:

"Yes, I have told her. Well, I have not told her I had sex with this girl. I told her there is this crazy bitch trying to get money out of me, and I don't know what to be bloody doing."

I almost laugh at how easily he can deny any wrong doing in this situation. He's lied to his wife to cover up his own lie to his wife. Mohammad is hardly smacking of honesty.

If you've got the wrong end of the stick upside down you've got the right end of the stick the wrong way round.

He said in his text message to Tracy he didn't want his wife to be hurt by this because she's a good person, but if that is the case he shouldn't be sleeping with prostitutes in the first place.

He's protecting himself.

Mohammad tells me his wife told him she already knows Tracy because she happens to live in the house opposite her.

Mohammad tells me his (ex) wife informed him Tracy is from a large family who are already known to the police.

Mohammad looks up at me and as he speaks he smiles and for a moment, just a moment, life returns to his heavy eyes:

"I found out Tracy's sister was actually born a man, you know? She had the sex changing with all the bits cuff off and tucked in so you cannot be telling the difference."

As Mohammad says *bits cut off* he moves his hand from his right shoulder to his right knee like he's swinging an imaginary axe. He winks at me, and I wonder if he had sex with the sister.

"My wife says the local people say they're bloody masochists, do you know this word, masochist?"

I nod.

"My wife says she heard a man scream from inside the house, and he ran out of the house and ran all the way down the bloody road and he was dressed all in leather, like they had been having the sexual intercourse but in a most peculiar way. Bloody maschochists is it so they are. And the next time the screaming man was seen he was covered all in bandages...*bandages*...wrapped up like a bloody mummy so he was."

I'm not sure why he repeats the words bandages, but the word gives him the most joy I've heard him get from any word he's spoken before.

Mohammad sits on the end of my bed and I watch his smile leave with the life in his eyes; his facial expression changes to one of an old man lost in the dark who has no memory of anything else other than being trapped.

Sometimes when he looks up at me with this wide-eyed expression, his big head, tanned skin, confused eyes, bulging belly on a too thin frame, long spindly fingers and a long neck he looks like ET.

A prostitute wanting to take his money who comes from a family known to the police, and recently a man was seen screaming in pain running from their house, and they know where Mohammad lives.

This is something out of a bad horror film.

Tracy is sounding like the type who would have no qualms in turning up on a Friday night with her family to beat Mohammad up on his own doorstep.

Mohammad also informs me Tracy has had many children, all of whom have been taken from her and placed into care.

Mohammad places his hands on his legs and turns his large head so he's facing me, he tells me he wants me to send a text to Tracy tonight, from my phone, telling her I've gone to the police.

He wants me to lie to Tracy, from my phone, because he's too scared to do it himself.

This is why he's still sitting on the end of the bed.

The reason he carried threats hiding as presents from the pound shop has nothing to do with kindness, he knew he was going to drop all his mess in my lap to sort out, then walk away.

I don't mind giving me phone number to a volatile female prostitute who has many brothers, comes from a tough family, can't look after her own children and knows where I live.

I should tell him no and demand he gets out of my home.

Mohammad repeats I should send Tracy a message.

He tells me to make sure my message has nothing to do with him, and does not mention him in any way.

His negative energy swamps into me.

He's bullying me.

I'm being used.

I suggest I should mention him, and he snaps back in anger he doesn't want anything to do with the bloody girl.

I *was* happy to help him.

I'm annoyed he's happy to put me in the firing line when what he should be doing is telling his wife what an arsehole he is.

Mohammad is old and scared and I know he is, but he will not admit to either. He won't even concede I'm the only person who can help him when we both know I am.

I tell Mohammad I'll help him, I'll send a text to Tracy and after I text her she'll never bother him again, but I know if I'm going to do this from my phone I'm going to do it my way;

there's no way I'm going to completely blame Tracy because it's not completely her fault.

Mohammad stands from sitting on my bed and doesn't thank me, but as he leaves my room he asks me if I would like another shelf. Which, in his own way, is him thanking me.

Mohammad leaves my flat with nothing to worry about.

I sit on my bed and try to think of the best way to deal with his stress he's left in my head.

First, I remove my phone number from Facebook.

Maybe I should go on-line and send the text from a website, but for the text message to be believable it's going to have to come from a real phone number and, if Tracy responds, I may need to open up a line of dialogue in order to completely sort everything.

On the upside if this goes wrong I'll finally have something in common with Mohammad; his enemies.

Enemies, who will have my phone number, know where I live and want to hurt me.

Choosing the right angle for the text message is important.

Mohammad told me not to use his name in the text, or to show any signs of weakness like calling him old or elderly. At the moment he's treating Tracy like a criminal and accepting no fault on his part like an old fool; if you treat someone like a criminal they behave like one.

I text the following from my phone, inciting possible retribution from a prostitute, her sister who used to be a man and the rest of her family:

I have phoned the police because my father told me what's going on. I am his daughter, and I'm concerned about your recent threats to my mum and dad so therefore I contacted the police regarding this and they have a report they've confirmed will lead to action against you should you continue to contact my father or mother. I do not wish to take this any further, but if you continue to harass my mum or dad I will be left with no choice.

I told Tracy I was Mohammad's daughter for three reasons:

Mohammad could deny he knew about the text message.

In a previous text message Tracy called Mohammad a dirty old man. That would imply (perhaps considering her profession) she may not respect men, or their ideas.

Mohammad has a son who visits and I don't want any retribution going to the son. Mohammad doesn't have a daughter, so it seems the safest approach all round should this entire thing head south; and if this does head south, it's going to head there fast.

My phone beeps.

This is a pivotal moment: if Tracy is raging I won't get through to her, if it's a calm response then with a bit of humble pie I might be able to save Mohammad from himself.

I open up the message from "Tracy Mohammad's Prostitute."

A name not in my phone yesterday.

"Ur dad has sent me perverted texts 2 my phone and my sisters so do wot u want coz I have the texts and all I wanted was 4 him to stop."

Mohammad would not agree with the message I type in response because he'd rather paint Tracy as a criminal and him as a shining light.

Mohammad called the prostitute, not the other way around.

Mohammad doesn't want his wife to know because it will look bad on him.

This is his fault but he will not apologise, when all Tracy *probably* wants is acknowledgement.

I send the below, with the intention of saving Mohammad from himself by giving Tracy what she wants to hear.

To me, they're just words, but Mohammad won't agree:

"I apologise for my dad Tracy, I really do. He's an old man and he's paid for his mistake. He told my mum earlier about it and it looks like she's left him, for good. I'm not defending whatever he's done. But all he has just walked out the door. Leave him be, he's too old and the stress could actually kill him. And whatever the text was, it's not worth anyone dying over."

I'm only telling Tracy what would be the likeliest conclusion if Mohammad had a wife in the first place.

I'm also telling Tracy what she wanted to happen has already happened so it's over.

I'm saying sorry, a word she needs to hear Mohammad would never say.

And I mention his age too, because he's an old man.

My phone beeps again.

The message that will either be a flag of peace, or show she's hell bent on hurting him:

"No problem all I said 2 him was if he did not stop sencing the text I would show them to his wife. He has made his own problems but thank u it ends now."

I reply thanking Tracy and feel a rush of joy as the feeling of doing a good thing for another human being, whilst at some potential risk to myself, washes over me.

Mohammad is safe.

I go downstairs to tell Mohammad the good news; we can go back to our lives before he angered a prostitute.

The bear has got away with stealing the honey.

Mohammad opens his door a little and pokes his head through the gap, he asks me how I sent the text message and I tell him I pretended to be his daughter; the safest approach because he doesn't have one.

Mohammad asks me what phone I text the message from and I tell him I text Tracy from my phone.

Mohammad's face glares at me from inside his dark door frame; he opens his door fully, and steps outside.

He stands in front of me visibly angered.

Mohammad says using my own phone means Tracy would know the message is from me, a man, and not his daughter.

I tell him of course it wouldn't, my phone would show up on her phone as just a number.

Mohammad snaps back with his voice raised, and tells me the message from me would show up with my name on her phone, because when anyone calls him their name comes up on his phone.

"Look, see you bloody Colossus...You call me now on your phone and I will be bloody showings to you."

He thinks because my name comes up on his phone when I call him my name will come up on Tracy's, because he doesn't understand the reason my name comes up on his phone is because he knows me, and at some point he told his phone what my name is.

All I want to do is tell him it's over but Mohammad wants to fight me.

I try to explain, but Mohammad talks over me in a fashion so rude I feel a spike of anger ,which I have to suppress, reminding myself to be patient because he's old; saving him from a beating only to beat him up myself would serve no purpose.

"No! Just bloody be calling me like I am telling you to do so."

I call Mohammad, I have to.

His phone rings, and as his phone rings my name flashes on the front of his phone.

"See, SEE! Your name comes on the display when you call...bloody be lookings."

"I see."

"She'll know somebody called Colossus sent the text message to her phone and that's not going to be my daughter's name! This is very bad. Everything is be ruined by you. This is so very much worse than when you didn't send your stupid bloody text messagings."

I want to tell Mohammad I've sorted out all his problems but instead I find myself explaining how mobile phones work to a guy who is 100% sure my name has come up on Tracy's phone.

I take a breath and tell Mohammad everything is fine and I've sorted it and Tracy won't be contacting him again.

He doesn't say thank you.

He's sure Tracy is going to come back to him and doesn't believe my name won't come up on her phone.

I'm annoyed with Mohammad and tell him I've done my bit; I told the girl what she needed to hear to get rid of her and it worked.

Mohammad is so full of pride he still doesn't want to concede any wrong doing.

I tell him his pride will lead to a gang of people on his doorstep threatening violence and trying to take his money from him.

He tells me it won't.

I tell him it will.

I tell him she won't contact him again.

He says he's not happy with me.

What a prick.

Don't bite the hand that needs you.

He demands to see what I text Tracy, I tell him it shouldn't matter, but he's so angry I show him.

He reads the text and shouts at me he wanted Tracy to think his marriage with his (ex) wife is strong.

I tell him it is whatever it really is, and a text message doesn't alter reality.

I ask him why it's so important to him Tracy thinks he has a strong marriage when he thinks of her as a common prostitute.

I tell him it's over, he should be grateful for my help.

I tell him he should be thankful he's got away with his mistake.

He stares at me.

He tells me Tracy knows he's weak because she knows a guy text her pretending to be his daughter.

He tells me he wished he'd never asked for my help.

He takes a step back and brings something up from his throat; quite possibly the most disgusting thing I've ever seen a human being do; a penguin about to feed its young.

He stares at me with eyes of fury, opens his mouth and shows me he's clenching between his teeth a small, hard looking ball; slightly bigger and rounder than a pip.

He spits the hard little ball at my feet, turns, shouts I had no right to send Tracy any text message without his permission, storms into his flat, and slams his door behind him.

He's forgotten he asked me to send a text message on his behalf, and it's not my fault he can't understand how a phone works.

I walk up the stairs feeling extremely agitated because he should be thanking me.

His door opens and I turn on the stairs, looking back down, hoping he doesn't leave his flat with an old pistol from a war he can't remember serving in.

His fat head pokes out of his door and he shouts at me:

"You bloody Somalian bastard! Tracy will know I don't have a daughter called Colossus! She will know because Colossus is not a girl's name you fucking bloody stupid bloody fucking Somalian!"

Mohammad's head disappears back into his flat and he slams his door with anger.

Locks, four or five, fasten behind his door.

I walk back up the stairs, enter my flat and sit on my bed angry with Mohammad for his short sightedness.

Only an idiot gets angry at being called stupid.

I remind myself he's an old man, but I'm angry and don't enjoy having to handle the emotion of anger when I shouldn't be feeling any negative emotions at all.

I hear the voice of wisdom enter my head reminding me anger is only putting lines on my face and no one else's; I try to relax.

I can't understand why he cares what Tracy thinks about his life.

Perhaps I've been manipulated into fighting the corner of a man in the wrong, and he sent more offensive text messages to Tracy he never showed me.

A thank you would have been nice.

He's not wanted to concede any truth to Tracy, preferring to
cover one lie with more lies; acting like an upstanding citizen.

He wanted to take the patronisingly moral high ground,
which would have continued a war he would lose.

But he can't see this, so I have no choice but to let it go.

Every time I see him he'll want to see the text message and
for the next year he'll shake his head every time he sees me.

He might evict me for being Somalian; cackling as he slides
his eviction notice under my door.

He who has the last laugh takes the laughter from everyone.

I look at the gap under my door, and wait for the white slip to
come under, telling me I can't live here anymore.

"I LOVED YOU"

June 23rd 2008

I wiped tears from my face, as I walked away, with vodka chased down by beers.

Falling in love is a bit like getting into bed, eventually you have to wake up and get out of it; and sometimes there's a cat on your face.

I landed in San Francisco and my drinking continued; no longer me drinking the drink but the drink drinking me. I drank on the plane, I drank at the San Francisco airport bar, I got to the hotel and cleaned out the spirits in my room, I drank at the hotel bar, I left the hotel bar and walked into a bar where I drank till I left that bar and found another; and another, and another.

My hotel was a desperately grey block made from paper and people's screams; at night the sound of strangers having icy sex echoed off the building and poured through the broken air conditioning like tiny daggers I couldn't see, reminding me of just the tip of what I was missing.

There was a small writing desk in my room along with a laptop and I had an internet connection. Three weeks before Lily and I split up I was told my UK agent had secured book deals with Scribner in America and Headline in the UK for a book called How to Hide From Humans.

Although my relationship had swallowed a grenade and ran across a field of landmines my professional life was finally shaping up. Perhaps Lily had tired of living with a dreamer and understandably; for years I'd been telling her I would be a published writer in a year's time, but each time I got close to my dream my dream disappeared in the wind.

I had a good agent and exchanged regular emails with the American publishers about what they wanted me to change before publication.

The only thing that could possibly ruin it was me.

Throw a grenade into a group of ducks and they regret not having a different word for take cover.

I was going to make it as a writer, but that would have to wait until I returned to England in a few short days.

All I wanted to do was drink, and so I did.

I remember little of my San Francisco binge.

Riding trams, steep roads like mountains, religious people wearing sandwich boards shouting the love of God will save us; thinking if they had been loved by their parents, they might understand they are the saviour of themselves.

Being lost, wandering beyond the two block tourist racius, stumbling upon rows and rows of derelict housing, homeless people in their masses. Every homeless person black, or *African* American; the word *African* separating from them white Americans, who are just called Americans, not African Americans, even though we all hail from Africa.

This is America.

I was shocked the richest country in the world spending billions of dollars on its war budget was letting its own people down massively; for a country meant to be multi-cultural and free thinking I took note all these people, rows and rows, *hundreds* of people were all black; not a single white face, except mine.

What kind of education had been provided to these people? What kind of social disadvantages are they been born into?

Their children would be born on the street.

What the fuck America?

Simplistic, moronic white people will question how the homeless can live in such conditions, putting it down to the colour of skin, because that kind of thinking ticks all the boxes and so everything neatly tucks in.

How dare America let down its black population so badly, and so obviously, by not providing the basic opportunities it claims to advocate so aggressively; land of the free and home of the brave? How can you be free if you are born beneath a class system that's recognised legally? Where's the bravery in obliterating far off enemies who live in caves with billion dollar weaponry whilst on the streets of San Francisco a mother can't afford to feed her baby?

Street became street after street, more homeless people; men women and children, all *African* American; is it any wonder people drink when born to a government who sweeps their hopes under the rug, whilst standing on the carpet above, in shiny shoes, shaking hands with other politicians in a large white office; signing autographs with the man holding African American children; in the hope the same people being oppressed vote the next shiny shoed man into office.

I found my way out from the skeleton closet of America and back into the central part of San Francisco, pockets rattling with mini vodka and whisky bottles from the hotel bar; *fuck this place, I thought, it's full of either racists or ignorant cunts.*

That was the whisky thinking, or the vodka, but it's a thought I kept having.

I recall walking along a boardwalk by the ocean and looking over a railing at fat sea-lions wallowing around on giant rocks, thrown food by people applauding who must have thought sea-lions understood the custodial implications of hand clapping, and would therefore reciprocate by bowing.

The sea-lions just sat on the rocks being sea-lions, but the people kept clapping and the clapping grated me.

I became confused as to whether the sea-lions were the fat things on the rocks, or the fat things in tourist hats eating ice cream cones and barking occasionally.

On the pier I looked, inebriated, through a telescope at Alcatraz and thought I should go but decided I was already spiritually incarcerated.

I walked past a homeless girl with a sign reading "hoping for a random act of kindness" and thought about the massve implications of asking for something non material; a thought, or a moment, or an act, or simply time.

I wonder if homeless people were more honest about what they needed, if they would be harder to step over or around.

I bought the homeless girl a sandwich and coffee; I lent her my ear and but didn't give her a chance to use it as, instead, I barked at her about cold pavements and people clapping like demented sea- lions until she ran away, and I continued ranting to a lamppost about how much love hurt and institutional racism was an act of hateful ventriloquism.

I ended up in another bar easy on history and class, but served beer and spirits in large glasses; quiet enough for me to drink myself silly, a good place to sit and burn images of Lily.

I sat desperately; convincing myself getting on my flight from San Francisco to England was an act of mercy and the right thing to do.

As seemed always the case in American bars somebody joined me before too long.

The guy seemed a character, dressed in leather with black hair and dark rings under his eyes, he looked edgy but seemed sincere enough, and we chatted about nothing in particular.

I got us a jug and he drank my beer.

The guy was drunk and his skin pasty, he was too thin, his fingers painted dark, a tattoo rose from somewhere on his body and stretched up the neck on his skin.

He nervously picked at a napkin, suppressing some kind of disposition; he looked up and explained what he did for a living.

"I work for tough people and sometimes I go with these people to collections, you know; here and there. On occasion I do things I want to forget, but I can't; some things, some images don't let you forget them. They absorb into your very fucking being, you know what I mean?"

I have no idea what you are talking about.

His voice was intense and he leant forwards and, whether he meant to or not, I was threatened.

"I've hurt people, sometimes just a slap, sometimes more. A broken arm or a leg with a baseball bat, you know? Other times... there are other times."

Instinctively I thought this was my life now.

Without Lily, who was all rainbows and flowers, this was the new kind of energy I was attracting.

Since Lily and I split up, even though it was only a few days ago, I had gone from our own place in Hawaii to a shitty hotel room with cum-stained carpets.

My only friend was the sound of cheap hotel sex and people screaming at each other in high pitched rows leading to slamming doors and bottles crashing against walls, and now I sat opposite a guy - who could be any guy in the world - but he had mental problems, and *wanted* to be in my company, wanted to tell me about snapping people's bones for money.

He leant in further, he wanted, needed, to get something off his chest and he picked me, from all the people in all the places, to unload onto.

"A man I killed watches me."

His pupils rolled in his head and I wondered what his brain was doing behind his eyes I couldn't see; this was the calm before his storm, and his storm wasn't going to be pretty.

We are the method of madness. With rigid claws and beady minds, gripped by vice and held up to the light.

He insisted on getting another drink for us both because my glass was coming to an end.

I tried to decline but he spoke over me, grabbed my wrist, and told me he insists.

He smiled as he spoke.

His eyes burning cities, names he put on gravestones.

I sat as he stood at the bar and wondered what I had managed to get myself into; my life was going downhill fast, but I wasn't quite at the stage where I wanted to get drunk with a psychopathic hit-man who thought dead people followed him.

He returned with two beers and two shots.

He put mine down in front of me with a big smile I didn't believe; his first words sent a genuine chill down my spine; if he was joking his timing was off.

"I want you to know when I was at the bar getting these drinks all I could think about was how much fun it would be to sneak up behind you, when you're getting the next round, place my hand over your mouth and snap your neck with my hands."

How lovely.

I wanted to tell him life is thinking you're a broken kettle until it rains, a fish falls from the sky and you realise you were always an awesome goldfish bowl.

He just needed to stop killing people until his fish fell from the sky.

His stare was naturally aggressive; I sensed he was about to jump at me from his side of the table so told him I needed to go to the toilet.

I walked around the bar, past the toilets, out of the pub and into the daylight.

I headed left and hurried towards the nearest crowd of people.

The last thing I wanted was an assassin after me in the middle of my alcoholic binge from reality.

Assassins are hard to see coming at the best of times, but floating in a vodka bubble my chances of escape were minimal.

From that moment, in every pub, in the back of my mind was the thought the crazy hit-man could sit down at my table demanding the round I owed him; a legitimate grudge.

A reason to kill me.

I woke up with the sun in my face; slumped at the base of a public payphone, the receiver dangling upside down by my head; swinging slightly in the breeze.

Hundreds of people walked over and around me, I was completely ignored by people in control of their own situations, and would be as long as my situation didn't alter their own.

I hadn't got through to her, but later, she got through to a different version of me.

I was in my hotel room at the time of the call; drinking the remaining contents of vodka from the small plastic bottles provided by the hotel that lived in the fridge under the faded redwood table.

Lily's voice was calm and she simply wanted to know how I was.

To hear my voice.

My mind was so sozzled with alcohol I completely lost control of myself and I was a complete and utter bastard; Lily was calling for a conversation, to find out how I was, to be nice, to talk for perhaps the start of a potential consolidation, but all I could think about as she spoke were her last words at the airport:

I love*d* you.

I was caught up in myself, again, rather than listen to Lily and help her save us I listened to my pride, my ego; I was more intent on shouting her down because of three stupid words I knew she didn't mean.

Lily's tiny voice drowned in the storm of my thundering rage; how dare she fall out of love with me before I was even on the plane.

Lily was trying to talk to Colossus but I was gone, replaced with some angry machine who wanted to make Lily hurt and feel the way her words made me feel.

How are you?

Why are you being like this?

I screamed down the phone at Lily and couldn't handle it, couldn't be man enough to talk the problems through; I hung up and threw my mobile phone across the room like some rock star whose only song was heard by his mum, who thought her son shouldn't give up his day job anytime soon.

I was just another lost soul screaming through the hotel paper walls into the ears of the lost and drunk.

I was staying in the right hotel for me, part of the fabric of a decaying society.

Wallpaper peeled from my eyes onto the walls, lay on torn carpet, grabbed my heels.

Wanted me to become part of it.

I stormed out of my shit-box hotel room and continued drinking, tried to bury the images of Lily crying on what was our sofa, in what was once our home.

I couldn't get out of my head her last words to me "I *loved* you" but if I just stopped to listen maybe I could have heard her explanation, maybe she hadn't meant to say them, maybe she meant them at the time, but those words were just one of those things people say when the person they love is leaving them forever to get on a plane.

How long hadn't she loved me?

I was twenty-seven, becoming an alcoholic; no job, no money and a one way ticket back to homelessness, poverty, the UK weather and a life I left.

I had one hope, my book deal, but no amount of what I could gain could fill what I was losing; never again would I have what I had been part of, unless I didn't get on the plane from San Francisco to the UK.

And that's what I thought about all night, sitting in the corner of dark bars, staring into the bottom of glass after glass; swallowing answers from poisoned questions.

What if I didn't get on the plane?

Could I win her back?

Could she forgive how I have behaved?

Could we get back to being each other's worlds, could I grow up and show Lily men mature slower but we get there in the end?

I calmed down at the bar and wanted to call her, if only to say sorry for my earlier behaviour.

How could I call her?

How could she call me?

If I hadn't thrown my phone across the hotel room there would be a chance of reconciliation but it lay rotting on the hotel floor along with the carpet.

And I was drinking.

I was going to the airport in the morning and knew if I got on the plane back to England I would never see Lily again, a world apart; a mind away.

"GO AWAY"

Sunday 21st November 2010

Mohammad is at my door clutching his phone; the world's oldest mobile. The phone itself is not much smaller than a brick and is only one step up the evolutionary ladder from the paper cup phone.

Mohammad asks me if typing 141 before a phone number when sending a text message means the person receiving the text won't know who sent the message.

He then asks me if he dialled 141 before calling someone if they would know it was him calling.

The only reason he would want to know this information is if he's planning on calling or texting messages he shouldn't be sending.

Either sexual texts to random phone numbers or, what I sense he may be thinking of doing, persisting on sending further messages to Tracy because he thinks he's untouchable.

I notice Mohammad is clean shaven, his pancake hair is now brushed back away from his saucepan forehead and, although he still looks over three hundred years old, I can tell he's worrying less in his brain.

I tell Mohammad if he puts 141 before he calls another phone the person receiving the call won't know who is calling, but if he does it with a text message the text message will fail and it won't work.

I tell him if this has anything to do with Tracy   don't want to know and I won't be helping him.

Mohammad smiles but says nothing.

The bastard; the smile lets me know he's probably up to no good but the lack of verbal response means I have nothing to go on.

Mohammad stands in front of me.

I stand in my door looking at Mohammad expecting him to leave.

Instead he stands, blinks Morse code; his eyes beg me to crawl into his ears and pull out the last remaining parts of Mohammad before he disappears.

He shakes his head, coughs phlegm into his hand, wipes the phlegm on the wall outside my door, looks up and shakes his head:

"No, no Colossus, I am thinking you are wrong about the text messagings with the numbers and so I am going to send you a text messaging now to your phone with the 141's before the number."

"Mohammad, there's no point. I know what I'm talking about. The text message will fail."

Fuck off.

Mohammad ignores me and brings his phone closer to his face, then moves his phone further away from his face, then moves his phone nearer his face, then away again as he tries to find the appropriate distance from his fat head to bring his screen into focus.

This is going to take at least half an hour.

The thought of standing in front of him as he finds the correct screen to write the text in, then finds my number, then has to alter the number to put 141 behind it, then writes the text message and sends it to me; all so he can get a fail message back, because it won't work, when I could be inside my flat doing something I want to be doing is beyond explainable frustration.

"Mohammad, really, this won't work."

Mohammad chuckles:

"I think it will."

Wanker.

I wait.

Rage boils inside me at the arrogance of the man who never listens and thinks he has a right to repeatedly encroach on my life.

I watch on as he hits the button on his phone, beginning the long scroll down to the text message icon.

Tap.

Tap.

For the love of god tap faster.

Tap.

Tap.

Mohammad looks from his phone and up at me, I look back at Mohammad and he raises his eyebrows, like *technclogy* is the stupid third wheel in this moment.

He looks back down at his phone.

Tap.

Tap.

"Here it is isn't it so? The home of the text messagings."

"Mohammad don't send me a full text message, just text me a full stop."

 Mohammad starts typing his text message and comp etely ignores me.

Tap.

Tap.

He very slowly types *"Hello Colossus, How are you?"*

Tap.

Tap.

This is like being in a pub with no music or atmosphere; forced to listen to the constant drone of people mumbling over other people mumbling.

Tap.

Tap.

"I need to be just puttings the numbers in here."

Oh, please, do take your time.

"One"

Patience.

"Four."

One, for fucks sake, just push one.

"One."

Push him down the stairs.

You could push him down the stairs.

"Ah, and now I am pushing the sending text messagings button and it is sending. This is where we have to wait a moment isn't it so?"

Mohammad pushes the send button.

"We won't have to wait long Mohammad because fail message are immediate."

"But it isn't going to be failings."

"Yes it is."

"No it isn't."

"Yes it is."

"Colossus, this is like you telling me the bloody prostitute woman didn't know you text her but we found out she bloody did."

That never happened because it's NOT POSSIBLE!

Oh, what's the point?

Mohammad's phone buzzes.

Mine does not.

He opens the text message and reads out the fail message saying his text could not be delivered.

"Like I said Mohammad, you're trying to text a number that doesn't exist."

"No, it's probably just because I put the number in wrong. Let us be trying again."

Dear God, grant me the serenity to accept the Mohammad I cannot change and the courage to change the Mohammad I can. And the wisdom to not shoot the Mohammad I know.

Mohammad takes another ten minutes to type out the message again; he places the 141 behind my phone number and hits send.

"This time it will be workings."

I roll my eyes and Mohammad's phone buzzes and he reads another text message telling him he's an idiot.

He looks up at me, smiles and shrugs his shoulders because to him this is killing time in a day he was going to spend doing nothing anyway.

"Oh, so it doesn't bloody work isn't it so?"

"No Mohammad, like I told you half an hour ago."

Mohammad starts telling me about the tenant who put up the "please respect our privacy we respect yours" sign.

He's already told me this story, but can't remember telling me, so I stand in front of Mohammad as he tells me a story I already know.

He forgets what he's telling me, peers into my room at my bed and then he's off again; this time telling me about dust protectors he recently purchased from the pound shop.

New game: Ides and Seek. I hide, you pretend you aren't playing. Then when I turn around you brutally stab me in front of the entire senate. That would be less painful.

I'm waiting for a chance to tell him I have to go, but he avoids the space bar in his story.

Mohammad says he showed two "homosexual" guys to one of his rooms and he deliberately showed them to a room with a single bed so he could ask them how they would sleep together; because in his head it's forever 1940 and he thought he would embarrass the guys.

The word 'bed' looks like a bed.

The guys said they would share.

Mohammad got angry they were not embarrassed and asked them to leave, then called the estate agents to complain about who they sent.

"Because I don't want a place like that, you know with the gays and the lesbians and the homosexuals, do you know the word homosexuals? I don't want that kind of place. I want a respectable place, with respectable being of people."

Close your mind too much and no good will fall from your mouth.

I'm anti-nothing but I'm starting to become anti Mohammad because he can't see his small mind is what's making the world seem so big and scary, and he won't leave me alone to just be.

I stand looking at Mohammad.

Mohammad looks back.

I raise my eyebrows and I'm about to tell him it's been a nice chat but I really must get on, but it's like he's some kind of machine sent back to this time from the future, and his only mission is to talk just before I'm about to say goodbye.

Mohammad tells me he's going to lock the washing machine door on Sundays because he doesn't like the noise it makes.

I tell him he isn't because Sunday is when I wash my clothes.

He wants to control when people use the washing machine and has decided he wants to give each tenant a day when they use the machine, so he knows when and who is doing their washing.

The girls in the building have agreed he says.

I bet they wouldn't agree if they knew the real reason you wanted to know who was washing their clothes, and when, is so you can masturbate over the twins bras once their load has finished.

We argue for a while about his stupid idea, which effectively means I'm about to be a thirty year old man who can't wash his clothes when he wants.

Mohammad shakes his head and says he doesn't think I understand his idea and he asks me to walk with him to the washing machine, which is just outside my door, in the cupboard to the left.

In his head I'll only fully understand his idea if it's explained to me again, for the third time, as he points to the machine itself.

Mohammad and I stand looking at the white washing machine.

He picks up a piece of paper on the washing machine and tells me he wrote down what settings the girl next door washed her clothes on, and tells me this is what he thinks everyone should use.

People should be able to choose their own settings, that aside, I'm aware it was me who told Mohammad about the settings I used, and a quick glance at the end of the note confirms it:

"...hope this helps Mohammad – Colossus."

I tell him I don't agree with him making us pick days to do our washing but it doesn't really affect me because I'm doing mine on Sunday like always.

Mohammad says he's tired and must sleep; his words are angels playing the violin with the eyelashes of fairies providing their hair willingly.

"YOUR RELATIONSHIP IS BOARDING NOW"

June 24th 2008

I was alone in San Francisco airport, the other side of security, sitting in the boarding lounge.

Nobody sat next to me; I was on the end of a row of three blue chairs.

Through the large windows to my right I could see the runway; a word too close to runaway.

The sky was blue and clear, a beautiful day.

My eyes darted from the people behind the desk calling out numbers on tickets, to the queue of people forming to my right waiting to get on the plane.

I watched the plane sitting on the concrete through the glass; the people had finished scurrying around its wheels and ferrying bags from the terminal into its belly; feeding a flying monster livestock hoping it would spare their children for another year.

The plane would take me home.

Home is where the heart is, but hearts don't belong to a place.

I looked at my ticket; the perforated bit at the end would be ripped off soon and handed to a stranger, confirming my imminent departure.

I looked between my legs, put my hands on either side of my head, stared down at my feet and played out images of us in my mind.

My heart sank in my chest and I drowned; held under by the invisible grip of the body I was trapped in.

I saw me and Lily on acid trapped in a van in daylight being attacked by a neighbour.

I saw us climbing a mountain and only just making it back without dying.

I saw us swimming across the ocean in Thailand fearing sharks.

I saw our home, us at festivals, her shadow walking over a hill in Blackheath and stopping for a moment to take her all in.

I saw us fighting until we started laughing because neither of us knew why we were.

I saw her sharing her hamburger with me; and me putting a flower in her hair.

I saw her crying in tears holding a letter I should never have given her.

Lily had not called since last night and I couldn't blame her.

I had nobody to blame but myself.

The people behind the desk called the next row of boarding numbers.

The time had come when I had to make a decision where the consequences were so massive I had no idea what to do.

Get on the plane, causing an irrevocable split between me and the girl I love and leave my life in Hawaii behind forever...

Or stay, and hope Lily and I can rekindle our love so utterly crazy yet undeniable.

I looked at my ticket and then out at the plane.

Tickets 12A though to 15C your time to board is now.

I should call.

I should call Lily.

I had to speak to Lily before I got on the plane, surely.

Call her.

Call her.

I stared at my phone; my time was running out and all I had to do was call Lily back and apologise.

Ticket 15C through to 17A your time is boarding now.

My ticket was 20C. I had at most five minutes.

I didn't know how to call. I don't know how to, or what to say to her.

My mouth was dry, I felt dead inside; a little boy with a red hat held his mother's hand and squealed:

"Hey mom, is that the plane that's gonna take us to Erg-err-land?"

I stared at the screen on my phone and it flashed.

Lily's name flashed on the screen and somehow she was calling me.

I spoke first, my voice sounding stronger than it felt to me.

"Hello."

Lily's voice was soft, full of emotion, bunnies feeding on rabbit stew.

"Hi."

There was a pause.

Lily spoke; unable to fight back tears, they spilled out of her mouth and through the phone and shattered my ears.

"I miss you. I miss you."

She missed me; I felt alive, a flicker of my former self sparked somewhere inside me and I thought perhaps, maybe, I am worth loving, all this can be resolved, I'll grow up, I'll mow the jungle, cook every night, bring Lily coffee in the morning and take a more active role in socialising.

I spoke and my voice broke with emotion, it just wasn't possible to hold back the impossible:

"I miss you too. I don't know what's happening. Where are you?"

"I'm at my mum's; I came here for a few days to clear my head."

I knew I had to apologise for the hotel phone call, I wanted to apologise for the hotel phone call.

That wasn't me.

"The hotel phone call, I am so sorry. That was, that was totally my fault."

Lily responded through sobs:

"I miss you."

Ticket 17A through to 20B your time to board is now.

My ticket was in the next batch to be called and I was at the front of the queue.

"Lily, I'm at the airport. I'm about to get on the plane."

I cried, tears so overwhelming I couldn't finish what I was trying to say.

Lily cried too, and we became the entwined expression of our pain born from our distance.

We listened to each other sob; our hearts desperately searched for a solution to the stupidity of the human condition. The cries of our hearts stamped out by the wishes of control, ego, and the fear of letting go.

I waited to be told not to get on the plane.

Lily waited for me to tell her I didn't want to get on the plane.

"Lily."

"Colossus?"

"I love you."

"I love you too."

Ticket 20B through to 20D your time to board is now.

"They're asking me to board Lily."

"How did we get here?"

"I don't know. Maybe I'll go home and see my family and then I'll come back?"

What was wrong with me?

I thought saying I would see my family *and come back* told Lily I saw my future in Hawaii with her, but all Lily heard was I was getting on the plane.

And she was right.

I should have just told her I didn't want to get on the plane.

"Colossus if you need to go, *you need to go*."

She wasn't talking about going to see my family.

"No, I mean, they're calling me I...I *have* to go, I think I have to go, I love you."

I cried.

And Lily cried too.

And through her tears she spoke:

"I love you too."

I moved my phone from my ear and down into my lap.

My tears fell from my eyes onto Lily's name, a screen with words on.

At her mum's house, most likely sitting on a wooden chair in the kitchen, Lily looked down at her phone displaying my name on her screen.

Her tears fell from her eyes onto my name.

Neither of us had ended the call.

Two lovers waiting for the other to hang up.

No, you hang up.

Both of us stared at our phones.

Neither wanted to hang up because we both knew once the call was over so were we.

If Lily hung up it would be her telling me to get on the plane, if I hung up it would be because I had decided to get on it.

I waited.

Lily waited.

It wasn't too late.

There was still one more chance, if I moved the phone to my ears and told her I wanted to come home.

And so I moved the phone up to my ear to tell her, but as I did I was struck with a thought.

What if she wasn't with me? It would be painful for her now but what about in a year or maybe more; could Lily find someone better, more employable, better looking, mature?

What if she could meet a man who was just like me but without insecurity?

What if you really do love someone but the only way you can love them is to set them free?

I moved the phone back from my ear and looked at her name on the screen.

I took a deep breath.

I whispered I hoped she would forgive me and one day my actions would make sense, to both us.

I moved my thumb over the button that would terminate the phone call and our love.

With an action so simple, but the echoing implications inexplicable, I pushed the button.

The end of me and Lily forever; the termination of all our aspirations and dreams as a couple, all boiled down to a button.

As I walked crying towards the plane I imagined Lily looking through tears at a little red icon on her mobile phone indicating I hung up on our hearts.

I knew once her tears dried and her anger dissipated she would never forgive or understand my reasons for leaving; it was inevitable a chance of a friendship was improbable.

I would never see her beautiful face again.

And so I thought, fuck it, I'll drink on the plane.

"YOU ARE NOT TALKING THE ENGLISH"

Friday 3rd December 2010

Voices hurl from the bottom of the stairs and bombard the silence of my room and snap my peace in half, one of the voices is Mohammad and the other is the voice of a girl.

I can't hear the words because my television is on, but I can tell they're arguing.

I hear Mohammad raise his voice in stress; I hit the mute button on my remote control, fearing he hasn't paid another prostitute and I'm going to have to go downstairs.

Then I recognise the voice he's talking rudely too, Alicia.

Alicia tries to speak but Mohammad cuts her off and shouts over her, his voice booming in the swirling cold, funnelling up the stairs and into my room where it fills the air with a sense of why do I live here?

"No, NO, you stop talking when I am talking. YOU listen to me. YOU LISTEN TO ME."

Both of their voices rise, neither is listening to the other so I go downstairs and act as a mediator; if I don't Mohammad is going to either have a heart attack or make Alicia cry.

I leave my flat and walk down the stairs; when they see me coming they stop talking and look to me with facial expressions expressing they each believe they are talking to madness.

Mohammad towers above Alicia and stands too close to her, attempting to physically bully his way out of whatever she's trying to ask him. I take a seat on the bottom step, which forces him away from her, creating a bit of breathing space; so we can go back a few moments to when the conversation might have made some sense.

By sitting on the bottom step I'm ensuring I'm beneath Mohammad so he still believes he's in full control of the conversation; my position of being lower than Mohammad is the same position children should be spoken to when being directed for their own good.

Mohammad, as charming as ever, is the first to speak.

His words are spat at me; they reek of impatience and old people complaining about how you can't leave your front door open when you go on holiday without being robbed by the youth of today.

"She, this bloody *woman*, she is talking at me and won't let me speak. SHE WONT LET ME SPEAK."

Alicia tries to say something but Mohammad talks over her:

"NO. YOU SEE COLOSSUS? YOU SEE – She doesn't be shutting up, this stupid woman. This annoying stupid bloody *woman*."

I speak; emphasizing Alicia's name, suggesting to Mohammad he should talk to Alicia like a person:

"Let's calm down. Mohammad, wait a second. *Alicia*, what is the problem?"

Alicia is close to tears.

"I want to know when I get my, how you say, my deposit back."

Mohammad's face wobbles as his anger rises; his ear lobes shake against the side of his head and his gibbly bits hanging from his neck lunge from side to side, the Snuffleupagus from Sesame Street runs from a pack of starving hyenas because they see an easy meal that will become a humorous story to tell their children.

"WHAT? I CANNOT UNDERSTAND YOU WOMAN. YOU ARE NOT TALKING THE ENGLISH."

Mohammad looks at me confused like he thinks Alicia is talking Spanish.

I look at Alicia and Alicia looks and talks to me.

"But, I am talking English no?"

Alicia looks skywards in despair.

I can't blame Alicia because, yes, she speaks quickly; but in this moment she is talking slowly and clearly so Mohammad can understand, and he's responding by being the rudest he could possibly be, by pretending she isn't talking English.

Alicia *is* speaking English.

I know this because it's the only language I speak.

Alicia looks at Mohammad and says to him directly and slowly:

"I am talking English Mohammad, this is English no?"

I look to Mohammad to respond to Alicia, he stares at me and growls; living in his throat are two cats fighting over the same territory:

"WHAT DOES SHE SAY?"

I look at Alicia and shrug my shoulders; Alicia's mouth is a little open, she cannot believe the audacity of Mohammad; the king of his own tiny home, and god, in his curiously upside-down looking head.

"Mohammad, her name is Alicia, stop calling her woman because it's disrespectful."

Mohammad smiles at me but says nothing; it's that sick smile he flashes when he's heard what I've said and wants to let me know he'll continue to do what he thinks best.

I sit on the step bewildered by the stance of Mohammad, digesting the dawning reality I'm about to translate English to English for Mohammad.

I'm not sure this has ever been done before.

"Alicia – you tell me what you want to say in English, and I'll translate to Mohammad in English. How does that sound?"

That sounds bloody crazy.

They both nod, happy to accept the terms of the discussion.

Alicia speaks to me:

"I am only asking how long I have to wait to get my deposit back. He says thirty days!?"

I look to Mohammad, who stares at me blankly waiting for me to translate.

"Alicia is asking how long it takes to get the rent back, is it thirty days?"

Mohammad speaks back to me, now refusing to even look at Alicia.

"The government has her bloody money and it takes me thirty days to get the money from the government. *The bloody government Colossus*. I cannot bloody be giving her the money without the signature of her friend. If she pays me thirty pounds maybe I can be getting her money quicker."

I look to Alicia, who although hearing what Mohammad just said doesn't seem to have understood what he's trying to get across, so I translate Mohammad's English into English Alicia can understand.

"You need the signature of the other person when you moved in, because the deposit is in two names. If you pay thirty pounds you can get the deposit sooner, if not it could take up to thirty days."

"Okay, buenos, so who is the scheme with, can I know?"

I turn to Mohammad and ask him if he has any paperwork on the scheme so Alicia can show her friend, so she can get him to send Mohammad a letter.

This angers Mohammad and I sense his frustration he has to explain where his tenant's money is going; a concern for me because he's holding my deposit which was two months' rent, over one and half thousand pounds.

Mohammad angrily disappears into the smoke behind his door like an evil cartoon wizard disappearing into another dimension after successfully stealing the dreams of children.

Alicia whispers to me:

"He is crazy Colossus, really *crazy* no?"

I let her by a small movement of my mouth and a slight repositioning of my eyes that I, in no uncertain terms, completely agree with her assessment of Mohammad's mental health.

Mohammad returns from the smoke, clasping a letter in one hand, and in his other, a knife.

He speaks angrily to Alicia, still calling her *woman*; he waves the knife around close to her face, subtly suggesting if she continues to harass him he will cut her.

I note the letter is already open, so the knife isn't needed.

"HERE, here is the bloody letter about the government scheme. You see, you have to give me a signature from both, it is the government. The GOVERNMENT."

"Mohammad, maybe you should put the knife back in your kitchen?"

He completely ignores me, suddenly unable to talk my version of English.

"The government are watching this scheme, so I can't just get back your bloody money as simply as you be thinkings because the government has it and they're watching the money."

Oh no; his crazy *government are all powerful and nobody can question them or anything they do* speech.

"The government ask me to ask you, you stupid bloody woman, to give me letter and I give you the money. This is THE GOVERNMENT, we *have* to do what they say because it is the law and they could be watching."

"Mohammad, the knife, stop waving it so close to Alicia, I'm telling you; put the knife back in the kitchen."

He ignores me.

"Before I give the money I will check your room. I need both keys. If you don't have both keys it costs me three hundred bloody pounds to get a new key. You understand? YOU UNDERSTAND?"

As he speaks he waves the knife till it's almost under her throat, I place my finger on Mohammad's wrist and move his hand and knife away from Alicia's face.

That was a threat, loud and clear as far as I'm concerned.

"You're talking to a twenty-three year old kid in a threatening manner holding a knife, calm down, and no key costs three hundred pounds to replace."

Alicia pulls my arm because she's taken offence at being called a child.

I ask Alicia if she understands about costs coming out for damages.

 "Si, yes. I understand."

"So Alicia, you need to get a letter with both signatures on to Mohammad instructing Mohammad to release your deposit. Then he will start the process. So, first thing is first, get the letter to Mohammad. Are you both happy?"

They both agree.

Alicia and I turn and walk up the stairs, Mohammad calls up to me and I turn:

"There's nothing you do not know Colossus. And you can speak Spanish too? I cannot believe in all of the things you know so it is."

Not quite a thank-you for coming out of my room at night to help him get out of another situation where he's upsetting someone who has the misfortune to be in contact with him.

As I walk up the stairs I smile because although Mohammad is annoying, and a bigot, he now believes I speak Spanish, and his English speaking Spanish tenant doesn't speak English.

Alicia is waiting for me at the top of the stairs. She asks in a whisper if she can come into my flat, darting her head left and right like a small piglet on the lookout for the big bad wolf.

I tell Alicia she's welcome and she pops up to her flat to grab her laptop; two minutes later Alicia is sitting on my floor with her back to the radiator and her computer on her lap.

I'm watching the television, but glancing at Alicia looking at her laptop sitting on my floor and wondering why she's here.

She's only twenty-three but I'm only thirty; so the age gap is fine.

I find myself wondering if maybe she's in my flat, again, because she fancies me.

I haven't had sexual contact with a woman for a long time, with the exception of the almost touching a nipple debacle a few weeks ago, and Alicia is quite attractive.

When I came back from San Francisco I blocked the idea of girls from my mind because I wanted to be alone until I knew what I was going to do with my life, or until I could have a shower without hearing waves crashing into my skin.

Then Alicia knocked for me.

And knocked for me again.

And again.

And here I am glancing at Alicia on my floor, through no action of my own, and wondering if she's here because she wants more.

Alicia is wearing her pyjamas and I can't help notice they're low cut. When she looks up to talk to me she leans forward, revealing cleavage, but I don't want to offend her so I don't look; then I think maybe she knows they're low cut but I can't remember how to turn flirting into something more.

Perhaps it's been too long for me, sometimes I get lonely; but it's peaceful and there are no arguments, no tears and just because other people don't condone being alone doesn't mean I have to find it weird.

Alicia asks me if she can sit on my bed and I tell her she can.

And so there we are me and Alicia; sitting on my bed watching TV and talking as I wonder if this is a subtext to bonking.

Alicia rubs her shoulders, her nightie slips off revealing her bra.

I want to hug her.

How do I get hugging to happen?

This would once have been a natural and instinctive act.

Don't think; just put your arm around her.

The longer I've been away from women the longer I've been left alone to over think every thought.

Now I find myself thinking about thinking about hugging Alicia and the more complicated I make it the more I tense.

I'm in a plane with all systems failing, the pilot has taken a bullet to his chest and he reads out a poem in broken English; *try and hug Alicia she's one in a million,* but his last words to me are instructions on how to land the plane but he only speaks Brazilian.

I'm going to try and hug her.

What if I have coffee breath?

What if she says yes to the hug and then tries to kiss me? She would think my face stinks.

I'm pretty sure asking a girl for a hug isn't the way to go, but at the same time I don't want to just go ahead.

If I was a girl and I didn't like a guy and that guy just hugged me out of the blue I might feel forced into the hug, but, if I don't try and instigate a hug soon she'll be gone and I'll never know.

Alicia has come to my room (not for the first time) and decided to hang out with me. So, on some level she must like me.

She's in my bed and unnecessarily touching me.

I don't want to make her feel uncomfortable by just going for a hug, so I ask if we can hug, in what is probably one of the most awkward plays by a man on a woman to be recorded in a book this side of the twenty first century.

"Alicia, do you fancy a hug?"

Alicia says yes but falls on me and squashes my left arm with her entire weight.

This isn't a hug, more a brief collapse, in order to retract away from hugging.

I lay in my bed with Alicia crushing me not complaining about the pain, whilst Alicia lays on me thinking of an excuse to get out of the hug.

There's a brief silence, the air screams of awkward.

Alicia says she can't see the television from where she's laying; I mumble something about nothing in particular.

Alicia gets off me and sits back up, ending the most awkward hug ever.

She isn't into me.

Our awkward hug tells me all I need to know.

We sit in a brief silence watching the television.

The male pride part of my brain talks to me:

Ask her again.

Maybe she really couldn't see the television from where she was laying.

Ask her again.

If she didn't like you she would just say so, or would not have said yes to the hug in the first place.

Go on Colossus, ask again.

We watch the television in silence.

For all I know Alicia is thinking of the most polite way to leave without hurting my feelings.

But what if she isn't?

What if she's thinking the same thing as me, and she actually quite liked the hug and regretted moving away?

I ask again.

"Would you like another hug?"

There is silence, the second a year struggling to breathe.

Alicia doesn't turn her head as she speaks, won't give the dignity of looking at me:

"I want to watch television."

I should leave, but I'm in my flat.

I'm confused.

Why are you here at night?

Is it really just to watch television?

I remember she doesn't have a television in her flat.

Am I being used?

I've reached the age all men have to one day face, the age girls see me as their older brother, or good mate as they're off shagging more successful men, then, when they're treated badly or not loved or listened to because they're only being used for sex, they run to me to off-load their problems, and talk about themselves so they can once again feel pretty.

I have better things to do than hang around a younger girl, feeding her positive male attention to keep her topped up with confidence, until a guy comes along who she goes out with, only to be completely ignored by her until the relationship goes wrong.

I am more than a shoulder to cry on, I can make people cry to.

Saturday 4th December 2010

I'm woken by a female pterodactyl yelling over the sound of a Scottish bank manager telling the dinosaur he has to repossess her nest through the medium of bagpipes.

The fire alarm screams into my ear in a high pitched, angry tone.

With the fire alarms in every room connected there's no chance of a fire destroying the building, but an equally small chance of anyone cooking something without setting off every alarm in every flat.

The time is six in the morning.

I hear someone running down the stairs, past my door, down the stairs outside my flat, to the ground floor.

The main alarm box is outside Mohammad's flat.

Whoever is pushing buttons and trying to turn it off is in a race against time.

They need to turn the alarms off before Mohammad leaves his flat, because if he opens his door it will be to find out who next receives a crudely written note slid under their door.

I know how to turn the alarm off and it's probably a new tenant, so I get out of bed and run down in the hope I can help.

At the bottom of the stairs I find Alicia; a look on her face like an old turtle blaming others for not being able to complete her jigsaw puzzle, forgetting she ate the last piece the night before.

Her eyes are wide, she shakes her head and I know she knows if Mohammad finds her, after last night, she would be dead.

He would come out, see Alicia, return into his smoky chamber and come out with the same knife he held last night; sliding it across her throat in one movement before calmly walking back inside to smoke cigarettes and rejoice in the death of another Somalian.

The alarm is so loud it's hard to hear each other, we shout at the tops of our voices, some words lost.

"I'M SO SORRY!"

"I CAN TURN IT OFF!"

There's a little key needed as well as an alarm code.

I trace my fingers along the top of the alarm box in search of the key.

"I WAS COOKING A SAUSAGE."

"Sausage can be tricky!"

My fingers find the key.

"WHAT?"

The sirens are so loud and piercing we shout louder to be heard:

"Sausages can be tricky!"

"I WAS IN THE SHOWER!"

She can't hear me.

Another alarm works in conjunction with the alarm already ringing; the loud shrilling noise is joined by a whooping circular yelp; the sound makes me think of a dolphin from the fourteenth century performing open brain surgery to a room of watching dogs in white coats making notes on canine lobotomy.

I put the key in the alarm, turn it and shout at Alicia:

"YOU WERE COOKING SAUSAGES IN THE SHOWER?!"

"I PUT A SAUSAGE IN THE OVEN THEN WENT TO HAVE A SHOWER NO?"

Alicia's shower is three floors beneath her studio flat.

She was never going to keep an eye on a sausage when having a shower three floors below.

"You idiot."

"WHAT YOU SAY?"

I punch the code into the alarm system followed by the star button.

The alarms silence.

Amazingly Mohammad has not left his flat.

We turn, head back up the steps and smile at the twins; they're in matching pyjamas at the top of the stairs with angry eyes and confused looks, two time travelling mimes who have travelled too far forward in time and find themselves hunted down by a society who thinks people who paint their faces white, and speak through action, should be outlawed and tortured into extinction.

Alicia goes to her flat and I sit in mine, unable to get back to sleep, because of the cold.

*

I'm now wearing two jumpers, a hat and I'm under the covers in my bed but my flat is freezing;

England is going through its coldest winter in twenty years and Mohammad has decided to turn the heating off.

I'm thirty years old and in full time employment but can't control the temperature around my own face, in my own home, because my landlord is an evil control freak.

I breathe out and the warm air from inside my body hits the cold air of my flat, forming an ice cube in midair which falls to the floor and shatters on impact.

I move to the kitchen and stand by the boiling kettle and make a coffee; I grip the cup with my hands for warmth.

I prefer not to be confrontational, but this is ridiculous; I'm paying almost eight hundred pounds a month for a room with a bed, a small lime green kitchen which never stays clean and a shower that's always either boiling hot or freezing cold.

I've had enough.

I send Mohammad a text asking him to turn the heating on in my flat.

If Mohammad had his way he would tell me when I could wash my clothes too.

In the words of Mohammad *it is unbelievable so it is*.

The silence in my room sounds louder today.

The heating does not turn on, but worse Mohammad hasn't bothered to respond to my text message.

My hands are and feet are cold.

I want to get ready for the day but that means taking my clothes off and there's no chance.

I send Mohammad a pretty blunt message:

"Mohammad, are you in? If so please come and feel how cold it is in my room. I need the heating on now. I can't live in a room this cold without heating. It's as simple as that. Many thanks."

I actually typed *many thanks you big headed tight bastard twat jockey* at the end of the text, but deleted it before hitting the send button.

Mohammad completely ignores my two text messages, so I go and knock for Mohammad; leaving my coffee on the side in the kitchen.

I walk down the stairs in a hat, two pairs of trousers, three pairs of socks, two t-shirts, two jumpers and my dressing gown.

I knock on his front door and wait.

I knock again.

I hear movement from the other side of the door and chains move from side to side; his door opens and Mohammad's face stares back.

A gust of warm smoky air ripples sarcastically over my cold, previously free from smoke, face.

I ask Mohammad to turn the heating on and he tells me the heating is coming on at six in the evening.

I look at the time.

Half past five.

Mohammad was planning on ignoring me completely, and no doubt the complaints of everyone else, until the heating went on at normal time.

All the while making sure he was extra toasty.

I tell Mohammad I'm freezing cold and want the heating on in my room now.

Mohammad stares at me with cold eyes from inside his warm flat, and smiles his stupid smile that reveals surprisingly white teeth, for a man who smokes more than his bodyweight in tar every day.

He keeps his door pulled tightly against his face, hoping to not let all his heat escape.

"This December is very cold, the coldest December in seventeen years isn't it so. I read this in the Evening Standard."

"That's why the heating needs to be turned *on*."

Mohammad's thinking the cold is not his fault, because the weather is colder this year than ever and that's why I feel colder.

Mohammad continues:

"So you see, I cannot be controlling the weather."

He smiles.

They must be dentures.

And his hair is so thick, still so thick at his age.

What a bastard.

I've had enough of his stupid smile.

"But we don't live outside do we? We can't control the weather but you do control the radiators in every room. So turn mine on. Turn it on now."

"It is bloody cold in here too so it is."

"No it's not Mohammad; I can feel your heat from here. Come to my room. Come to my room now and feel for yourself how cold it is."

"No no... I will turn the heat on for you. The heating always be comings on now anyway."

He gives me an all knowing nod, the subtext to his nod is him jumping around me with his arms in the air chanting over and over again how the heating came on when he wanted, even though I complained.

I head back upstairs.

I'm sitting on my bed angry despite sending two text messages I'm still freezing cold and being made to wait until Mohammad wants the heating on.

The heating doesn't turn on and I know the heating will turn on at six o clock on the dot.

Mohammad knocks on my door and tells me he wants to check the temperature of my flat, he walks into my kitchen, which is so cold the floor is starting to curl up around the edges.

Mohammad tells me he can't feel any cold.

I put his hand on the kitchen window so he can feel the cold breeze pouring through the edges; predictably, he gives me his smile and says there is no breeze.

Mohammad would make a terrible poker player because when he smiled the other players would know he was bluffing.

I tell him there's no way he can't feel the breeze coming through the window and my kitchen is freezing.

In response Mohammad looks around my kitchen for something he can attack me about, instead of defend ng himself.

He looks at my cooker and pulls a face like a crow has shot up his nose and is knitting a small jumper two other crows are trying to drag out of his left ear.

He hobbles over to it, points a long spindly finger at the marks around the edge of the hot plates and tells me my cooker isn't clean enough.

A watch the end of his finger point to the cooker, and as my eyes trace up his arm to the face I hate his arm changes, his skin lightens, and by the time I stare into his brown eyes they have turned blue.

His hair is longer and blonde.

I'm in Hawaii again, by the kitchen, and Mohammad has turned into Lily.

I love his face, for a moment.

I close my eyes, try and get a grip, try and ground myself in the here and now.

Forget the face I didn't do enough for. Remember the one in front of me, the face of the man who despite how much he irritates, I seemingly can't do enough for.

The people we bend over backwards for are the people who are the meanest, and those we love and let in close we stand up to.

I clean my flat every Sunday and I'm a pretty tidy person along the way so it's never bad. I take offence Mohammad is pointing out marks around my cooker when the reason the marks are irremovable is because they're on the world's cheapest material on top of the world's cheapest oven.

Mohammad's ovens are essentially fireproof boxes sitting perilously beneath the flashing lights of giant alarms.

I focus on Mohammad; try to see him for who he really is.

He tells me when he was in my room during the week the oven was in the same condition, implying I don't tidy.

I see Lily opening the oven in Kauai, pointing inside at the areas she wants me to scrub and clean.

I tell Mohammad I pay him rent and expect privacy.

Lily stands in front of me and tells me I need to sort out the front lawn because the leaves are building up.

I tell Mohammad I'm renting the cooker from him and don't appreciate him thinking he can go anywhere he wants.

He tells me his builder was in my room recently and remarked my place was untidy.

I shake my head because Lily is asking me what I do all day, and I'm telling her look, look at all this writing, but she doesn't read, doesn't want to know. She doesn't understand, she thinks I'm mental, a man in a hotel in a horror book, repeating the same phrases over and over again.

Repeating the same phrases over and over again.

I'm frustrated at Lily, the same frustration, the exact same frustration I now feel towards Mohammad.

I steady myself; put my hand on the side.

I don't love Mohammad, surely.

I'm stunned by how, in his brain, he thinks ignoring my request for warmth can be appeased by telling me he's broken into my flat twice.

Mohammad continues his attack:

"When I came in here you had a t-towel over your cooker which is a bloody fire hazard. You could have started a bloody fire."

How many times has he been in my flat without me knowing?

"So even if the cooker is off, and off at the wall, so it's not even plugged in; you still think it's a fire hazard?"

He ignores me; like he always does when he hears what he doesn't like.

Like Lily did, when things weren't going her way.

Mohammad walks into my front room, on a mission to lay down the law and remind me of who is boss so I never complain about the cold again.

He comments on three work shirts crying on my curtain rail.

He points at them, shakes his head and tells me he's told the builder to put a drying rack up in my kitchen because it would be better for me.

I don't want to dry my shirts in my freezing cold kitchen.

"Better for you, you mean."

"No, better for you."

"No, Mohammad, better for you."

"No Colossus, BETTER FOR YOU."

Give me strength.

I should write him a letter, I should write him a letter from my heart with good intention, and one morning I'll walk down to the bottom of the stairs and he'll be crying over my words.

"I'm happy drying my three shirts where I dry them and I never asked you to put a rail up in my kitchen. I don't want to dry shirts in my kitchen. You never asked me if I wanted to dry shirts in my kitchen... So the rack is clearly something better for you."

456

Mohammad shouts at me, a vein in his neck bulges like a slug under his skin:

"NO BETTER FOR YOU!"

I don't respond.

We stare at each other in silence.

I look behind him, and through the doors on the kitchen side I see the coffee I made, colder, dying.

He speaks again, as he does the slug in his neck slithers away:

"Who dries their shirts on a curtain rail? Nobody does this."

"I do it. Look...

I step aside so he can see my three shirts drying on the curtain rail.

...That's how I dry my three works shirts. I don't appreciate your comments on my private life, I don't appreciate you dictating I become like you. You're making it impossible for any tenant to live here. First you say you want good people, then people who work, then people who pay rent on time; well I'm all of those people but now you're saying you only want people who keep the oven like new."

Tension sucks our air from the room, pulling the steam from the cooling coffee, making it hard to breathe. I feel my neck closing, a familiar feeling.

"Yes, I want the oven to be like new. And also why I am bloody telling you these things, I want you to clean the bloody taps, you do not polish the taps, and if you don't be polishing them they will be rustings, and these are my bloody taps so they are."

The taps, the *fucking* taps.

I feel my heart beating faster in my chest, a dizzy feeling tingles in my stomach; the base of my lower spine turns to ice.

I breathe in.

Not now.

Not fucking now.

"Well that's impossible. I can't see how I'm MEANT TO LIVE SOMEWHERE when the landlord is entering the rooms when the tenants are out on a regular basis and breaking the law! THIS IS MY HOME TOO!"

Mohammad's ear lobes do the familiar dance on the side of his head and his voice rises; he can't stand his authority being challenged.

My heart, Lily is in my room, what is going on, my heart is breaking again.

This time I want to drink the coffee, devour it, smash the cup into Mohammad's face, tell him some people are tidier than others, but the tidy people don't have the right to make other people like them, just because they want things to be a certain way.

Tell him if messy people didn't exist, people who demand a certain level of cleanliness would be exposed as the unimaginative boring people they have let themselves become.

Tell him I want him back; want us back like the way we were before.

Before I knocked on his door and complained about the heating.

Before I gave Lily my letter.

"This room was meant to be for ten bloody pounds more a week, but when I met you I put it down to one hundred and seventy five pounds because you were not part of a couple?"

A lie.

My forehead is sweating; my t-shirt is sticking to my back.

"That isn't true. I replied to an advert for one hundred and seventy five pounds a week, *your* advert. It was always one hundred and seventy five pounds."

"No, it was more."

"If you want, I can show you your own advert."

Challenged he runs away into another subject.

Runs away.

Runway.

An airport, tears falling onto a phone.

Drinking on the plane, trying to fly away from the pain.

"Do you remember Amit, Colossus? He lived upstairs and he put shit, fucking shit down the drains and now I have to pay hundreds of bloody pounds to get the drains cleared. I paid fifty thousand pounds to create the rooms. Do you think this is fair? That I have to pay out more bloody money?"

Never has a man so old taken such little responsibility.

Maybe I'm the same, maybe that's why I feel pushed against the wall.

Why do I care? Mohammad is the landlord. If he budgeted badly, that's his fault.

He continues, sensing my weakness.

I look down, trying to get hold of my breathing, trying to think of happy thoughts.

I close my eyes and I'm sitting in a car, and Lily is in the driving seat, and all of paradise is in front of us, but inside the car our lives are draining us.

"Amit was Indian, and in India they're not civilised like us, they shit in their roads, do you know this Colossus? How people in India are is how Amit was; I was very much happy to be able to give him a note under his door telling him he was no longer welcome."

Hidden under a stream of racist hate preaching is the real reason he's come upstairs into my flat: to threaten me.

To suggest if I keep complaining about his failures and his cruelties to his tenants I'll find a note under my door.

He embellishes division of his own making because the smaller the room he creates the bigger in that room he becomes; but outside, the world is laughing.

I wonder if being homeless would be so bad.

To live in a park, to simply sit on the grass; if I had a sleeping bag and wrapped up warm it would be no colder than living in Mohammad's flat.

I could walk away from him and all of his negative thoughts.

Get on a plane, not deal with anything.

Fly away.

Mohammad tells me he sent Amit a letter telling him to tidy his studio, that he told Amit if he didn't tidy his room he would get a cleaner in to tidy it for him, and charge Amit three hundred pounds for the cleaner.

Mohammad is threatening again; implying if he wanted to he could get a cleaner in without my consent and then charge me whatever he wanted.

I blink, green trees and blue seas, and stare back at Mohammad.

His face, but with long blonde hair I can't shake.

And her eyes.

"And his food, I did not like his bloody food, with all the spices and the smells; you know he only ever cooked rice, cooked it with every meal like a simple minded bloody heathen. I know you be knowing this word."

The way Mohammad says heathen feels like another dig at me; perhaps he's been through my food cupboards and noted I mainly eat rice, though I can't know for sure.

He smiles a boastful smile then tells me his cooker is always tidy and he would never let his cooker get in a state like mine.

My breathing is under control for now, shallower, my heart is still beating fast, but I feel a little stronger than I did a minute ago.

Two furry dice swing under the mirror of a car, and I wonder what invisible wind moves them.

I recall Mohammad's flat; plates of royalty stuffed between stacks of papers and pornography. Yellow nicotine stained walls and ancient bottles of clear liquid from a previous life when he was interested in holistic medicine.

His entire flat is an untidy mess, but yet here he is; throwing stones again; a God amongst men.

"My flat and my cooker are always spotless because after my wife has cooked for me she always tidies afterwards."

Poor woman; she probably met him young and never knew what life could have been.

She still feeds and tidies him, even though they're divorced, and then she's told to leave him so he can get back to his porn.

I've had enough of his nonsense, and I want him out of my room before I have a full blown panic attack.

I tell him I'm not even getting heating, and he's left me with no choice but to look for somewhere else to live.

I tell him I'm not comfortable handing my money over in return for no privacy, an impossible list of instructions on how to live and all whilst having to constantly handle his dark judgemental views on life.

And Lily sobs into her hands and there is no hope; no hope for us.

I watch Lily cry and want to go to her but can't. I want to make it better but I'm not sure I know how.

I'll leave and go and live in a park; I'll be free from his rubbish and I won't have to go to work where I'm equally as unfulfilled as a receptionist bringing coffee to people with IQ's lower than dead fish.

I was meant to be a writer, what happened to being a writer?

They say life is what happens when you're busy making other plans but it doesn't have to be; life can be what you always wished, if you don't stop believing in dreaming.

What if I took a pad and pen with me to be homeless and spent every day trying to write my way out of the park?

I would have to write.

I would be forced to.

Mohammad responds by telling me he'll find people to live in his home who live to his standards and will tidy before and after every meal.

I think he means he wants to only have tenants he can bully, manipulate and dictate like his poor wife.

Be seen and not heard.

Mohammad heads to my door clearly angered.

I can't believe I ever found this guy funny, even from a distance.

Once I have my deposit back I can use that money for food whilst living in the park.

Or is this a crazy idea crazy people think?

I don't think so, maybe I'm meant to go and live in a park.

Or maybe I'm losing my mind.

At my door Mohammadily turns, blue eyes still bright, blonde hair falling down to his waist.

"This isn't at you. Not specifically. Not really."

Mohammad smiles, so I know what he's about to say is aimed directly at me and nobody else:

"Supposing I hired out the room upstairs to a single man and this single man started seeing one of the other women here. And they started to be having a bloody affair...

If he's talking about Alicia he means a relationship not an affair; but such is his controlling nature in his mind the affair he's talking about is against him.

Here it comes, he's about to tell me I can't have sex, or have a girlfriend, as long as I'm under his roof.

"I could not accept that because I couldn't have this place turning into a brothel. If you go to Cricklewood and ring a door number you can go into a room and have sex for forty pounds with a girl. I have plenty of bloody rooms and I could turn this place into a brothel very easily. And you know, these women would pay me seven hundred pounds a bloody week, because they make three thousand pounds a week just from their pussy."

As Mohammadily says the word "pussy" he makes a triangle with his two hands and places the triangle over his groin.

Lily fades away from his face, leaving just an old man in her place.

By his maths I calculate a girl would have to have sex with seventy five different men every seven days, or eleven men every twelve hours.

I have no idea what he's going on about. He's telling me I can't get involved with any girl in the building, which is fine; I have no plans to do that anyway.

This must be because Alicia has been seen going into my room, or he's been listening to our conversations somehow, but it's all ridiculous because Alicia and I are friends.

I wouldn't be surprised if he's installed secret cameras in each room.

That's the insanity of this man; he's leapt from me talking to Alicia to running a brothel, complete with charges and final profit after reduction of the prostitutes share.

Content he's warned me I'll be evicted if I have sex, don't clean my flat, continue eating rice or refuse to accept where he wants me to dry my clothes he finally leaves me alone.

Home is meant to be a place where I can relax but I have no heat, I can't have friends, I can't have anything hanging up where I want it and I can't have a cooker that looks like I've cooked from it after I just have.

I close the door behind Mohammad and lay on my bed.

I feel my breathing no longer mine to control, my wind pipe closes up and no air fits in through my nose. My stomach turns and fingers tighten.

My back is heavy and my lungs can't do their job properly.

My body leaks water from every pore and sweat drips from my forehead and crawls down my skin, compounding the state my system is putting me in.

The panic attack is not mine to control, and all I can do is stare at the corner of the room and wait for it to be over.

Feeling like death is upon me, knowing in a few minutes, if I'm lucky, death will be off again to touch someone else, to remind another of their fragility.

I stare into the corner and Lily is putting her hand on my face, telling me she'll love me forever.

She holds me close and tells me I'll never be alone.

She tells me there's nothing I could ever do that would make us fall apart.

And I close my eyes and feel sand in my fingers and water between my toes.

But the coffee cup still sits on the side.

In present day and in memory.

And as I begin to get control of my breathing there is nothing I can do, but ponder if all of this is because I'm meant to write a book, or if all of this is just because I don't like polishing taps as much as two other people.

My heart slows.

And as my heart slows, the rest of me jumps back on.

*

The freezing cold day has turned into an almost warm evening; my radiator is on but struggling to catch up with the seven hour head-start the cold had over it.

It is sometime around nine in the evening.

Alicia and I are sitting in bed watching television again; and again through no instigation of my own.

She keeps touching me unnecessarily, when she laughs she leans into me and, at one point, she leans into me laughing and feels the muscle on my arm.

I pass her the remote control and as I do she holds onto my fingers for half a second longer than necessary, looks into my eyes, and doesn't look away until I do.

Maybe she does like me.

There's no way I can ask for a hug for a third time.

This makes me happy because there's no pressure on me; if Alicia wants something to happen she'll have to instigate it.

A kitten appears on the television trying to sell cat food and Alicia squeals like a piglet rolling toward a bowling pin formation of children on Christmas morning.

I glance to the right of my bed.

There are some books on the shelf.

At exactly our eye height is a bit of tissue I ejaculated into this morning.

I lean over Alicia, she asks me what I'm doing, and I say I'm just getting some water and she asks why I don't just ask her to pass it to her.

I say I don't want to trouble her, and just before picking up the water I knock a book over the tissue so it's covered and cannot be seen.

I lean back away from her with the glass in my hand.

Alicia, in turn, leans across me to take the same glass of water from my hand; as she does her breasts push into my face and, once she has the water, she sits back up holding eye contact.

Kiss her.

She's gone away and decided to come back and start something with me.

This is it.

She thought when I leant over her to get the glass of water I was flirting, not destroying the evidence of an earlier wank, and she's reciprocated.

Perhaps I could have a girlfriend again; perhaps tonight will be our first kiss.

How do I kiss again?

I should probably hug her first.

Just relax; this is all going to happen naturally.

This is excellent.

This balances out my earlier panic attack.

There's a knock on my door.

Mohammad must have heard Alicia is in my room and is knocking on my door to tell her to leave my flat, but I'm not going to let him; he can't stop me from having my first kiss in years.

I open the door but it's not Mohammad.

It's a guy I've never seen before in my life.

He's young, intelligent and expensive looking; his hair is neatly side parted, his clothes ironed and safe. His smile is a little arrogant, but also goofy enough to let me know he's more of a fool than he allows himself to recognise.

The sharpest tools in the box are not always the best tools for the job.

He tries to carry himself as older than his years but when he travels back home (often) his mum dresses him and makes him eat his greens.

He looks like a rich goose; I'm naturally curious to know who his is and what he wants.

He speaks in a Swiss accent, his first words surprise me:

"Is Alicia here?"

What?

"Yeah, sure, come in."

This is interesting.

The goose from Switzerland walks into my flat, his walk is regal; his back stiff and tall. He was never allowed to slouch in his family home. He walks through the main room, ignoring Alicia, and into my kitchen where he turns around and inspects the room with a look of disgust on his face.

He returns to the main room and talks to Alicia:

'I don't mind if you stay here honey, I'll see you later."

Honey?

And he leaves.

And just like that, he's gone.

This is the last thing I expected.

The truth of the situation is immediately clear.

Alicia's *friend* that was staying with her never left and this *friend* is actually a boyfriend; which Alicia has failed to mention.

Telling me she has a boyfriend, and is living with him, should have been one of the first things to crop up in conversation.

When Mohammad told me earlier about having girls n my flat and he used the world "affair" he wasn't talking about me cheating on him, he was talking about Alicia and her boyfriend.

I've been used.

A good relationship is all about give and fake.

Perhaps not deliberately; Alicia and her boyfriend are probably having arguments at the moment and what better way to get a reaction from your boyfriend than go and hang out with another man in the same building.

I thought she liked me; I even checked her facebook status and it says she's single.

Rather than apologise Alicia cries and tells me about the worst aspects of her boyfriend.

I don't mean to be cruel, but I don't fancy being the emotional battering ram for a young girl who has displayed clear comfort at receiving the attentions from two men at once, along with the capacity for promoting confusion by not being open.

I'm sure her reasons are buried in her past, but I have no interest in justifying them.

"I SHOULD HAVE MOWED THE JUNGLE"

15th December 2008

Love involves evolving loving.

I landed back in England without much clue of what to do or where to go, so I went straight to a place where I knew people, a community/art project in East London. A place always full of lively vibrant people; a place if I'm feeling alone I can go and be part of everything else.

I sat in the garden by the fire and the first friend I met ribbed me *I had fucked it up,* but I wasn't sure what *it* was meant to be; my relationship, my life; probably both. He was right, I had messed everything up. I sat around a fire in east London, under grey London skies, leaning back on a bin, imagining the bark of a palm tree pushing into my back, trying to see paradise through the new holes in my life: but we are not our location, our location is us; something for all the governments invading others to philosophise and discuss.

I wasn't ready to talk about what happened because I was still trying to process it myself.

In groups everyone wants to know what's happening with everyone else; there's a subtle expectation to provide information about your life, and information is currency; the more you give the richer in the group you become, but where did I start? *How* did I start?

I could no more explain what made us fall out of love than I could explain what made us fall in.

I returned from Hawaii with nothing, no big bags of clothes or suitcases full of sea-shells for family members, so when I went to the community in East London I entered not knowing where to go when I left.

I caught up with my friends; one day stretched to two until some of my friends told me they had a garage I was welcome to move into, until I found a job and got back on my feet.

In the time I'd been away the party scene of London had changed somewhat with the introduction of a new drug called Ketamine. Ketamine had been around before I left but back then it was more of an afterthought, whereas now it was the drug of choice for a lot of people.

I was about to move into a garage and my life was in disarray, so I decided I might as well take truck loads of this horse tranquiliser to see if, by exploring the universe inside my brain, I might be able to untangle some of the complications of pain.

Ketamine was, over the next year, a drug I would fall in and out of love with; a drug that would, in hindsight, mirror my relationship with Lily and lead me to understand who I relate to is dictated by how I do.

At first Ketamine was a blissful escape, initially I created worlds within my mind, with oceans I didn't have to leave; I felt a warming comfort and sensation, a relief almost of being home; drowning was fun.

I sat and closed my eyes and travelled back or forward through time; the drug coloured the dark unlit paths of my imagination and united subconsci; showed me rainbows exist in the dark and you don't have to see them, if you close your eyes you can be them.

Entering a K-hole is one of the most bizarre experiences a person can have. A rollercoaster for the brain; I sank into the floor and melted behind the curtain of the universe. I travelled to places inside my mind, on many occasions I was a second behind an important answer, a thought behind the biggest thought ever had but simultaneously a donkey chasing a carrot, a chicken playing chess with pieces made from wolf heads. Slow hand clapped by fat poultry.

There were times I knew the secrets to the universe; when I woke up I remembered I found them, but had no idea how to recall what I found.

Consciousness starts with a con.

Ketamine however is the fast food way to obtain these states of mind, and eventually my mind grew fat, my thoughts leaked chicken nuggets, and I sat in a garage all day clucking at bricks.

The ketamine lines grew longer to achieve the same states, I spent day's unconscious with a television watching me, the images flashed from the screen to my eyes, but there was no brain inside to store the memory.

Eventually the drug that was a friend became a dark passenger who whispered negative thoughts in my ear as I lay semi-conscious and highly susceptible to brain waves altering.

My brain hid beneath the windows of the house my garage attached to, peeked out from behind curtains at friends seen as strangers, and strangers seen as government agents.

Repetitive ketamine abuse darkened colours, narrowed corridors, cut me off from my family and friends, sent sparks of panic flying though me when my phone rang, divided me eternally and caused chaos internally; ketamine became the thought I can't downstairs because someone might want to talk to me.

I took a line, waited twenty minutes then took another.

Waited twenty minutes, took another line, waited twenty minutes and took another.

There's no time for sleeping, or for regular sleeping patterns; even though the drug is a horse tranquiliser, so I was never really awake either.

Days that used to be a day drinking on my own became days of going out drinking and taking ketamine in toilets on my own.

I walked into a pub in Blackheath and the guy serving me was talking to the girl behind the bar about how he was happy to serve someone on drugs, as long as they didn't cause any trouble or take any on the premises.

Drugs have the reputation everything expands and contracts, but when you take them every day there's no great impact, no high or low, everything becomes the same; life through cling film.

My brain was confused; harder to think, I was slower; stupid.

Hills became mountains, and when I looked back from base camp, I realised all the effort was to climb over a paving slab.

I sat down and thought what an amazing coincidence, the guy behind the bar happened to be talking about serving someone on drugs as he served me.

I went to the toilet and looked in the mirror; the lower half of my face was covered in white powder.

I had no idea how I managed to walk to this pub and not be arrested.

I cleaned my face and stared in the mirror.

A mirror does not judge our reflection, but our thoughts.

I moved the bullet from inside my pocket to my nose and snorted more.

A pinch in the nose of relief.

A trickle of peace down the back of the throat, reached by removing a little bit more of me.

I sat back down, my face now free from white powder; I looked out of the window with my beer and watched my thoughts look back into the window at me.

I thought I was lucky the guy had been talking about drugs because I might not have gone to the toilet.

I had no idea he was talking about me.

I left the pub and sat on Blackheath common, the place I met Lily years before.

There was no sun; the wind bit my face and I was alone.

As my journey around the edges of addiction took hold I moved into my friend's garage, which they kindly offered me, saving me from the streets.

I was, am and will always be extremely grateful to my great friends; Danny, Rob and Max; without their help, without them offering me the garage I'm not sure where I would have ended up.

I had a bed in a garage, my new life.

Bikes pinned to the brick wall, tools sat in boxes overflowing with nails, an old lawnmower full of dead grass from lost summers rusted in the corner, a concrete floor embellished the cold, empty spider webs loomed in every nook and cranny, the garage not good enough for them to stay in.

The garage wasn't much to look at, but it was a step up from not having a garage.

I put fairy lights up, because fairy lights make everything better.

Two large double doors, the type found in every garage, sat at the opposite end to my bed; a continuous two inch gap between the doors and concrete floor meant there was no escape from the elements.

A single white door directly connected the garage to the house.

During the day, due to the kindness of my friends, I was able to use the house like everyone else; so I only had to sleep in the garage at night.

The garage was in Blackheath, a ten minute walk from Blackheath common; the field where Lily and I first met; so in a strange way I had come full circle.

I should have mowed the jungle.

I was adjusting to being back in a big city with no job, and with no idea how to get one.

I had no bank account and couldn't get one without an address, but I had no proof of address because I was homeless.

Without any identification I couldn't get a bank account and, I thought at the time, I couldn't get a job because I couldn't get a bank account to get a salary paid into.

So I stared at bricks and took ketamine hits.

I still had two international book deals for How to Hide from Humans, and once the money came in I would be able to move out of the garage; my name would be out in the public domain.

I would write endless silly books and live as an author.

I was poor, but if I could cling onto my dream for a little longer eventually I would turn the corner.

The downside to living the dream is you can't afford to be awake.

I emailed my agent to ask on the progress of my book deals, but he never came back to me.

So I emailed him again and again; the longer the quiet, the more concerned I became.

I emailed the publishers directly, one in the UK and one in the United States, asking what the plans were with my book and they both responded with apologies; they sent the contract to my agent, and when he failed to respond they took my book deals away and gave the publishing slot to somebody else.

What?

They told me they sent my agent contracts months before but, because he hadn't responded, both publishers assumed I had received better deals from elsewhere.

I asked if they could send me another deal and they said no.

The people who offered me a light in dark times changed their minds to conserve batteries.

There was no point in blaming, no point in getting angry; it was over.

In two emails I lost over fifty thousand pounds, but more importantly, I lost my name that would have provided my future as a writer.

My agent was meant to forward me the contracts, but, he never did. He was a good guy. Later on I found out we had been living parallel lives at similar times.

His marriage had failed, so he flew from London to Australia to sit on a beach and pick up the bits of his brain that were left at the same time as I returned to the city to blow my brains up with drugs; rather than gather the bits of my brain remaining.

Our two breaking points mirrored each others.

In Hawaii I had a home, a girlfriend and international book deals, since leaving Hawaii I had met an assassin who wanted to kill me, I now lived in a garage, struggled with drugs and lost my book deals.

The lost book deals turned into another object for life to break over my head.

Cars drove by outside in the street and sounded like the sea.

A bottle of wine.

I closed my eyes and heard waterfalls.

A line of ketamine.

I dreamt of beaches.

A line of ketamine.

Lily smiling.

A bag of ketamine.

The garage was cold at night, especially over Christmas, but I grew to love it. The garage wasn't without moments of hilarity; I shared moments with my garage I couldn't have shared with a normal bedroom.

Late at night I drank bottles of wine and snorted ketamine. Before blacking out I swallowed a few pints of water to prevent waking up with a goat in my mouth, teaching the vagina monologues in Chinese, to a group of confused Japanese tourists.

The garage was pitch black at night when I turned off my fairy lights because there was no natural light or windows.

With the lights off I couldn't see my hand in front of my face and the darkness I lived in, at times, put me out of sense with my own space.

I opened my eyes and needed to go to the toilet; the matter was most pressing.

I couldn't see an inch in front of me, I was swallowed by darkness.

I shuffled to the end of my bed as fast as I could; in slow motion because ketamine changes the pace of time as we believe we move through it.

I moved my feet over the edge of the bed and onto the floor.

I stood up and my legs wobbled as the horse tranquiliser made jelly of the muscles inside me; I took a couple of steps forward in the general direction of the door connecting the garage to the main house.

I walked forward thinking I will get to brick, and when I reach brick I can follow it along to find the door and let myself into the house, but as I reached out I didn't touch brick, I touched plant pot.

I never knew I had plant pots in the garage.

Was this even my garage?

I searched the wall with my hands and found the rubber handle of the rusting lawnmower; old dead grass from lost summers.

I should have mowed the jungle.

I was back in a festival toilet.

I was lost in the most shit-covered festival toilet to ever exist again.

I turned around and tried what had to be the door, but I pushed, and it wouldn't move.

I stopped panicking and thought logically.

Bewildered, confused, not sure what way to move.

I was lost, unable to find a way out from my darkness.

I walked forward straight into a shelf, pain shot up my knee.

My life was repeating, only now I was stuck in the darkness, and Lily wasn't outside wondering if she should help me.

This time nobody was coming.

I was in the darkness of my own making.

I put my hands out and touched the heads of several garden gnomes.

This time I needed to get out of the darkness to go to the toilet, at least at the festival I had already been.

My mind, dazzled and frazzled from wine and blunted by Ketamine replayed me pulling a glow stick from my pocket.

I moved the glow stick along the wall in the thick darkness.

A yellow glow against close brick, silent around me. Nothing to hear, only my breathing.

I moved the light over two red shoes, new to me.

Two dangling red shoes, reflecting a little of the warm yellow light from the glow stick in my mind.

I moved the glow stick up from the shoes to ankle, to skin, and discovered the shoes had legs in.

I moved the glow stick further up from the legs to bare chest, took a step backwards, took a step backwards and stared up at a pale face in the darkness.

A naked man hung from a rope attached to the top of the garage, his neck slumped against his chest, slowly dangling from left to right.

A breeze moved him I couldn't see.

Two furry dice dangling from the mirror of a red car.

He breathed in, a huge breath, his legs dangled and kicked, he was still alive, struggling to breathe; having a panic attack, having a panic attack as he died by his own means.

His eyes bulged and he reached out to me, his legs kicked out hard in panic, one kick removed the glow stick from my hands and dropped it to the garage floor where it disappeared, leaving me back in the darkness.

Completely alone again, and nobody was coming to help me.

I couldn't even help myself, the man hanging was me.

A call from my body, a call of nature happening outside of me brought me back down to earth, my new Lily, a man trying not to piss himself.

I Jigged up and down on the spot disorientated; my time running out; my plan of urinating like a normal person in a normal toilet had to change to something entirely less ordinary.

Plan B was annoying.

Plan B I didn't want to do.

My few life belongings sat on one side of the garage.

Fortunately my entire life was two black bin liners of clothes and a book titled 'photo-shop for dummies' that Rob bought for me because he was trying to convince me it was no longer 1985.

I also had a little USB camera. A key-ring which hooked to my belt and took bad photographs because it was so small I had no idea what I was pointing it at; and my laptop.

The laptop was the only possession I cared about because it contained all of my books and documents.

I had most of my writing saved, but the laptop was my one shot of a happy life; if I couldn't type my way out of this hell then I was going to end up in a park, living under a tree, probably writing on paper.

On the other side of the garage were Max's tools.

Plan B was pissing in the garage.

The garage was small and I couldn't in good conscience urinate on Max's work tools. Without him and my friends I would be homeless and I refused to repay his kindness and big heart by covering his favourite work tools in hot urine.

Plan B was my only option.

I couldn't find my way out of the darkness.

I couldn't find the light.

I had to piss over my stuff.

My jig was now a full on jog, my hands searched in panic for the door handle, I was desperate and my body was now the boss of me.

I found an area away from my laptop and clothes, an area far away from Max's tools.

I pulled Professor MerryDinkle out of my jogging bottoms and relieved myself.

Urine splashed indiscriminately across darkness, I heard piss hitting plastic and objects I couldn't define by the noise they made when piss hit them.

Once relieved I found my bed and sat down; from the bed I found the door and eventually I found the light switch.

I turned the light on and turned around to survey the damage.

I was no longer hanging from the garage ceiling, which was a relief, but I had urinated over the plastic bin bag containing all of my clothes.

But I wasn't dead.

Then I noticed next to my bag, the object I couldn't define by the sound it made when pissed on.

The object most covered by my urine, the only thing in the world I needed; my laptop.

But I wasn't hanging from the ceiling.

The clothes could be washed and would dry but my laptop took the brunt of my urine and was dead.

Killed by piss.

Without my laptop I was as good as dead.

I looked up to the corner of the garage, a red shelf ran along a wall; dangling over the edge was a rope, the same rope I imagined myself hanging from earlier.

Two dice dangling from the mirror of a car.

That's why the dice stuck in my mind.

They never fascinated me because they were dice, not even because they were moving, they fascinated me because they were hanging.

Two fluffy dice, meant to be fluffy, intended for fun, hanging from their throats at the front of every drive.

I needed towels; I needed tissues and had to get them fast because I needed to dry out the garage.

With the light on I turned and pulled down the handle on the door connecting the garage to the house, I pushed the door inwards but nothing happened.

I tried the door again but it wouldn't budge.

And then I realised.

I checked the time and it was half seven in the morning.

The reason I woke up was because somebody, when they left the house that morning, had without thinking shut the door connecting the garage to the house on their way out to work.

The garage door was always left slightly open because it could only be opened from inside the house.

It wasn't a problem; in fact, it was a good thing because I could let myself out of the main garage doors and back into the house through the front door, and because everyone was out nobody would ever have to know I destroyed my laptop.

I breathed shallow, the smell not pleasant, and grabbed my keys.

I pulled the large main garage doors towards me using the bit of string dangling from the ceiling and the garage door raised an inch, hit something, and then stopped.

I pulled the string again, and nothing.

I pulled it harder and nothing.

I got on my hands and knees and looked under the gap where the garage door raised an inch and discovered Max had parked his van closer to the garage door than usual.

Close enough so I had no chance of getting out through the front doors.

I couldn't get out through the connecting door either.

I looked around the garage making a face like a duck chewing gum, my eyes narrowed then enlarged.

I was locked in the stinking garage.

I was going to have to watch my laptop die.

The captain was going down with his ship.

I was trapped in a box with my piss.

Somebody had to be in.

Max should be in because his van was parked in the driveway, so I knocked on the door that led into the house.

And I knocked again.

I was still expecting to see Max, and Max would laugh at my predicament, and then laugh harder when he found out I couldn't find the door when I needed to use the toilet.

And so I knocked again.

Nobody came.

I put my ear to the door hoping to hear sounds of life from the house and heard none; no sounds of footsteps coming from the kitchen above, no television on in the front room, no music from Danny (a music producer) coming from his room.

The only sound was the odd whistle or click from Dave, the African grey Parrot Max rescued from a home years before who lived in our front room; although Dave was a good parrot the chances of him helping me get out of a locked garage were slim.

Nobody was in.

I had pissed all over my life and was unable to help myself.

On the plus side, I had marked my territory; there was no chance of being mauled by a bear or surrounded by a pack of lions.

I was the biggest loser on the planet.

I had taken the last of my ketamine.

Any wine was upstairs in the fridge in the kitchen.

There was no way I could use my laptop.

My phone was upstairs charging.

The only possible source of entertainment I had in the garage not covered in wee was Photoshop for Dummies.

I had no food either, or water, so I sat on my bed and waited.

I spent the day sleeping as much as I could and trying to look for objects in the garage I could stick up my nose to b ock the smell, but it was hopeless, so I sat with my pants on my head and sulked at my prognosis.

Danny came home and rescued me at six in the evening.

I was locked in a stinking garage watching my laptop slowly die for just over ten hours.

Still, I had to laugh, and so I did.

We all did.

The beauty of having nothing to lose is you learn the beauty of having everything to gain.

"HERBIE GOES HASTA LA MANANAS"

Saturday 10th December 2010

The winter has well and truly landed in London and snow has settled. Children throw snowballs at each other on the way to school, men in suits wearing long brown coats slip as they walk up curbs and barely stand tall whilst their arms wave around like mini helicopters too close to the ground, the national rail service has ground to a halt and on the front page of every newspaper is a story about how many people today the snow has killed.

The white snow looks beautiful, covering everything my eyes can see; but beneath the incomprehensible beauty the snow is freezing greenery struggling to breathe.

Green leaves freeze from existence as children scream *go faster* to fathers pushing them along in upside down bin lids as they make the most of their schools being closed.

I walk up the driveway, snow crunched steps, and Mohammad is outside smoking a cigarette.

I haven't seen him since we fought about the heating in my room and we seem to have reached a truce. Since our argument he hasn't come to my room or randomly knocked or called me at night, and nor has he put a notice under my door telling me he wants me to leave.

Sometimes Mohammad looks strong to me, and other times he looks like a baby.

As I approach him his large square head seems lower than his shoulders and he looks small, he has been ordered back into his box by his invisible Somalian masters.

The heating has been on in my room since we argued, so in the end I think he conceded, though without telling me.

Mohammad smiles, looks up at me with large eyes screaming paranoia and loneliness and I wonder if the reason I recognise those qualities is because when I look into him it's really me I'm seeing.

He takes a large drag on his cigarette and looks away from me breaking our look. He brings his hand to his lips to cough up black bits, his new custom after each drag of a cigarette.

He asks me in a weak voice if it's been warm enough in my room; I tell him it has and thank him for leaving the heating on.

"Colossus, did you notice a sign on the bathroom door one of the bloody tenants put up? A bloody notice saying I should respect their privacy? It has been up for many months so it has."

I tell Mohammad he should go inside because it's cold.

Mohammad tells me there is something he needs to say and I turn, smile, and wait patiently to be told again about the sign on the bathroom door.

He looks back into the house to make sure we're alone, and then swings his low head towards me till the top of his head is beneath the end of my chin.

He moves his head back, and straightens up so he's a little shorter than me; a cobra preparing to strike.

His voice is a whisper, the government might be up the nearby tree and recording everything we say.

"It is something very serious in its beginnings and possible endings."

I nod my head and wait, half interested and half wondering if Mohammad feels the cold in the same way I do.

"The bloody Moroccan couple."

I've never met or heard a Moroccan couple.

"I cannot say anything more because I don't know what is happening yet, so it is, but when I do know for sure I will be coming to you with the findings of these people. They are bloody sneaky bastards so they are being isn't it so…but keep that between you and me."

Mohammad smiles and winks and takes another puff of his cigarette and coughs out dead air which, after leaving his lungs and hitting the outside world, takes its first breath and starts a journey to life.

Mohammad drops his cigarette into the snow, places his foot over the burning end, twists his shoe to make sure it's out, and tells me he's trusting me with this.

I have no idea what he's trusting me with, but whatever *it* is, it's so dangerous or evil he can't bring himself to speak of it out loud.

Hitler has just shared with me his plans for the final solution and I've been subtly informed I have no choice but to come along for the ride.

Night falls and more snow comes; I'm bored of being alone in my flat.

I go to The Queensbury because it's closer; to be alone, but nearer to other people who have nobody to share their life with.

I walk up to The Queensbury and walk past; once I'm past the pub I turn back around to try again.

I can do this.

The second time wields similar results, I walk past again; watching my destination fall behind me to my right.

I turn around.

You want to go in, so just go in.

I cross the road and pass The Queensbury again, only this time from further away.

I turn and walk back.

I stop.

Just cross the road and walk up the steps and go in.

I walk back across the road; as I'm about to walk up the steps I look up and notice the bouncer outside is watching me, he's probably seen me pacing both sides of the street and is questioning my mental health.

What if he talks to you and you have nothing interesting to say?

There's no way I can go in now, not with him at the bottom of the steps.

I turn my back on the bouncer and cross back to the other side of the road.

Sometimes I want to go out but end up walking in big circles until I return back home having gone nowhere.

Small reasons not to go inside somewhere make complete sense; that man has a wonky moustache, there aren't enough sharpened pencils in the white cup sitting in the window of the Willesden Green coffee shop.

I decide my indecision means I don't really want to go out, so I head to the off-licence to buy some alcohol and plan to then head back to my flat.

No circling the shop; I go straight in with unbridled determination.

I pick up a bottle of red wine and wander up and down food aisles for no reason; for five minutes I stare at olives and tuna asking myself why I'm staring at bits of food.

I pick up a chicken wrap sitting above pints of milk and, with the chicken wrap in my hand, I think to myself I don't really drink milk anymore and put the chicken wrap back down.

I catch my reflection in the fridge door and shout at myself, in my head, I did want to go out and once I'm inside a pub it will be full of chairs; so I'll be able to sit down like I can't do at home.

I return the red wine to the shelf and head to The Windmill.

I will stay for one drink.

The pub will be so busy nobody will have time to talk to me because it's Saturday night.

I walk into The Windmill and it's empty.

Tom the manager is standing behind the bar reading a newspaper.

He looks up and smiles; his Greek statuesque beard does not move, complimenting the freedom of his warm eyes and smile.

Tom doesn't ask what I want to drink; instead we have a conversation.

On the fourth minute of Tom talking my mind slows down and, through listening, I return to normal and I'm reminded talking to people is a good thing.

Go and sit in the corner away from everyone.

Take your drink and sit in the corner.

I order a red wine and sit at the bar because sitting away from the bar would make Tom feel like I don't want to talk to him.

An older guy maybe in his mid sixties walks in.

He looks like an old actor, with slightly tanned skin and a chiselled jaw-line, although he's old now I can tell in his day he was another James Dean.

He's wearing a flat cap which he keeps on; nature has been kind to him so I get the feeling under his cap is a thick bunch of grey hair slicked back with gel, same way he's styled his hair since he was fourteen.

He has a pencil thin moustache immaculately groomed, as white as the snow melting fast on the shoulders of his coat.

He says hi to Tom and his accent is strange, I can't place it; he sounds like he was born in South Africa but moved to America then Spain then somewhere odd like Sweden for ages.

He's a larger than life character; his voice is deep, booming.

A guy people would turn and listen to even if he was in a crowded room.

He hugs Tom and tells three jokes that get Tom laughing, and me smiling, before he's ordered his first drink.

He doesn't sit down, I notice, preferring to stand.

He's a natural in front of people, completely comfortable in company; coming to the bar to seek conversation; he no doubt has stories to tell.

The opposite of me, I think.

He stands at the bar and begins a story.

I know we're going to talk so I draw up mental plans to finish my drink and excuse myself so I'm not revealed as boring.

His story is about somebody stealing one of his gloves from a bar.

As the story moves on he looks over at me and smiles, letting me know we're going to talk.

I smile back and when he looks at me I laugh a little; letting him know we share the same sense of humour.

At the end of his story he turns and raises his glass to me.

He's drinking vodka and soda; in return I raise my red wine to him.

He speaks to me directly; his movie star looks make it hard to know how much he is acting.

I recognise sadness in his eyes; maybe he has a son he doesn't know as well as he should.

He can be open to strangers but not always so open to those he has loved.

There's an echo to his voice I hadn't noticed before, like another voice is beneath his deep voice following a second behind all of his words; making him sound like a choir of builders trying to sing the perfect harmony for a figure, never seen, standing behind a curtain of mystery.

"Who steals one glove?"

He laughs at his own question.

He has a laugh full of heart but there's a wheezy sound in his chest cutting his laugh short and hiding his true mean ng; a child hiding a frog he wants to save from biology in his pocket who has to pretend he's enjoying his lesson to get away with it.

"Well, you can cross off your potential suspect list any octopi."

He smiles at me but says nothing, urging me to fill the silence with something humorous for his mind to lighten up to.

"Who you're looking for is someone with one hand ar d they shouldn't be too hard to find. In the film The Fugitive Harrison Ford looked for a guy with a missing limb and all he did was check local hospital records."

I lean closer to the movie star at the bar, saying the rest in a whisper, like I don't want Tom to hear.

"I know people, in the hospital; if you need me to get you on the inside."

For a second he doesn't know how to react; like my words have taken the wind from his tongue.

Then I wink, to let him know I'm joking.

His laugh sounds like a wheezy roar that's been on the road hitchhiking to his mouth for months and has finally found a lift; I sense in his laugh relief he feels he's not the only comedian at the bar.

He saddles up next to me, still standing, and raises his glass to me again.

I raise mine to him and we talk.

He seems quite drunk but at the same time remarkably astute and although his words slur on occasion the language he uses, and the colour of his projection, leave me confused as to the nature of his inebriation.

He tells me he used to be a hippy and smoke a lot of weed, but these days he smokes the occasional cigarette even though his doctor doesn't agree.

I tell him if the definition of a hippy is someone who lives outside of the normal parameters of society; I tell him I've been one during periods of my life.

I tell him not long ago I was living in a garage in Blackheath.

I tell him I hold the world record for being locked in a garage in Blackheath.

He laughs and tells me he knew I looked interesting, he says he'll be back in a minute and heads out into the snow to smoke his small roll-up cigarette.

I drum my fingers on the bar and bring red glass to my lips.

I place my glass back on the bar and move it up on its edges, so it's slightly teetering, then look around for a moment but decide to look back at my glass, in case I catch the eye of anyone behind me who might also think I look interesting.

I go back to drumming my fingers on the bar, observing mentally the contrast between wanting to leave earlier and now impatiently waiting.

The movie star who speaks six languages returns from the outside darkness rubbing his hands with an expression on his face like nobody told him snow was cold.

He doesn't look as young as he did before he left, with his face now slightly red and his hands turned pink.

He finally sits next to me.

He seems distracted a little and takes a sip from his drink, puts his glass back down on the bar and stares straight at me:

"Here it is. This is the thing. I'm dying."

I hold his look.

We are all born on our last legs.

I don't even know his name.

"The doctors say I have three to nine months to live. I've beat this thing three times before. I've kicked its motherfucking arse three times and I'm going to beat it again."

I ask him what he's dying from and he tells me pulmonary lung disease.

Nature has not been kind to him; I realise nature can only be cruel to us all.

"I had something in my body and they froze it so it couldn't grow, and it worked...but it caused complications and the problem moved, now it's in my lungs kid, my fucking lungs."

I like how he calls me kid. It's not patronising; he says it in a father and son way.

I ask him if he has any children and he says he has four daughters and a son.

He tells me how he had a lot of money taken from him because of complications with the drugs he's on because they make him forgets things, which has made him vulnerable to fraud.

He tells me he often repeats back entire sentences, but he hasn't repeated anything back to me.

He tells me he's getting tired and when he's tired his symptoms get worse.

I tell him I never got his name.

He apologises and we raise glasses.

"Herbie, call me Herbert of Herbie, I never liked Herb."

"I'll call you Herbie, I'm Colossus."

"Pleasure kid, some name you got."

"Likewise old timer."

He hiccups and says they're a symptom of his disease.

Herbie tells me he's writing a book, I tell him I'm writing one too.

Herbie flies in conversation from Parisian writers in the 1940's to German literature in the 1960's. He ice skates for fun over the surface of massive issues like an elephant skating across the arctic in the summer, daring the ice to break; daring me to question him so he can drown us both in the unexplored depths of his knowledge.

A conversation with him is like being on the magical mystery tour of literature. He's a raconteur; as he speaks he's so full of life.

Was he ever this alive before being so close to death?

Candles burn brightest surrounded by darkness.

Herbie tells me he has to remember to eat all the time, because a consequence of the drug he is on is he loses his appetite and another consequence is he can't remember if he's eaten.

Then he stands and says he's tired and he better be getting home.

He tells me maybe London hasn't changed after all, maybe you can still meet a complete stranger at a bar and they can become a friend.

I give him my card and I joke he'll wake up in the morning and not remember who gave it to him.

He smiles and says he doesn't remember who I am now.

Then he calls me kid and gives me a wink, to affirm he's joking.

His language is splattered with swear words he relishes wrapping his tongue around; I've never heard swear words used with such class or savoir vivre.

Herbie tells me if I can't be good be careful, odd phrase; if I'm going to shoot an innocent person make sure I wear a seatbelt.

We shake hands and I watch Herbie shuffle out of the door and into the snow.

A person dies every second; but there's also a six year old somewhere, every second, trying to move an apple with his mind.

I wonder what it must be like to sense living life as a ghost.

I won't have to wonder for always.

Our lives are spent with the people we get closest too perpetually trying to get us to behave more in accordance with their expectations and beliefs.

There is a freedom in death, a freedom we cannot have in life.

In death nobody tells us how to behave, the arrogance of the people around us telling us how to exist in life fades away as everyone is joined by the same fate; nobody knows what comes next, or if there is even a next at all and so finally, through the eyes of those watching, there's at last no wrong way to be, no judgment, just the simple beauty of previously unknown universal sympathy.

Religion says death is when we are judged, but that's not true to me; life is when we are judged, death is when we are finally free from that simple human inadequacy.

Our problems come not from what we believe, but from how we relate to how we believe in what we do.

Herbie walks away into the snow a prisoner to his own sentence, but perhaps he also walks away a free man beyond my comprehension.

"JOB SEEKERS DEFIANCE"

27th February 2009

Life is a belly dancing robot elephant. First you accept it, then you question it, then you're mad at it because it's impossible.

The morning of the 27th February was my first meeting at the jobseekers allowance building in Woolwich Arsenal.

I got out of bed, patted my concrete garden gnome on the head, wondered where the plant pots had gone and double dropped some acid.

I don't know why, or even what I thought I could possibly achieve from being on acid in a job centre, but it was the beginning of an experience I wouldn't recommend anyone repeating.

I got to Blackheath station wired on the acid, paid for a travelcard and felt my way onto the train.

I found a two seated chair, sat in the window seat and looked down at the grey concrete pavement waving at me.

A tiny voice told me I would be fortunate to get through the day without being arrested.

I looked around the train and caught the eye of an old lady, I looked away as she smiled at me, then thought I looked rude because I hadn't smiled back, so I looked back at her to smile but she was looking the other way, then, sensing she was being watched, she looked back at me and I freaked out and looked out of my window.

I want to ask the old lady why she won't roll down her socks.

I managed to get an ipod from Amazon for seventeen pounds but when it turned up it was a fake Chinese copy which failed to play any music.

Maybe it will work now, I should listen to something, distract my thoughts from wanting to grab the old lady be her ankles.

I pushed play and it worked.

My fake ipod managed to find one song in the thousands I installed.

I looked out of the window, Fix You by Coldplay rang into my ears and my mind wandered.

I stood up to take my applause for performing Fix You and I was told God wanted to give me an award.

God came onto the stage but he didn't look like God, he was holding a mop and wearing blue overalls. He was short with large back legs which he rubbed together to translate he was a Mexican grasshopper called Bob.

I accepted my reward, overcome with emotion; in my imagination and on the train.

On the train, tears streamed down my face.

The power of any great song or literary work is to make the listener or reader respectfully wish for a moment they could share the brain of the creator; and so there I was on the train, crying because I was given a prize by Bob for writing a song by Chris Martin.

I snapped out of my imagination as the train pulled into Woolwich Arsenal station, wiped tears from my face and turned off my fake Chinese ipod to try and get a handle on my emotional state.

I was crying to Coldplay on a public train and having imaginary awards given to me by God.

The drugs were working.

I wasn't mentally in a stable place for a serious meeting with people government affiliated.

I got off the train and tried my ticket in the machine but my ticket wouldn't go through, I tried it again and again.

I didn't want to be part of a scene caused by a ticket I couldn't control; perpetuated by a machine programmed to ruin my morning, but it was happening.

The bastard machine bleeped loudly enough to burst skulls, and the ticket inspector walked towards me, drool falling from fat frog lips, slime trailing behind him.

He stood in front of me, the ticket inspector, as welcome as Elmer Fudd at an opening ceremony for an orphaned bunny sanctuary.

He stood too close to me.

The type of guy who failed school, not brave enough for the army, not intelligent enough for the police force.

He was short; his face softened by Christmas fat from 1987.

From over a mile away he could smell flour; his insides collapsed inwards from weight, forcing blood to push his insides outwards from beneath; making his skin red and his breath hard to reach.

His feet were small and his shoes shiny and cubed; tiny hoofs.

His eyes bulged from his sockets; someone held a large vacuum a foot from his face, permanently sucking his eyeballs away from his head.

Real slime fell from his lips and skin, and dribbled to the floor beneath.

His eyebrows were too thin, he shaved them, the lines on his forehead moved like waves; snakes dangled from his nose and he wore a hat he never removed because it filled him with the sensation of being powerful, which in-turn fed his state of delusion.

His nose was two square blocks, a wall; the same wall suspiciously not incriminated in the trial of Humpty Dumpty.

His voice was red like his face, his words heated because he thought we'd already had an exchange.

"Ticket please?"

"It's not *my* ticket."

"What?"

He didn't understand my philosophical point about the nature of ownership.

If our life on this earth is temporary and the material objects we allure to be ours live on without us then who is really the keeper in the concept of "my."

Did I own the ticket or did the ticket own me?

"Your ticket."

He peered over every aspect of my ticket like an archaeologist deciphering ancient hieroglyphics.

The inspector wanted to make me think he was intelligent, which in turn only served my belief in his mental malevolence.

The machine already told him my ticket was not valid, this part, the *inspection*, was all for show.

I paid for a daily travelcard which was more expensive than if I had paid for a single ticket from Blackheath to where I was.

He stared boggle-eyed at the ticket; I was having trouble keeping my thoughts behind my mouth, so I mocked him casually, and regretted it afterwards.

"It's not a Rubik's cube."

"What?"

He removed the ticket from his face.

His red face, bulging eyes, hoofs and snakes dangling from his hat and nose made him look like Lucifer with Medusa hair.

Lucifer Medusa.

"You haven't got the right ticket."

He has no active social life or wife.

The ticket inspector had taken five minutes to establish what the beep knew ten minutes ago.

"Where did you travel from?"

The very ticket you've been staring at for years tells you.

"Blackheath."

He looks at the ticket again.

"And you planned on coming here to Woolwich Arsenal?"

No. I got off here for kicks because I heard Woolwich is the land of tomorrow.

"Yes."

"You've got the ticket going the same amount of stops but in the opposite direction."

"Sorry, it's been a long night."

An odd thing to say at nine thirty in the morning.

"I thought I had a travelcard?"

"I'm sorry but I have to fine you."

Don't apologise, you live for this moment.

I explained I've paid for a ticket; my intention was to pay for a ticket, I've made a mistake.

He writes out a twenty pound fine, gripping his free rail pen in his cubby claw, ignoring me.

A twenty pound fine for me was the equivalent of a week's wages for him, I was pretty sure he wouldn't appreciate having a week's wages taken away from him by someone who thought reading was a weapon to use to intimidate the intellect of others.

"What's your address?"

Venomous bile dripped from his chin and landed on the swirling floor then continued to melt straight through, leaving pin-sized holes in the concrete red light beamed back up through; he was calling on spirits from hell.

Snakes crawled out of his nose, up his face and under his hat.

The ground swirled at his feet; I tried hard to concentrate on the notion of location.

This wasn't going to go down well because I was homeless, living in a garage and had no place of residence.

And then there was the small matter of my name.

"I don't have an address."

"Don't be funny with me. What's your address?"

"I'm not being funny with you. I live in a garage and, it being a garage, it doesn't have a number."

"I'll call the police."

Lucifer Medusa spoke into his walkie talkie to someone who had the better job and was sitting down responding from the warm drinking coffee.

Lucifer asked for my name:

"Colossus."

He raised a shaved eyebrow.

"My name is Colossus."

He asked for my second name; I had been found guilty and had to prove my innocence, completely against how the legal system in England is meant to work.

"Colossus Sosloss."

He raised both shaved eyebrows.

"That's my name."

"Can I get a check for any people by the name of Colossus Sosloss registered to addresses in Blackheath please?"

He smiled.

He goes out for drinks with his few friends once a month but always leaves before buying his round.

He cuts his crusts off his bread and masturbates to the five minute free view on porn channels because he hasn't figured out how to obtain it for free from the internet; his mouth never laughs, but when he does it's at someone's pain because that's how he feels alive again.

We stared at each other as he waited for the person sitting in the warm with the better job and the better pay to come back to him.

The silence was too tense to accept.

I had to fill the silence because the floor swirled beneath us; I took a breath and tried talking sense into the man with snakes dangling from his head, devil horns gone wrong.

"I'm homeless; I'm on my way to the job centre. I have no money to pay any fine so even if I'm found it's not going to make any difference; I can't pay what I don't have."

"I hear that all the time mate."

Prick.

The radio guy returns with information stating he can find no Colossus Sosloss in Blackheath.

"Can I see some ID because your name is obviously not Colossus Sosloss and you don't live in a garage."

How can I prove who I am if I don't know why?

Identification; so much trust is invested in something so easily fabricated. Our society is so fractured we have to root through wallets until we find irrelevances validating our paranoia, facts falsehoods worn with pride and honour.

I had no identification; Lucifer didn't care, he was looking for something to back up his belief system programmed to only see the worst in people.

"Is that your bank card?"

Adrian leant me his bank card so I had a bank account to receive money.

So I had a chance at starting over.

I had not offered the card to him voluntarily; his right to question what I had not surrendered freely was probably putting him on ground where he was the man acting illegally.

I wasn't even sure if the police had powers to stop and search without suspicion or proof of a crime, but here was the devil, his ignorance creating within him a foolish belief in his own self significance.

"No, it's not my bank card, it belongs to a friend."

Lucifer studied the name on the card and slowly the thought sunk in the name did not match the name I had given.

His brain made false connections supporting wrong judgements; Lucifer had caught Americas most wanted.

He smiled again; he knew something I didn't, and spoke into his radio:

"Don't worry, *I've got him*. Check Adrian Seale Blackheath?"

I had taken enough of being bullied by an idiot who wasn't listening to truth or reason.

I took a step back, reclaimed my personal space, put my arm up towards his chest and showed him my palm in the internationally recognised symbol for STOP.

"You needn't bother checking that name Lucifer Medusa."

He looked up, left then right; he was uncertain of what was happening.

"I'm exercising my rights as a citizen in this country and I'm arresting you on encroachment of personal space, failure to disclose clear evidence you're legally allowed to look into my wallet, contempt of my rights as a fare paying traveller on the rail network, wrongfully accusing me of fare evading and for offending my honour."

Lucifer Medusa looked bewildered and his snakes bit each other, forced into frenzy by truth.

He looked at me, spoke, but as he said something about calling the police, I screamed over him a lot louder CITIZEN ARREST!

A voice like a robot reading out the back of a cereal packet in a cave spoke as I paused to breathe.

"There's no Adrian Seale registered in Blackheath."

Lucifer Medusa looked at me with uncertain eyes.

You've got nothing on me, you bastard.

Lucifer Medusa looked like he thought he may be dea ing with the unbalanced mind of a dangerous stranger.

"Listen, sir, calm do..."

...CITIZEN ARREST!"

My entire counter argument had boiled down to shouting CITIZEN ARREST very loudly over anything he said.

My counter argument was unarguable.

Sir, much better considering I was a patron of the company he was representing.

At last, we found ourselves on a mutual playing field of respect.

We stared at each other, two cowboys reaching for weapons.

There was no way I was backing down; I was armed with infinite ammo, there was literally no end to how many times I felt I could scream CITIZEN ARREST over anything he said.

I told him to say something with my eyes, anything.

A church bell rang in the distance.

Women gathered children away from the sun and took them into the shade, clearing the street, only dust and me.

And him.

Horses were freed from stables.

A storm was coming.

Make your move Lucifer Medusa.

Go ahead, make my day.

"You haven't got a vali...

CITIZEN ARREST!

"This is ridiculo...

CITIZEN ARREST!

"What are you trying to achie...

CITIZEN ARREST!

Another silence fell between us.

He was evaluating his position, weighing up the embarrassment of continuing this argument in public; he wanted to beat me intellectually, with people watching on.

He wanted to be the man in uniform, in control, powerful.

Instead, he had been dragged into the type of argument two five year olds might have, people had gathered around.

Nobody knew what was going on.

Neither did I, but nor did he.

I waited, prepared to shout CITIZEN ARREST again and again until he let me go; or one or both of us was arrested.

We held eye contact.

Air burst from his lips, his jelly lips wobbled up and down and he made a sound like life was too short and his coffee was getting cold.

"Pay the rest of what's owed on your ticket over at the booth and be on your way."

*

Fifteen minutes later I sat in an office waiting to see Sarah from recruitment.

The office was huge; full of wooden desks, bland floors and wallpaper intended to eat hope and throw up repetition repeatedly.

I sat on my chair staring at carpet; the pattern swirled around my feet, the walls breathed in and out and I felt amazing, but at the same time claustrophobic, because acid soars where people do; and neither thrive in an office with rules.

Tapping keys, hollow rings, and people bleating tired phrases repeated a hundred times daily clouded the air with dead ends and hangovers from drinking too much the night before to forget the horror of their days.

I needed to leave before I was infected, but as I stood a girl called my name and because I was standing she looked up, we made eye contact and that was that; I had to go to her, see this through, but I was over-thinking and had no idea what I would say or do; in a panic I decided as I sat down opposite her I would just be honest.

She said *hello Mr Sosloss* but that didn't sound like my name, she asked me if she could call me by my first name but my mind went blank and I couldn't remember my name or what the word was for yes.

Sarah stared at me.

I stared at Sarah and blinked in slow motion at the straight forward question.

My mind raced diatribes about what names really mean when we're all the same; labels to divide and incite.

Not very good things, the evil of being polite.

"Why can't we both be called Sarah, Sarah?"

Sarah was unsure whether to laugh or call security.

I caught my philosophy and managed to tie it down with some borrowed rope to a tree called reality.

"I'm too wasted to talk to you."

Sarah smiled, remarkably; I was no doubt fortunate she seemed around my age, she bit her lip, moved her head to one side and reached a decision based on the information I kindly provided.

"Would you like to make another appointment?"

"That would be great."

"Next week will you be more normal?"

Not likely Sarah, perhaps next week you could be more on acid?

*

Thankfully the next week I arrived sober and left with an approved job seekers allowance agreement.

I had money coming in at last, and evidence I was alive, which I could provide to future employers.

This was the beginning of the end of living in a garage, and the end of the beginning of securing a job and moving to Willesden Green in South East London.

"BLOODY BONKERS ISN'T IT SO?"

Sunday 17th December 2010

There's a knock at my door, I look at the time and it's nine in the evening on Sunday night.

I get out of bed, put on my dressing gown and answer the door.

Answering the door takes me eight seconds.

Mohammad stands in front of me.

I'm tempted to close the door straight into his stupid block head but I don't; instead I activate patience mode, and remind myself he's old and lonely.

"Were you asleep?"

"No."

His first question is annoying; he's subtly complaining I don't answer my own door quick enough.

Maybe I should tell him the truth; most times he knocks I'm naked and think it's best for all concerned my landlord doesn't see my penis.

Mohammad walks into my flat without being invited in and begins talking:

"Do you know the Moroccans upstairs?"

Mohammad is slightly out of breath, the few steps to my room are beginning to take their toll on him.

He reminds me each day we are a step closer to becoming that bit of the banana nobody wants.

If I lived in the room with the Moroccans I wouldn't have to have these chats because he can't make it to the top of the stairs.

"I have never seen them."

"They have been there for many months. Anyway, this is very serious. The builder, you know him, he is a good man. I have worked with him for two years. He still only knows four words of the English and instead of be saying the word *months* he be sayings *missions*."

Fascinating.

I nod.

"I had to go out to get filters for the ovens so the bloody fire alarms don't be making their ringing noises. I bought the filters home, one bloody pound each from the pound shop; a bloody bargain isn't it so? Then I went out again and told the builder to fix the filters above the ovens in all of the rooms."

A story about purchasing oven filters.

This must be hell.

I must have died in the snow one night coming back from the pub and this is my purgatory.

"I wasn't sure if I wanted to get the bus into Cricklewood or not. In the end I decided to wait for the bus. There were three buses at the bus stop when I got there but I bloody missed them. The bus stop said it was seventeen bloody minutes until the next bus. The buses 102, 113, 226..."

The brass symbol bashing monkey who lives in my brain is eating popcorn.

What has any of this got to do with me?

Mohammad chats aimlessly about buses, then about the heating costs and finally, he gets back onto topic about the Moroccan couple:

"He works in an embassy, for the embassy. You know a very professional job, because that's what I want here Colossus, professional people, very much like yourself being."

My monkey puts down his symbols and picks up a shotgun I never knew he had.

"The wife is always in, *always*; she never leaves her bloody room, I think he goes to the gym during the day. I was out and told the builder to be going into the rooms to install the filters above the ovens."

My monkey puts his shotgun into his mouth and pulls the trigger.

I don't blame him.

As Mohammad is telling the story I notice his head is waggling from side to side as he does, like a cat purring at getting its belly rubbed.

Something in this story excites him.

He tells me his builder knocked on the Moroccan wife's door and stood in the doorway holding the oven filter. The wife ran across the room, opened the window, and screamed she was being raped by the builder.

He is excited by rape.

Great.

I might have known.

I don't know what to say, I stand there, watching him enjoy me listening to his twisted words sliding out of his mouth like an out of kilter helter skelter.

"The builder runs downstairs and makes the crazy sign to my wife. Do you know the crazy sign Colossus? The sign with the wiggly finger by the temple."

Mohammad points his forefinger to his temple and waggles it around in a small circle.

Nothing I have ever seen, or will see, will seem so poignant; so in its right place, as Mohammad making the signal for bonkers.

He tells me the man outside ran to the front door, and asked Alicia if he should call the police. Mohammad was out in the shops and his phone rang and it was the husband of the Moroccan woman shouting at him his builder tried to rape his wife.

His head waggles the most when he says the words *rape* and *wife*.

Mohammad tells me the husband said he was coming to the house to kill the builder.

Bloody kill Colossus, can you be imagining?

I have no idea if I even live in the real world anymore.

An irate husband is coming to the house to kill a man who may or may not be a sexual predator.

Brilliant.

Mohammad is on a roll now and his waggling head is feverish.

He doesn't care I'm so tired a slug could crawl over my head, steal my left eyeball and escape in an ice-cream cone converted into a motorised wheelchair.

This has nothing to do with me.

He tells me he got back to the house as fast as he could, tells me the builder has run away, tells me the builder only speaks four words of English so probably doesn't know what's going on.

"The bloody Moroccan woman says the bloody builder did not enter her bloody room or be touching her, but he made a rude sexual gesture."

Mohammad's tongue falls out of his bottom lip when he says the word sexual.

He's telling the story like nothing happened to the girl, but at this point there's no way of knowing. I ask Mohammad what the sexual gesture was, in case I need to tell him to call the police.

Mohammad pulls out his phone and, completely changing the subject, asks me if I can make it ring for longer.

"Because you see I never be having the time to answer it."

Inside a die, just a little. I feel it, and it's a piece of me gone that will never return.

I take Mohammad's old Nokia phone and go through the settings.

I turn on the vibrate mode and end call diverts.

This fixes the problem.

He asks me to call him to check if it works.

I call him.

He's thinking.

He asks me if I can turn the ring volume up a bit because he can't hear it.

I go into the settings. The ringing volume is currently on level four.

I put it up to level five, the highest level.

Mohammad asks me to ring him so he can hear it.

I ring him.

Mohammad says the ring is too loud now, just by a little bit. Could I turn it down just a touch?

Even I smile inside at this.

He never says please and he never says thank-you.

I change the volume to level four and then call Mohammad so he can hear the ring.

Mohammad thinks the ring is still too loud, and could I turn it down one more level.

I turn the volume down to level three and ring Mohammad again.

Mohammad thinks the ring isn't loud enough and asks me if I can take it up, just a notch.

I put the volume on level four, the same level the phone was set to when Mohammad gave me the phone to change the volume settings, and call him.

"Yes, Colossus, now my ringing is the perfect volume."

Mohammad stands in my room looking a little bewildered as to why he's in my flat; I prod him by asking him about the sexual gesture the Moroccan girl accused the builder of making.

Mohammad looks at me and thinks for a moment, then rubs his chin unable to remember anything.

I wait for the gesture.

I wait for him to remember what he's trying to think of.

We stand looking at each other, him waiting for me to speak because he can't remember what he was doing, and me waiting for him to do what he only just said he would.

This is awkward.

"That was me be showing you so it was."

"What was what?"

"That was me showing you the sexual gesture the builder be making to the bloody Moroccan woman."

I ask Mohammad to show me again, thinking the world's gone mad.

Mohammad rubs his chin to think, and stands still.

We look at each other.

This time Mohammad prompts me.

"That was the sexual gesture. He be stroking of his beard Colossus."

It was me being stupid. Not Mohammad.

Oh god, what shame.

"Mohammad, stroking a beard like you're thinking is not sexual."

"He be doing this all the time, when he's thinking or doesn't know how to respond. He strokes his beard. I think this Moroccan bitch went crazy when she answered the door to him and he panicked and stroked his beard."

"But that's not sexual Mohammad."

"Well, I don't be knowing. Maybe in Morocco if a man strokes his beard it means he wants to be having the sexual intercoursing with the ladies."

"Well Mohammad, I've stroked my beard several times talking to you, and it's not because I want to rape you."

He chuckles.

It's because I want to kill you.

I chuckle.

We chuckle together.

Mohammad tells me the Moroccan wife has changed her story since her husband came home, now saying the Polish builder tried to push his way into the flat.

If the builder wanted to get into the flat, he would have brushed the wife aside like an elephant pushing into a queue of ants.

Mohammad tells me he checked with Alicia, because f Alicia thought the builder was creepy then the builder might be, but he says Alicia thinks the Moroccan woman is strange.

He tells me she never leaves her flat, that in two months she's never left the flat, he thinks she's kept prisoner in her room by the husband and has gone crazy from being alone.

"She has gone bloody *bonkers* so she has Colossus."

I can't believe a couple have lived in the building for two months and I've never seen them.

A picture paints a thousand words but a thousand words paint a million pictures.

"Anyway Colossus, what are your thinkings on what should I be doing?"

Finally after all the diversions with bus stops and mobile phones Mohammad has reached the reason he knocked on my door.

He wants my help, of course.

I tell Mohammad he should get a translator so the builder can be heard, because if he's being accused of a crime he has a right to defend himself; and until the truth is unearthed the builder should not be allowed in the property.

Mohammad tells me the husband is saying he will kill the builder if he sets foot in the house, and then tells me he has essential house repairs to perform and he needs the builder.

I tell Mohammad he should try and find a day when the couple are out for the repairs, or at the very least the builder needs to know his life is under threat if he returns to work.

Mohammad says this doesn't suit him because he has essential house repairs.

I repeat it's hard to see a resolution without a translator, and the husband needs to calm down so the voice of his wife can be listened to and the truth heard and dealt with.

Mohammad nods his head and says he thinks the builder will come back.

I hope I'm not here when he does because I would rather not have to stop two men from killing each other.

Two large men, standing along the shoreline, shouted at the top of their voices so they could hear each other against the high winds and crashing waves.

Rain whipped around in circles of wind trapped inside the night, but I couldn't feel water hitting my skin, or the true temperature beyond the false heat of the booze I was in.

The two men were closer to the sea than I was and walking into the ocean; they would be killed.

I tell Mohammad I'm tired and want to go to bed.

The time is now half past ten.

I've been more than accommodating.

Mohammad finally leaves my flat.

He stands in the dark corridor alone for a moment with his back to me; a metaphor for his life journey.

Perhaps a metaphor for mine, and all of ours.

Walk down the stairs Mohammad, please walk down the stairs.

He turns to face me and asks if I really go to bed at this time.

I tell Mohammad I do when I'm tired; he shakes his head.

His pupils look whiter surrounded by the darkness of night.

His last words to me are creepier than an old man desperate to show a young girl his book of pressed flowers:

"I know you don't go to sleep this early because at night I listen to you walking across your floor."

"Goodnight Mohammad."

I close the door.

I breathe out twice as much air as my lungs can contain in relief he's on the other side of a closed door.

Seeing is deceiving.

There's a knock at my door.

I open the door and it's Mohammac.

"I was downstairs today in the front garden, at about ten o clock this morning, and I was cleaning the leaves. You know...they are falling from the trees but never straight down, do you know these things Colossus?"

He has knocked back on my door to ask me if I know what leaves are.

I could just make a run for it.

Push him aside; run down the stairs, out of the main front doors and across the road and into the night.

I could hide under a bush in the church over the road and he would never find me.

I blink, raise my eyebrows, and feel my forehead rise.

My bottom lip covers my top as I give the face that asks: no, please go on...explain.

"They are the brown ones that fall on the floor and they fall in number of many so they do. I am thinking they be calling themselves *leaves* Colossus. I was sweeping away the *leaves* with that thing, what is it called now? Like it comes over with its spikiness?"

"A rake."

Sarcasm may be the lowest form of wit; but it's the highest form of telling someone to fuck off before you stab them.

"Yes, Colossus, very good. A rake. I was getting all the *leaves* and some had gone down the side, down the side of the edge where they are hard to be getting to."

If I punched him in the face he would go away; but then I could never begin to explain all of this to the police.

"The Moroccan couple come out of the house, walk past me and up the road. Now they are up the road, a little way, and I am thinking why is it taking them so long to cross the bloody road? You know, because to cross that road it only takes two minutes, not *five* minutes. Sometimes it takes two minutes to cross because there's traffic coming both ways but five bloody minutes? Nobody takes five minutes to cross the road. So I was thinking with my leaves watching them something is funny very going on with this couple you know?"

People cross the road at different times according to an entire range of uncontrollable variables and specific parameters, you idiot.

Mohammad's eyes widen in excitement as he reaches the point of his story.

I hold my breath.

"A *car* came and picked them up."

He ears waggle in joy and his eyebrows move in unison like he's just finished telling me the greatest tale ever told.

Please tell me there's more.

No, wait, actually, tell me there isn't.

"I was only downstairs picking up the leaves because they keep falling this time of year. I wasn't spying on them."

Please God I just want to be alone.

Make Mohammad think he should have another best friend.

Then a miracle happens.

As Mohammad is distracted by his tales of highly adventurous leaves he coughs.

As he coughs he farts at the same time.

Loudly.

Being thirty years old and pretty immature I find this hilarious, but Mohammad, being a head strong old man finds his own gift to his story most awkward.

His nose wrinkles, his confidence is notably wobbled and his face turns to one side.

I know if I laugh it would be rude, but that knowledge is making it harder for me to contain my laughter.

He continues with his story.

"So whilst they were gone I went into their room...

Don't laugh.

Please don't laugh.

I smile.

"And they have a heater on in their room."

Mohammad tells me he found a heater in their room, during the middle of the coldest winter in seventeen years, like he has caught Jack the Ripper.

I can't hold my laugh in anymore because he farted when he coughed. His face is still so embarrassed and he's trying to talk over the embarrassment, but I heard his fart and he knows I heard his fart, and his awkwardness just makes the situation funnier.

Don't laugh.

I laugh.

I can't help it, the laugh starts as a sound I try and hide as a cough but then there I am, laughing into Mohammad's face at a point in his story where there's nothing to laugh at.

Mohammad perseveres and explains he phoned the government, and the government told him the heater would cost him ten ponds a day to run.

Yeah but Mohammad why don't you call them and tell them you farted when you coughed?

I'm laughing so hard he stops talking.

He stands in the corridor looking at me and I laugh in his face.

He knows why I'm laughing and I know he knows why I'm laughing but neither of us can acknowledge why I'm laughing, so we both have to think of something else, and fast, to justify the laughter.

"What is the funny so much you are having?"

"Nothing Mohammad, nothing, well...I was just thinking about the leaves, they do get everywhere don't they?"

Mohammad smiles, as if sharing for a moment my joy in leaf dispersion.

Leaves aren't funny you idiot, I'm laughing because you farted when you coughed and you know I am.

Mohammad tells me he's feeling tired, but I know what he means is he wants to leave because, if the smell in the hallway is anything to go by, he needs to do downstairs to check he hasn't just shat in his pants.

He turns and walks back downstairs to his flat and, as I watch him go, all my frustrations at the patience I have to show him on an hourly basis are replaced with the simple pleasure of a single thought:

He farted when he coughed.

I close the door and eventually stop laughing.

I imagine myself, again, homeless under a tree in park; curling up in a ball and growing a beard.

I have this thought often and it seems rational; I have no fear when I think it.

I would only need warm clothes.

I open my cupboard and look at my large bag

The park near to where I live, Gladstone Park, has no barriers so it's accessible twenty four seven, so I couldn't get kicked out.

The council wants more money from Mohammad for his council tax, my job is refusing to help me and the council are refusing to help me help them; Mohammad is insisting his backdated council tax bill, from before I was in the property, is mine.

Nobody is helping me, nobody is listening to me and so the park option is looking increasingly likely.

The bastard even called the council to give them my name and details, so I have his bill in my name.

I can't afford my home and the only logical outcome I can see is leaving.

I could try and move in with other people but the more I think about it, the more I find appealing the idea of finding out if dreams, hopes and aspirations can come true in this life.

Life is not about making your ideas become dreams, but about giving your dreams the chance to become ideas.

I can't see them coming true if I get myself too comfortable and emotionally entangled with the ridiculous notion of safety.

How bad would it be to give up what I don't like?

No more alarm clocks, wearing suits, bosses, hierarchy, subservience, failing, pressure to succeed, comparisons, competition, drifting, hoping, when will I find a girlfriends, how much is the council tax, taking the bins out, disappointments, illusions, shaving, evenings spent waiting for tomorrow, being ignored because I don't look like the good looking guy with the big mouth who has nothing to say but doesn't stop talking but always has an audience; no more struggling to keep myself floating above the water, just acceptance I wasn't born to float, no more news, newspapers, ignorant opinions masked as facts, telephone calls, internet, Facebook, Twitter, no more how's the job going, how are yous, don't mind if I dos, invites to places, queues, drunk people shouting out fuck you and fuck you too's, no more buzzing electricity eroding away my minds natural vibrancy, no more computer fans, people complaining about what they don't have instead of enjoying what they do, no more talking about the weather, trying to avoid phone calls, being crushed in underground tube trains staring at the advert of the beach reminding me I can't afford to escape reaffirming there is a better life for everybody; no more packages never delivered, bills chasing me down and squeezing out the last of my living, fake smiles to people on higher pay grades and patronising conversations about them remembering what it was like to be in my position, no more repeating moments getting me down and getting in the way of the life I should have had.

Time to take a step away from the stage and change the way my cycle spins, draw a line in the sand and say thank-you, but fuck you, I'm taking my life back.

Who thought let's work them, let's work them until they break and they'll teach their children to do the same; why are we all so instinctively subservient? Why are we afraid? This is the same way they built the pyramids; nothing's changed. Why are we teaching our children not to talk to strangers?

When did children who wanted to grow up to be vets turn grey and become over fed bankers pretending to hate animals because their boss does?

The person you haven't met yet is far likelier statistically to be just like you in every single way; to be loving and kind, to be able to make the odd mistake, and not be the embodiment of all of the worst things created by the images the news has implanted into our brains.

Individuality is born from a connecting block that through war and divide we have forgotten.

Despite water separating ground, despite different languages and passports dividing there's a fact never marketed; the foundation to all, before government and power coerced to make us try and forget is one single truth that, if we stop to think, brings everything we are ever told by the powers that be to shame: we are the same.

We are humans being and not human beings.

I will do something different.

I will do something drastic.

I will do something people will question.

I will live in a park, and what I write will become my movement, my ballet.

After all, what's "here" anyway?

"ONE IN THE BUSH IS INVALUABLE"

24TH October 2009

Ketamine was scrambling communication with me and making it tricky to know what thoughts were mine and what thoughts I was taking from the back of dishwasher tab ets.

I doubted whether I should express my thoughts because I constantly second guessed they were not worth repeating; my relationship with ketamine was a walrus drawing an upside-down stick man on a mirror with paints extracted from dead poisonous frogs.

Ketamine was a suit that didn't quite fit but everyone kept telling me how good I looked in it; the drug had become the emperor's clothes, everyone was taking it, few were discussing it killed parties for fun.

I decided to have one pint at the small pub in Charing Cross train station; this pub usually houses more flies than customers.

In this pub stale beer sticks to wobbling tables and the cigarette machine flashes in the corner mocking smokers who never have any change on them.

There's no natural light in the pub so it's dark, gloomy and the pain on the face of the staff tells its own story; overworked, underpaid, exploited and treated as expendable; I feel at home with them.

They're so scared they will be fired from their terrible jobs *every* time I order a beer they ask me if I want any peanuts or crisps, in case between drinks I've turned into the dreaded mystery shopper.

The air is chewy and weighs heavy on skin; the fruit machines in the corners don't make a sound, aware this is the last stop saloon for the drunk few who can't afford to gamble properly, down to their last pint and pound.

My intention was to have one pint before heading back to my garage in Blackheath.

However as I was finishing my first and last beer someone walked in and insisted on buying me another one, then, as that person left another joined me and insisted on buying me a beer before they left to catch their train too.

A conveyer belt of people wanting to fill my glass to justify their own, or wanting an ear to chew before getting on the train home, thinking the cost of a pint was a small price to pay.

In the space of time I stood by the bar waiting for my beer to finish my pint glass was filled up by three different people all with a story to tell. I met a crack addict destroying the woman he loved, a guy who almost died in a horrific car accident, a woman made redundant and scared of tomorrow.

I explained to her the philosophy any fear is self creation; and feeling fear, thinking fear, becoming afraid; all of these self created thoughts are there to build us up to challenge our own minds, because once we have conquered our own fears life is a ride and the rush is a joy.

I left the pub and sat on the train with no unusual events or people or emotions or thoughts to explain.

When I reached Blackheath village I took the usual route down the usual road; a ten minute walk from the usual train station to my usual garage.

The road itself was beautiful, as usual, trees lined either side and large walls stood proudly at the end of long driveways leading to the front doors of large homes housing the fortunate few who had taken their opportunities, and turned them into success.

As usual.

Warm lights poured from these homes on cold nights and expensive cars sat in silence conserving mileage.

Some drives contained central fountains you could drive around, and others I couldn't see because large gates kept out the likes of people like me.

The walk was beautiful, as usual.

The walk was peaceful, as usual.

That's when I was suddenly aware of something highly unusual; an acute need to defecate.

This has not happened before (or since thankfully) and I put it down to a combination of ketamine and alcohol abuse.

I was only three minutes from my garage but knew I wasn't going to make it.

I was either going to have to defecate in my own trousers and have the most uncomfortable three minute walk back to my house trying to walk normally, or have to go in one of the beautiful driveways and hope no poor soul was looking out of their large bay windows as I succumbed to the irregular call of my body on their property.

I was outside a beautiful house.

I had no choice.

I'm not proud of this story, and include it because drugs and alcohol can be massive fun, but taken over a long period for ages and they might make you lose control of your bodily functions in public.

The driveway was paved; cobbled stones tumbled to the house and two large bay windows designed to let light in allowed the people inside to marvel at the pleasantness of the outside of their home.

The windows usually afforded the master of the house views fitting with his or her achievements, but they were about to reveal an act at the other end of the success spectrum.

The large fir trees, cobbled paving, immaculately kept gardens and water feature were all about to be upstaged by a drunken man having a poo.

The lights were off in the beautiful house and it was midnight so there was a good chance I could get away with my tactical poo.

I crouched low and moved into the property, crossing the line from drunk walking home to disturber of the peace and trespasser.

Half way up the drive, adjacent to the water feature, was a bush meaning passing cars couldn't easily spot me; but it also meant I was a lot closer to the house than ideal.

If indeed there is an "ideal" in such situations.

The cobble paving may have been good to look at, but it was loud. I stepped slowly, but quickly, in an attempt to make the long driveway seem shorter and the bush of relief arrive sooner.

The next part, you may want to look away for.

I made it to the bush, walked behind it, pulled down my trousers, then my boxer shorts and literally exploded.

This had arrived from nowhere; it was unlike any toilet experience I have had before or since and I was only thankful I had chosen the bush, because there was no way I would have been able to walk the rest of the way home looking normal if I hadn't.

I crouched behind the bush, relieving myself; such was my euphoria the devil was leaving me I sent a text message to Danny letting him know what was happening.

"Topping breaking my laptop with piss. Will explain later. Prepare the bath."

I looked around for debris I could use to wipe myself with but everything was too neatly clipped.

Perfect rocks, pinecones and sticks surrounded me; but none of those could be considered serious options when wiping one's bottom.

I felt the ground in front of me, still squatting down with my trousers around my ankles, and in the darkness I found leaves.

The security lights turned on in the driveway.

I froze.

After thirty seconds, I slowly moved a leaf back and forward silently.

The light in the front room of the house turned on and that was it, I was done for.

The lights from the front room coupled with the security lights completely exposed me; I had no time to finish wiping.

I would have to save up to buy new clothes.

I stood up, the bedroom light in the top corner of the house turned on; the house that moments before sat in darkness, was now the most lit house in the world.

Men in tweed jackets would soon be running towards me with torches, bloodhounds and shotguns.

Without looking behind me I moved my trousers and underwear back up to my waist and made a run for it.

Ideally I would have removed my underwear and disposed of them separately but it wasn't to be, I ran out of the driveway, turned left and hobbled down the road back to my garage feeling like someone had poured a bowl of ice-cream into my underwear and thrown in a couple of lesbian eels.

*

The next day I got a phone call from a friend called Phoebe and she told me the company she worked for were looking for someone to go in and work the odd Saturday and she put my name forward and they wanted to meet me.

I thanked Phoebe, said yes and the company asked me to work for them full time.

As I reached my new lowest moment by passing a motion in the driveway of a nice person's home other happier motions were already in action, without my knowledge, to pull me back from where I was going.

With regular nine till five work I found a routine, and with money I was able to move out of the garage.

I found a small studio flat in Willesden Green, only a few tube stops from work.

The place looked new, the landlord, a man called Mohammad, seemed friendly enough.

He lived downstairs in the same building, which would be handy if anything went wrong.

I was pretty sure, like most landlords, I would probably never see him.

My drug use naturally took care of itself because I worked every day.

Bit by bit my body and mind repaired itself; it was never like I quit, or felt I needed to, I just moved on.

"BILLIONS OF BLOODY PAPERS"

Saturday 15th January 2011

Mohammad is standing outside my door on the landing and whispering my name.

The last few days he's been trying to call me and text me so I've stayed in my room with my phone off and my television low, but the more I try and avoid him the more determined he is to find me.

We haven't spoken for a few weeks, though he did text me a picture of a radio on Boxing Day.

This is the first time in my life I've heard an old man whisper my name outside my front door and it's genuinely disturbing.

Mohammad doesn't leave.

He paces back and forth outside my door, a troll, and when he speaks his words sound like a snake enticing a mouse from its hole:

"Colossussssssssss. Colossusssssss are you in there?"

The television screen flashes across my dark room and I think, maybe, Mohammad can see the light from under my door so I pick up the remote control and turn my television off.

Silence.

His ear is against my door listening for me.

I remain dead silent trying to listen to him.

I hold my breath, I sense he's about to knock.

I hear the beautiful sound of him walking away and heading back down the stairs.

This is now three phone calls at midnight and an outside my door whispering my name session in four days.

The more I hope he'll go away the more determined he becomes to be noticed.

I worry I'll wake up in the morning to find him sleeping next to me.

If Mohammad wasn't my landlord I wouldn't have anything to worry about.

I turn my television back on and as I do I hear Mohammad climbing the stairs back up to my room.

This time Mohammad is more determined, there's no whispering my name outside of my flat.

He doesn't knock.

The time is midnight.

I hear a key in the lock of my own flat, it turns, and he opens my front door and enters.

I sit up in bed; Mohammad is in the shadow of my room staring at me with a face full of frown.

"You see, I knew you were in, I bloody knew you were in so I did."

"I'm in my home and in bed! If I want to open my own front door then that's my choice!"

"No, THIS is not why I am here; I need to be talking to you."

"But you can't break into my flat! You need to respect my right not to see you!"

Mohammad takes a step forward into the flashing light projected by my television screen.

He says nothing.

He simply stares.

He looks tired like he did during the prostitute sage. His hair, normally brushed neatly, falls down onto his forehead. Two tufts of white hair stick out of his temples like ghosts fighting over the last lifejacket.

He's unshaven and I wonder if this is the start of *new movement* Mohammad.

I briefly picture me putting a bright yellow flower behind his ear and giving him a little tender kiss on the end of his nose.

Then his eyes fix on mine and I see the anger and impatience and ego, and my eyes are drawn to his ghosts and there's no doubt in my mind if there were any hippies in the building Mohammad would evict them for being too colourful.

Because of the cold light flashing over his face, against a backdrop of darkness, compounded by his sudden eerie silence I imagine him pulling a knife from the pocket in his pyjamas, walking towards me whispering *Somalian* as he slides the blade into my throat; nobody could hear my gargled scream as blood poured across my bed.

"Turn my light on Mohammad, you're freaking me out."

He flicks the light switch on.

I'm moving out, there's not a doubt in my mind I'm moving out.

I don't care if it's to Gladstone Park.

"I wanted to say I've been bloody trying to contact you so I have, I tried to knock on your door a few times but you didn't bloody answer. And then I tried to call you several, *many* times but you did not answer."

The way he says *many* is flustered, but there's also an undercurrent of arrogance like he genuinely believes he's my boss, and when he calls I have to answer.

"It was a bit too late when you called, like now actually."

He doesn't respond to my words, instead they wash over him like wind under the wings of dead birds.

"I got your text messages Colossus."

I haven't sent Mohammad any text messages.

I've never sent Mohammad a text message.

Mohammad sits on my bed; I sit up to allow him more space.

At least I'm not naked.

I prepare myself for losing hours of my private life.

"I've been very sick Colossus, you know. I have had dizzy spells and sleep all the bloody time. Sometimes I will fall asleep you know, for something like anything up to *thirteen* hours. I will wake up, and go back to sleep. I have a lot of phlegm, and a cough. And well...I am forgetting many of the things I am doing as I am bloody doing them."

This is the first time I've ever heard Mohammad admit to weakness.

Suddenly, he's an old man wanting company, and not a landlord overstepping boundaries.

I ask him if he has any help downstairs and he tells me his wife comes every day to help him and to cook for him.

"You see Colossus. I have all these papers I need to throw out that are from my years of accounting because I gave up my accounting for holistic medicine. You see because I know a lot about holistic medicine. Did I tell you that? It's when you use natural remedies to...

I'm not sitting through the half hour holistic medicine story for the fifth time.

"The *papers* Mohammad? You were talking about papers?"

"I have these papers, these papers from my days before I studied holistic medicine, which I am very well scholared in, it can take many years to study because there are thousands and thousands of different combinations. Did I tell you about my holistic medicine?"

"The *papers* you had to sort through?"

Please don't try and tell me the holistic medicine story for the third time.

"Literally *billions* of papers."

His eyes light up as he says *billions* and his stupid big head waggles in joy, he actually thinks he has billions of papers and this amuses me no end.

I share his excitement at having a billion pieces of paper.

It's quite a simple thing but I imagine a billion pieces of paper and my eyes light up too.

He does have a lot of papers; hundreds, perhaps a few thousand, but never *billions*.

"I have to throw every single piece of paper away; but in all of these billions of pieces of paper there may be one or two pages I want to keep so I have to check each individual sheet then put the sheets in a box to throw away."

"Could someone help you check?"

"No, I am the only one who knows what I want to be keeping. I will not let anyone check. I pick up a sheet of paper, read it and then put it in a box but sometimes I forget if I have read the paper or not. So I recheck the box that I may have already decided to throw away. Sometimes when I recheck I find a piece of paper I want to keep so I move it; but then I cannot remember if I wanted to keep it. It's taking a very long time."

"How many boxes have you thrown out so far?"

"None because I can't remember what boxes are which. Sometimes when I'm checking I get tired and fall asleep. Because, you know, it's quite boring isn't it so?"

He chuckles to himself.

I chuckle with him.

We are chuckling together.

"Well Colossus I won't keep you longer. I wanted to tell you I haven't ignored your text messagings."

He broke into my flat, when I was in, to tell me he hasn't ignored a text message I never sent him.

"I never sent you a text message."

He ignores me, making me think there was never a text message.

Mohammad stands up and shuffles towards the door.

He turns the light off before he leaves, returning my light to how I had it before.

He opens the door and turns to face me.

The light from the landing reflects on his face, looking like angels are coming to take him away.

"I am old Colossus."

Mohammad has never recognised his age before.

I tell him I know he is; the oldest person I have ever known.

He looks at me and tears well up in his eyes and he shakes his head and looks at the floor.

I want to go to him but I can't.

Tears drop from his eyes and land on his shoes.

He looks up, making fists with his hands, like he's going to punch an invisible enemy only he can see.

"Colossus, you are being like my very own son to me."

I don't know what to say, I don't say anything.

He turns back around to leave; not wanting me to see his tears, then thinks twice, puts his hand on the door frame and stops.

With his back to me, he asks if he can ask me a question.

I say of course, ask me anything.

He asks me if we are friends.

He turns around, and asks me again.

"No Mohammad, you old bastard. We are enemies."

We both smile and he shakes his head.

"Then we are friends Colossus, the very best of friends, because we only get close enough to call someone an enemy to their face, if we are the closest person to them."

Mohammad smiles, tells me he'll bring me a new shelf soon, turns, leaves and closes the door behind him.

He is a friend, in the rare moments he shows his human side, his softer side, when he lets down his guard and becomes himself.

My racist, crazy, annoying, bastard best friend who I hate.

There's no other man on this planet moving *billions* of pieces of paper from one box to another and back again to find one single piece of paper he can't remember if he wants or doesn't want and then sleeping between shifts because he doesn't enjoy the process he's making himself do.

An all too familiar knock at my door.

He's only just left.

I open the door and he stands in front of me, telling me he has something in his eye, his manner suggests in his mind he's meeting me for the first time tonight.

He either can't remember his display of emotion, or is trying to cover it up.

He says he tried to call me twice last night and when I didn't answer he knocked on my door.

Then he called me twice then knocked twice more.

Mohammad, my landlord is back.

Eventually when I didn't answer he let himself into my flat and all because, he explains, he made me a bowl of soup.

"I wasn't in and never asked for soup Mohammad."

"I know, but I was thinking you may have needings for some."

What? Why would I want soup?

"If I don't answer my door I'm asleep."

 "Would you like some soup now?"

No, I don't want soup. I want to do what I was doing, which was why I was doing it. If I wanted some soup I would have been eating soup when you broke into my flat for the second time in two days.

"I don't want some soup, it's gone midnight."

Please don't walk into my flat.

You already left.

Stay in the corridor.

You are so close to leaving.

"You can come downstairs to my place if you want?"

"No thank-you Mohammad."

"I won't keep you long then."

Mohammad walks into my flat, brushing me aside, and sits back down on my bed.

NOOOOOOOOOOOOOOOOOOOOOOOOOOOOOooooooooooooooo oo!

"I used to have this pain in my ankles, such agonising pain. So painful it would make me cry...

Mohammad tells me about the agonising pain in his ankles and tells me the medical name the doctor diagnosed him with. This was about twenty years ago. He tells me about his migraines and pains up his legs.

As he's telling me in graphic detail I'm trying out varicus imaginary energy blocks between us.

I'm doing this because he's telling me in detail things that went wrong with him and therefore making me aware of things that could go wrong with me.

I try and think of another conversation I can have in my head with myself, but he's too close to me and his words are too clear.

I imagine a rainbow between us deflecting his negative energy back to him so I don't absorb it, but my rainbow isn't working.

I feel the cells in my body holding tiny cups up to their ears so they can hear the words of Mohammad and be influenced by tears.

"They would inject me with steroids, but when they have to inject steroids near the bone later this can give you brittle bones...you know the word, brittle?"

Rainbow. RAINBOW. RAINBOW.

"Do you know brittle*?*"

Why is he asking me if I know what the word brittle means?

Quick, say something.

"Yes."

"You know, like broken."

"Yes."

"They used to inject me once every six months but do you know what happened? I got headaches. Migraines. Sometimes they would be on one side of my brain. Either the left or the right and they would stop everything they were so painful, I once told a doctor I would pay him five thousand pounds in cash if he could get rid of it, in bloody cash isn't it so?"

I imagine a shield, a large roman type shield. This works.

I imagine my Roman shield in rainbow colours and for some reason, I feel less stressed; I can listen to Mohammad now without being subconsciously influenced in a negative way.

I know he doesn't mean it, but, like it or not, he's telling me things I don't want to know about or hear.

Thoughts influence subconscious workings and I could be susceptible.

"I solved all the problems with holistic medicine, but one day I woke up with a lump. A pea, you know pea? The vegetable. I woke up with a pea side lump on my left testicle."

As Mohammad says left testicle he points to his left testicle; he touches the tip of his penis to highlight the area he's talking about. Mohammad is only wearing pyjamas and without thinking my eyes follow his finger and I notice the outline of his penis.

I look away immediately and tell myself to NEVER follow his finger anywhere ever again.

I build a rainbow castle between us and withdraw the rainbow bridge and leave Mohammad on the other side; in his weird world.

I don't want to hear this story, but I can't get a word in and whether I like it or not I'm going to hear it.

I count back from ten, telling myself when I get to zero I'll ask him to leave, but, as I get to zero, I rationalise the end could be merely minutes away and hold on.

"This pea size lump on my left testicle caused me great pain, agonising pain. I went back to my doctors to find out what it bloody was."

Rainbow castle rainbow castle rainbow castle.

"The doctor told me the name of this lump, it's a known condition in the medical world and he told me I could either leave it or I could have surgery to have it removed, you be knowings...from my testicle."

Mohammad points a long spindling finger at his left testicle.

I notice out of the corner of my eye his finger touches his penis again.

Rainbow castle rainbow castle rainbow castle.

"The lump was in one of the tubes the man's sperm travels though. His semen. You know semen? It shoots out from the man's penis when entering the female's vagina. And then the sperm travels up the vagina. You know? There are millions of sperm in one bloody ejaculation so it is."

I am 30. I am aware of semen. I have also seen a vagina.

"These millions of sperm shoot up like a race. You know, like a bloody motor race. Or a horse race. And you know the jockey that's at the front of the horse race; he is the one who is going to have the baby. And the sperm gets to the woman's egg; she has hundreds of eggs."

Not sure about that Mohammad, women aren't spiders.

"Then I don't know what happens but I think one of the eggs somehow be openings up and eating one of the sperm."

The egg isn't Pac-man. The sperm eat into the egg, where they attach.

566

"Just one tiny sperm, and then that's it. And this is how babies are made, did you be knowing this?"

"Yes."

Wow.

Gone midnight on a Saturday and I'm listening to my ancient landlord give me sex education.

"I went to a hospital and decided to have the operation to remove my testicle, this would mean I could still produce semen, you know, to be shooting from the tip of my penis."

Mohammad places his finger on the end of his penis and makes a long arch from the tip of his penis away from him, illustrating his standard ejaculating sperm trajectory, which is very thoughtful of him.

"I would be left with one testicle. My right testicle would go but my left testicle would remain. I went to the hospital and met my surgeon before the operation and he was Egyptian. Bastards. And I said I was having doubts because I wasn't bloody sure and the surgeon told me I had to make up my mind. He put me under pressure. You know. The Egyptian. Bastards."

He hates Egyptians too, a new one.

Mohammad brings something up from his throat, or from somewhere inside of him; a pip.

He picks it from his tongue and flicks it onto my floor.

I remember the pip he spat at my feet after I saved him from the prostitute.

Flick weird tiny bits from your face onto your own floor, no problem; don't do it on mine.

"I had the operation and when I woke up I found out the surgeon had taken out *both* testicles *and* the tubes for both of my testicles."

Rainbow world rainbow world rainbow world.

"I could not have children and it was all because of this Egyptian."

Wait, surely you are meant to say bastards now?

"Bastards."

There you go.

I don't know what to say, I'm used to hearing the same two stories from Mohammad.

I'm sure there's a lot more to this story and if the doctor's version could be heard I'm certain it would be different but I do sympathise with Mohammad.

He touches his penis again and I ask him if he sued for medical malpractice.

He tells me he did but the courts dragged out the case for ten years until he was too tired to keep fighting, and he thinks the judges and doctors all golf together on weekends so his fight was hopeless.

Mohammad does not say bastards.

So I say it.

Not because I think Egyptians are bastards, I love Egypt and from my experience the people are wonderful.

I say it to try and comfort Mohammad, to try, for one second, to sing from his hymn sheet as one.

"Bastards."

"What did you say Colossus?"

"Bastards."

"What?"

"Not very good people, you know, because they got away with taking your testicles."

"Yes, yes, I know. Call them bastards because that's what they bloody are."

Mohammad sounds angry at me for not calling them bastards, I roll my eyes at the hopelessness of my attempt to try and make him feel good about something.

Mohammad yawns, stands, tells me he has to leave and I shouldn't be up so late.

I smile and tell him I would normally be in bed.

I open the door and resist the urge to kick him down the stairs.

I close my door behind him, glance up at the top shelf of my cupboard and look at my large bag.

A sleeping bag would fit.

No more Mohammad, no more work, no more stress; no more so many negatives.

He would miss me, and I him.

My shoes would be my plane; he would be another failed relationship I walk away from.

The lowest common denominator is me, I know; but Mohammad is an extreme case, not many people could live with their landlord interfering so often in their life.

And he's getting worse.

If he's breaking and entering now, twice in one weekend, I'm not sure I want to know what he could be doing in a month

Dear Colossus.

I really want to make peace with you.

I see too many people holding grudges for such a long time and I don't want to be like that.

I am working on understanding myself better and coming to a place of acceptance. I think I understand some of the reasons why our relationship didn't work out, at least from my end.

I'm sorry you had to deal with starting again when returning to England. I don't want to over analyze our relationship or put blame on either one of us and I don't want to stir up bad feelings.

I'll take the good memories and the lessons I have learnt about myself over everything else.

I have no regrets.

I really hope you are doing well and wish you all the best in everything you do.

Love and aloha,

Lily.

Hi Lily.

I do not hold, and will never hold anything against you.

When I speak of you it's only in glowing terms.

I know you are a good person and that doesn't change just because a relationship has failed.

It takes two to make a relationship and two to end one.

I'm glad you found happiness and are engaged.

He's a lucky man and I'm sure you are a lucky girl and I wish you both a wonderful and happy sparkly marriage which I know it will be.

Of course I want a truce; I have no ill feeling towards you and never will.

There is nothing to stir, the fact you have found your partner forever means ultimately we were right to split and in the big picture of life I guess in a small way I had some part in the path leading you to your husband.

I lived in paradise for a long time with a girl I loved and it was beautiful.

No regrets here either.

Together we shared some moments I will never top, and for those memories I will always be grateful to you and your influence on my life.

Peace.

Colossus.

"THE PROMISED LAND"

10th August 2010

Four days after today I sat and began the first day of this book; searching through old e-mails to see if I could find the email I sent to a global banking audience back in 2004.

I did, and so my e-mail became the first chapter of this story.

Then, on the fourteenth of August 2010, I wrote about being kidnapped by Mohammad and taken to a bar in his smoky car to watch him ogle young ladies he had no chance of dating.

And the rest of the story brings you to here: The end of Life Knocks four days before it began.

*

My mum and I stand in the main room of my small but clean studio flat.

The studio has a main room, a kitchen and my own shower.

The landlord has told me the oven is new and state of the art and the shower is a power shower.

There are large windows in the kitchen letting light through so the room has a good feel.

Some may think it's too small, but to me it's not a garage.

I'm working full time and have stopped taking Ketamine.

My life is going in the same direction as everyone else's; and I guess in time that might be enough.

I have made it; I'm just not sure where I have made it to.

My mum and I leave and we're called into the landlords flat at the bottom of the stairs; which is a little too close to mine.

We squeeze through a smoky room and manoeuvre around several stacks of paper, I can already tell my mum is trying to stifle a laugh behind me because she shares the same habit I have at laughing in inappropriate situations; like funerals, or when you're trying to make a good impression on your new landlord.

We sit in Mohammad's peculiar lime green kitchen and he asks us if we would like some tea which we say yes to out of politeness.

As he turns my mum makes a face and points to a plate that has a picture of Prince Charles waving and I note it's odd, giving my mum a look telling her we can talk about this later, when we aren't waiting to be given the keys to my new home.

Mohammad gives us two coffees which my mum and I both note aren't teas.

He sits down at the table with us and lights up a cigarette.

My mum coughs which is a little frustrating because I think the coughing might make Mohammad feel uncomfortable in his own home; I need to cough but I'm able to maintain a polite status quo.

Mohammad does not ask if my mum is okay, or if she would prefer it he didn't smoke, he jumps right in with what seems to be a story he wants to tell:

"I used to practice, and still be doing the art of holistic medicine. This is an amazing, spiritual way of combating all kinds of diseases and illnesses from the human body so it is; holistic medicine cleanses the soul, is very much treating beyond the symptom and looking at the cause, unlike any of the bloody useless hospitals we have today on the NHS."

I know my mum is trying not to laugh.

My mum went from being a nurse to being offered her own doctors surgery in a career spanning over thirty years within the NHS.

If he had tried to pick a story more likely to start an argument, he couldn't have.

"Normal medicine stops what we see so it does, but holistic medicine also treats the mind and it's the mind creating all of the negative things we think and have wrong with us isn't it so? Holistic medicine pours away the darkness inside of us and pours back in white light. Do you know the word light?"

He's partly right, the mind does have an influence on our being and our being consists of far more than how we feel and think; but if struck with cancer I would rather take my chances with proven medical practices than dropping plant juice into my eyeball and really believing it's going to work.

My mum, to my surprise says nothing.

"Yes Mohammad, I know what light is."

Does he honestly think I don't know what light is?

"Do you have the knowings of the light Mrs Sosloss?"

"Yes, yes Mohammad I know what light is."

Our confirmation we know what light is seems to charge his patter and he switches conversation.

"You see Colossus I'm happy for you to live here because you are a professional person isn't it so? But I won't let anyone in here. You know, none of them homosexuals or the lesoians, none of the bloody black people. No no...I'm not happy with them."

Great, my landlord is a racist, sexist idiot.

Don't say anything Mum, just smile and nod. I need the keys!

"You see the black people are so lazy, especially the Caribbean ones, you know they isn't be doing any of the things."

I want to laugh.

I know my mum is trying not to laugh too.

My step-dad is black; my entire step family are black.

My step-dad, Henry, is from the Caribbean island of Grenada.

I was wrong before, there was one more subject more argumentative than the NHS and proven medical practices versus exploratory practices; and Mohammad has found it.

Thankfully my mum is seemingly with me on thinking Mohammad is a different generation, different mindset entirely, and disagreeing with him isn't going to get him to change his mind; it's just going to start a fight when I still haven't been handed the keys.

"Caribbean's with the laziness, and also Indians, Indians are so much trouble with their dramatising of all of the actions."

I thought he was Indian.

My mum laughs but tries to make it sound like a cough, she stands with her hand over her mouth and speaks; as she does it's clear she's trying to keep it together and failing:

"Mohammad, I'm sorry to stop you, it's been fascinating but I have to get home. I have a lazy husband to feed!"

My mum laughs at her private joke.

I'm thankful my mum found an excuse to stop him because if it was me on my own I have the feeling I may have been sitting down for hours as he poured out his mind of poison over me.

"Thanks Mohammad, I'm going back with my mum in her car for now."

"Mrs Sosloss, you can come back any time. You know, I am always in my flat. You could just come and see me sometimes because I think you are a very beautiful woman."

Oh, Jesus, he's hitting on my mum in front of me.

My mum smiles, I laugh and tell Mohammad she's a married woman but I'll try and put a good word in.

Mohammad smiles, we all stand; as we walk to the door he puffs on his cigarette.

"When you come back knock on my door Colossus because I would very much like to teach you about holistic medicine, you know, holistic medicine is all about treat'ng the mind, not the bloody affect you see? The cause isn't it so?"

"Yes Mohammad."

Mohammad hands me the keys.

As Mohammad drops my keys into my hand they symbolise change and survival.

They symbolise the beginning of my life again.

A base, a place. An alarm clock, dressing how the system tells me to dress, A television set, a computer, a bed, home comforts, nine till five work, early morning tube journeys packed with people, lunches in Prêt D Manger, Sky Sports, wooden floors, using coffee in the mornings to wake up instead of sleeping eight hours like we're meant to, emails, the internet, cash points, fruit machines, long queues, night buses, Wednesday night drinks, pillow cases, cutlery, trying to meet a girl, ambitions, competition, success, comparisons, having, having not, hope, paying the council tax, taking the bins out, disappointments, shaving, evenings waiting for tomorrow, being ignored in crowded rooms, newspapers, false opinions hiding as facts, invites to places, being part of a group, sitting down, going out and plugging back in.

I want these things again.

I've missed these things; the daily routine of normal.

Life is long enough to get stuck in a revolving door and forget if you're coming or going yet short enough to regret not taking the stairs.

I walk my mum to her car and we sit in the front seats and Mohammad waves at us from the steps of his house.

We look out the car at my crazy, racist and still horny landlord.

My mum starts the car and we drive away laughing.

I put my hand in my inside pocket and feel my new keys and hold onto them tightly.

As my mum drives I look out of the window and think back on the festivals and friends, Kauai, Robert and Roberto, lost up a mountain, almost drowning in Thailand, walking home with a chicken head from the Cambodian Mafia in my pocket, meeting Lily on a sunny day in Blackheath and losing her years later, addiction, living in a garage, unemployment, finding work; and now finally I'm about to embark on peace and quiet living with Mohammad; with my own place and full time job, and I think maybe there's a philosophy to the knocks in life.

No matter where we go and what we say, no matter what knocks we give and what knocks we take, as long as we are alive to experience we can overcome, change and learn how to let go.

Letting go teaches us how not to hate; which is how we learn how to love.

We try to avoid the knocks; as adults we run around after our children hoping they don't fall over; but they're fearless and it's only by falling they learn how to stand.

Life is about the fall, life *is* the fall nobody gets back up from; but if we live our lives being held up, or running after others making sure they don't fall, then we'll never know what it's like to stand tall.

Life will knock you, but those knocks will take you to places your fears wouldn't allow you to go.

Without life knocks we would all be the same; and if we never thought to stand, maybe we wouldn't think at all.

THE END

Author Interview - Craig Stone

Today's Interview is with Author *Craig Stone*, Author of the True-Life Book '*The Squirrel that Dreamt of Madness*'. His debut novel has received excellent reviews.

Craig Stone has just released his second book *Life Knocks* - the prequel to *Squirrel that Dreamt of Madness.*

He is currently finishing up his third, a silly book, called How to Hide from Humans.

***Alan Kealey (Indie Author News):* What is your (writing) background?**

Craig Stone: I spent 90% of every job I ever had writing a book and the other 10% waving my arms around proclaiming how stressed my workload was making me. The downside; I was writing for a minute then interrupted for ten, writing for fifteen minutes then being interrupted for twenty. Not good for a writer, or employer.

Years ago, I worked for a bank, and a thought built up in my head:

You should be writing.

So I walked out.

That's the start of my second book *Life Knocks*.

Oddly, years later, my life had turned full circle and I was back at a desk and the thought returned. I had the thought over and over until eventually I walked out on my job again.

I left work one Friday afternoon, and just kept walking. That's the start of my first book *The Squirrel that Dreamt of Madness*.

This time when I walked out of a job to write I couldn't afford my rent as a consequence; so I left my job, went home, packed a bag full of clothes and moved to my local park.

I lived under a tree until I finished my first book: *The Squirrel that Dreamt of Madness*.

Once I emerged from the park I discovered I could self publish and had a weird website called twitter as my helpful robot sidekick.

Who are your favourite writers, your favourite book, and who or what are your writing influences?

I don't think I have a favourite writer and can't say I've been influenced by another writer's voice. I read a fair bit of Roald Dahl and Stephen King as a child but my main influence for writing The Squirrel that Dreamt of Madness was my brain telling me if I don't write, just because I'm scared of living under a tree, then I lose the right to complain I feel like I'm living someone else's life;

because the reason I would feel I was living someone else's life would be I had chosen to let my fear decide I was never going to live mine.

Anything you want to do is possible; fear is not meant to prevent but to motivate your heart into the life you naturally think is improbable.

Tell us about your writing process. Do you have a writing routine?

I would prefer to write in a white house on an oceanfront with a beautiful wife and a dog that knows where to poo and does so discreetly.

Alas, I write in a little room with a cat that takes great pleasure in pooing at the end of my bed at four in the morning, minus the wife.

I don't really have a routine, much like how I write my books; nothing is planned; I just do.

What do you find easiest about writing? What the hardest?

The easiest part about writing is writing; I find writing effortless, I always have.

The hardest part is the complete poverty I live in; the problem with living the dream is you can't afford to be awake.

Poverty and isolation: since I started this process I've seen my friends maybe twice in over a year.

I could go out this weekend, but nope – bank account says no. Repeat.

When did you first know that you wanted to be a writer?

I was eight years old.

Evil Ms. Goodrich asked the class to write a story about whatever we wanted over one weekend.

Most kids wrote a few pages, I wrote an entire book and the evil teacher told me to try and get it published whilst she pushed smoke rings into my young face; aging my skin slightly.

When I wrote that story I was buzzing, rushing full of energy; over the years that sensation has turned into something more akin to having my balls caught in a tennis racket mid serve, but the original feeling returns when I finish a book.

Craig, tell us a little about your first novel 'The Squirrel That Dreamt of Madness'.

I quit my job and my house and went and lived under a tree in Gladstone Park in Kilburn, London.

I had a pad and a pen and I started writing.

I told myself there was only one way I could ever get my life back on track and that was by writing my way out of it.

The book itself is set across eleven days; each day in the park in the book was a real day in real life in the park for me.

The book merges what was happening to me in the park with fantasy, as I write a book to escape my very real park environment.

The book is essentially a guy losing his mind in a park, caught up in a race to find a parrot.

What inspired you to write the book?
The mounting pressure of 3,652.42 days of denial.

...45,000 followers on Twitter..."

How would you describe the success of your book? (Sales, Awards, Reviews)
So far, the *Squirrel that Dreamt of Madness* has had over eighty 5-Star Amazon reviews and everyone loves it.
Not bad for someone with no help.
Not amazing, not life changing...but proof I'm right to try and fight to make it as a writer.
I was unable to find an agent because they're all running scared and playing safe and publishing boring books by the likes of Jordan and Peter Andre; ultimately destroying the business they think they're saving in the process.
However, it was a success because I found Kindle; I have over 45,000 followers on Twitter and I'm bloody lucky to have lots of lovely people send me messages of encouragement about my books.
Life Knocks has moved me closer to mainstream success. Life Knocks found me an agent, Sonia Land, from Sheil Land Associates in London and was shortlisted for the Dundee Book Prize.

In life all we can do is give our dreams the platform to fly but the wind is not ours to control. Dreams of the individual do not come true without the intervention of the inexplicable; that person who is a stranger when you put your dream into the public arena, who is touched on some level enough to send an email or a message saying they think your ideas have legs.
I have kept up my end; I now have two books available, and a third *How to Hide from Humans*, on the way.
I will get on with my life and if somebody wants to make my dream come true, if a wind is on its way I cannot see, then wonderful.

What did you do to promote yourself and your book?
Twitter has been my main source of promotion and Facebook, of course. I was fortunate everyone who read Squirrel loved it; the consequence being a few people who read my book had blogs and interviewed authors, so they helped me spread the word.
Recently I gave Squirrel away for free, just for a couple of days.
Squirrel was top of the free list, and has stayed in the bestsellers list since.

How long did it take it to write the book?
The Squirrel that Dreamt of Madness took ten days; ten days in the park, ten days in the real world.
I then had to type it up from a hand-written scrawl on a pad of paper to a PC, which took months. The whole time I was homeless, each day my pad would be expanding with more and more words and each day I

was thinking, "what if someone beats me up and steals it now?"

To others I was a bearded homeless madman clutching a shoe believing it to be gold.

As a consequence the closer I got to the end of the book the more desperate I was to get out of the book to save my material.

Life Knocks has been a labour of love; the stories have been in my head for years so the process for *Life Knocks* was entirely different.

I waited for a time to write it.

All in all, I sat down and spent three months recently refining it; and before that I spent perhaps three or four months writing the initial draft so perhaps maybe seven months in total.

Recently I have gone over it again and will be releasing the second, and final, edition soon.

Please, tell us where you self-published the book.
The Squirrel that Dreamt of Madness and *Life Knocks* are both available for Kindle on Amazon.com and Amazon.co.uk

How to Hide from Humans will be released on Amazon soon.

I am seeking a publisher for all of my books.

How smooth was the self-publishing process? Any issues? What are things to look for when self-publishing a book?
With self-publishing, the only hurdle to publishing is your self. So I guess it depends on how stupid you are. Because I'm very stupid, it took me ages.

I read all these websites making it sound so complicated; websites offering 20 steps to self publishing and blogs blathering on for ages about how to get a book onto Kindle; I found out people like to make it sound complicated to sell their intelligence.
Not one website simply said:
Download mobi pocket creator, put your word document through it and then it's done.
I had to find that out for myself.
Once I'd found that out, by an exhausting process of reading nonsense on websites and downloading pointless programme after programme, it took ten minutes.

Did you hire an editor and/or Cover Designer for your book?

The Squirrel that Dreamt of Madness was edited by a stranger who became a strange friend called Dionne Lister. If you are a writer reading this and want your book edited she is an editor, she charges, of course – but she's good. Her twitter handle is *@DionneLister* Dionne found out about my circumstances and loved my book so much she edited it for free.
The front cover for *The Squirrel that Dreamt of Madness* is my idea and creation.
The front cover for *Life Knocks* again is my idea and my design, and I completely edited Life Knocks.
The front cover, editing and artwork for my future book How to Hide from Humans is all me.
I always wanted the two front covers to go together for Squirrel and Life Knocks.
I needed help with finding the right beach picture and

with getting the writing correct on the sand in the image of the beach on the front cover of *Life Knocks* – Mark Bowler is one of London's finest photographers and he came up with the picture and design for the writing in the sand, I recommend people follow him on Twitter too *@One_Glass_Eye*

"...ignore what everyone else thinks and do it your way."

Can you give some tips for other Indie Authors regarding the writing and self-publishing process?
When I was starting to write I wouldn't listen to anyone's advice and so my advice would be to ignore what everyone else thinks and do it your way. Don't try and fit your words or your thoughts into boxes other people try to throw around them. If people don't understand, they aren't your reader, but if you change your voice to sound like what they expect for the rest of your life you will sound like everyone else. Although that may placate the one person telling you what they want to hear; you'll end up blending in to white noise.

Write your own way in, it's the chance you have of standing out.

Are you working on another book project? Can you tell us a little about it?
I've just released the prequel to *The Squirrel that Dreamt of Madness* called *Life Knocks*–out now available for Kindle.

Life Knocks is a story about a recluse who ends up living with a landlord with boundary issues.

Life Knocks is about love lost, and found in mysterious places; of light found in darkness, companionship found in isolation.

The more Colossus Sosloss shuts himself off from the world, the more people knock on his door, hence, Life Knocks.

The story confronts, challenges, evokes laughter, tears and, in parts, might offend...But then life never claimed to be Disney world.

Look out for How to Hide from Humans; it's a silly picture/philosophy book, written by a sheep, telling other sheep how to hide from humans.

It's not really for people.

Are you planning to move forward as an Indie author or are you looking forward to have one of your next books to be traditionally published?

I want all of my books published traditionally, and it will be a crying shame to my bank account if I only become known after I am dead.

"Kindle will not kill the book; but eventually it's going to kill the agent..."

Where do you see the book market in 5 or 10 years? Will there be only 99cent eBooks or do you see this just as a marketing phase of the book sellers to move

readers into the digital book market in a fight for future market shares?

Video didn't kill the radio star; it merely made the radio star a known face on Video and set fire to a lot of deadwood. Likewise, Kindle will not kill the book; but eventually it's going to kill the agent because Amazon reviews are doing their job for them and the publishers know it.

And the agents know it.

Has anyone tried emailing a first email to a literary agent in the past 6 months? They have never been ruder or more out of the office; and that's because they know they are Dodo's.

The power is now in the hands of the author, with social media not only are we the creators but we now have the potential to steer our own creativity towards the destiny we seek. The publishing industry is scared and rightly so. With Twitter readers can, at last, get to read the thoughts of a writer before buying.

If you like the thoughts of the writer then buy their book; if you think the writer has nothing to say, hey, maybe that's reflective of their material.

I don't agree Kindle and social media is a way for weak writers to rise to the top; I think with social media and Kindle we finally have the fairest way to find the world's best writers chosen from a pool of millions – rather than what we have had traditionally– the best writers presented to us by the publishing industry who choose for us from a limited pool.

Is Stephen King the best horror writer in the world? Probably not, but he's the best horror writer from a small pool printed by the publishing industry whc resist other writers to maintain the reputation of writers who are household names.

In this new dawn, those previously thought of as writing gods are going to be revealed as just writers. Good writers, perhaps, but not the best because for the one Stephen King published there are hundreds ignored to sustain his reputation as the best because it's easier and more profitable to publish a terrible Stephen King book than a great new book by an unknown writer.

At last, no more will an aging publisher or agent cut of touch with young talent be able to prevent the talent they are out of touch with from being read.

This is the time for writers the publishing industry has feared people will find out about: Game. On.

Do you write full-time or do you have a day job?

I write full time; though the system has its hands around my throat and is starting to squeeze me...so I might not be able to write full time much longer.

I'm a copywriter too, making average words shine for websites.

How can readers connect with you?

Via Twitter - @robolollycop - And anyone is welcome to find me on Facebook. I mean, if someone wants to come to my house that's fine too.

Just let me know so I'm in and wearing something decent.

Thank you so much for the Interview, Craig. Good Luck with your future book projects.

Link to the Book _The Squirrel that Dreamt of Madness_ with Excerpt

Link to the Book _Life Knocks_ with Excerpt

Connect with **_Craig Stone_** via Twitter: **@robolollycop**

*

My other book is The Squirrel that Dreamt of Madness:

"Craig's writing is in-your-face funny and genius. He has a fan for life because I loved, loved, loved this book. One of my top ten best books of all time."

"I find it hard to find books that genuinely make me laugh and this book is without a doubt the funniest thing I've ever read. I laughed so much that I had tears in my eyes."

"Throughout the book I had to stifle guffaws so as not to disturb those around me."

"Absolutely one of the best books I have ever read. He is not only hilarious in his story telling, but he describes things in a most creative way you would never imagine"

"His disjointed, stream-of-consciousness writing reminded me of Hunter S. Thompson on a drug-induced rant."

"I have given to it 5 stars, but only because I cannot give it 10. One of the best books I have read this year so far"

"I smile whenever I think about this book!"

"If Jonathan Winters, Robin Williams AND Tibor Fischer married and had a child, this author would be their son."

"Craig Stone is one of the most promising young writers to grace the indie and self-publishing world."

"There should be a warning on the cover about reading it in the presence of others because you will end up laughing raucously at the turn of every page."

"One of the strangest, yet most compelling books that I've read in a long time. Sort of like Odd Thomas had a nervous breakdown, and was being written by Robert Rankin after someone had given him a cup of tea laced with magic mushrooms."

"I won't give a synopsis here except to say it's based on Stone's own vagrant experience and if you ever wondered what the beardy dude on the park bench was thinking, you can bet you wouldn't think it was this."

"If you happen to be taking a sip when you hit one of those ridiculously ingenious images that come from the clever mind of Mr. Stone, whatever you're drinking will end up coming out your nose."

"A delightful read. The Squirrel That Dreamt Of Madness is brilliantly creative, often delightfully irrational, with a humorous look at the harshness of reality."

Coming Soon...

How to Hide from Humans: A manual by a sheep, telling sheep how to hide from humans.